Continuing Education of Reference Librarians

Forthcoming topics in *The Reference Librarian* series:

- The Reference Library User: Problems and Solutions, Number 31
- Government Documents and Reference Services, Number 32
- The Bright Side of Reference Services, Number 33

Authors: See *MANUSCRIPT INQUIRIES*, copyright page.

Published:

Reference Services in the 1980s, Numbers 1/2
Reference Services Administration and Management, Number 3
Ethics and Reference Services, Number 4
Video to Online: Reference Services and the New Technology,
    Numbers 5/6
Reference Services for Children and Young Adults, Numbers 7/8
Reference Services and Technical Services: Interactions in Library
    Practice, Number 9
Library Instruction and Reference Services, Number 10
Evaluation of Reference Services, Number 11
Conflicts in Reference Services, Number 12
Reference Services in Archives, Number 13
Personnel Issues in Reference Services, Number 14
The Publishing and Review of Reference Sources, Number 15
Reference Services Today: From Interview to Burnout,
    Number 16
International Aspects of Reference and Information Services,
    Number 17
Current Trends in Information: Research and Theory, Number 18
Finance, Budget, and Management for Reference Services,
    Number 19
Reference Services and Public Policy, Number 20
Information and Referral in Reference Services, Number 21
Information Brokers and Reference Services, Number 22
Expert Systems in Reference Services, Number 23
Integrating Library Use Skills into the General Education
    Curriculum, Number 24
Rothstein on Reference . . . with some help from friends,
    Numbers 25/26
Serials and Reference Services, Numbers 27/28
Weeding and Maintenance of Reference Collections, Number 29
Continuing Education of Reference Librarians, Number 30

Continuing Education of Reference Librarians

Edited by
Bill Katz

School of Library & Information Science
State University of New York at Albany

The Haworth Press
New York • London

41-8

Continuing Education of Reference Librarians has also been published as *The Reference Librarian*, Number 30.

The Haworth Press, Inc., 10 Alice Street, Binghamton, NY 13904-1580
EUROSPAN/Haworth, 3 Henrietta Street, London WC2E 8LU England

Library of Congress Cataloging-in-Publication Data

Continuing education of reference librarians / edited by Bill Katz.
    p. cm.
    "Also published as The reference librarian, no. 30, 1990" — T.p. verso.
    ISBN 1-56024-020-2 (alk. paper) : $34.95
    1. Reference librarians — Training of. 2. Library education (Continuing education) I. Katz,
William A., 1924- .
Z682.4.R44C65 1990
020'.71'55 — dc20
                                                                            90-4302
                                                                            CIP

Continuing Education
of Reference Librarians

CONTENTS

ABOUT THE EDITOR

Bill Katz, editor of *The Reference Librarian*, is internationally known as one of the leading specialists in reference work today. He is currently a professor at the School of Library and Information Science, State University of New York at Albany. In addition to the two-volume *Introduction to Reference Work*, he is the author of *Magazines for Libraries* and *Reference and On-line Services: A Handbook*. Past editor of *RQ*, the journal of the Reference and Adult Services Division of the American Library Association, Bill Katz currently edits a magazine column in *Library Journal*. He is also the editor of a new Haworth journal, *The Acquisitions Librarian*.

Introduction

Sam Johnson once said, "Everyone has a lurking wish to appear considerable in his native place."

That fairly well summarizes the continuing education desire, at least for those who don't wish to be accused of being deficient in their native place, in their library. Long ago, the reference librarian discovered an M.L.S. alone is not enough. Progress, forward movement continues when the degree is given. And in this day of fax, online, electronic garage openers and car sirens one has to keep up in order to stand in place.

Well bred librarians are sometimes scornful of the mad wish to add credits to one's record, but it seems necessary lest one perish under the terminal. One hardly has to be self righteous to recognize the prophets of the future are here and now, raging up and down the library looking for quick, efficient and accurate reference service.

So what does one do? The paths are varied, and help is on every hand. Unfortunately, a good deal of the assistance in continuing education is more furious than useful. Unless one perish both from boredom and awe at the possibilities, it is suggested that careful attention be given to this issue which is devoted to continuing education of the best sort.

Our first author, Dottie Hiebing, summarizes a general attitude of all contributors — "An increased need for non-traditional approaches to continuing education and training of reference staff is felt by supervisors, managers and trainers alike." She, as several other on-the-job librarians, offers practical ways of making the training both useful and relatively easy to carry out within the library setting. On the other side of the education wall are the good teachers of reference (bias showing, of course). Louise Sherby is representative of the group who are given this task within the library itself and who have to contend with current formal courses. She offers a number of excellent suggestions, including some sensible views on the "pathfinder." In this broad based look at continuing education, Mary

1

Ellen Collins looks at the responsibilities not only of the reference librarian, but also the bibliographer and faculty member in staying abreast of current trends.

Thanks to a survey of university and public libraries, Ruth Bauner is able to give a listing of skills most librarians expect of their reference people. Needs vary between type of library, but high on the list of both public and academic are reference interview techniques, mastery of basic reference sources and an understanding of new technologies. The interests are reflected in almost all the papers in this issue. Charlaine Ezell, for example, shows what the new technologies have done to training, and she has a typical, most useful philosophy — the willingness to take risks. Read on and you will see what she means.

What, asks Threasa Wesley, is a librarian's "most critical skill"? Fortunately, she not only stays about to hear the answer, but does much to explain why critical thinking ranks as one of the most important, if not the master skill. Patterson carries this notion to a logical conclusion in his advice about library use instruction. His major contribution is his historical appreciation of what is involved and the arguments and problems met along the way. It is a closely reasoned, well researched point of view which indicated the importance of the topic to many reference librarians.

Ahh, and at this point we enter directly into the electronic library. Much has been said about technology along the way, but with Mary Ellen Larson and later Anne Mosby and Glenda Hughes and the article by Linda Friend, one comes across the most revolutionary change in teaching reference librarianship in the past 100 years. That, of course, is the online search and all that it implies. All three papers more than fulfill the promise of giving the kind of advice everyone needs in education and training.

Karen Stabler's paper might have come first in this series, but it is saved for a middle slot to make the point that librarians are different, do have specific roles and, above all else, must be deeply involved. Training and everything it means is discussed in detail. And it is not easy, as Phoebe Janes and Ellen Meltzer explain. "For many librarians, the values with which we were raised and which were reinforced in library schools are no longer valid in today's pluralistic setting." That may be today's understatement, and the two authors explain why.

Fay Ann Golden reaches a parallel conclusion about ethics. She discusses the need for the librarian to be aware of the basic docu- ments of the American Library Association. More importantly, li- brarians must find the means possible to treat all library users equally, in terms of access and service, regardless of status and personal prejudice. This is the type of article which should be re- quired reading for all librarians—and students in library school.

To remind us about the "basics" Mary Layman and Sharon Van- dercook explain the pioneering program in California. The wide net cast by the program is one which could be followed in almost all other states and regions. Ellen Berkov and Betty Morganstern offer a look at a suburban library system in Arundel County, Maryland which deals specifically with teaching basic reference tools with beginning librarians and paraprofessionals. Sara Laughlin and Ka- ren Nissen consider the role of multitype networks in continuing education, perhaps the most cost- and time efficient means avail- able today. Ruth Patrick takes a look at self directed contract learn- ing as a method that requires long-term planning and rewards, an approach she prefers to the immediate results of a short term plan of education.

Administration and management is part of all education, particu- larly in the library itself, but with the last two papers we get down to the nitty gritty of particulars. Both authors—Helen Spalding in one case and Rose Albritton in the other—are working directors who can neatly separate the hot air from the reality of administration. They both offer sound, even inspirational approaches. It is the final paper by Tara Lynn Fulton, however, which examines the critical role department heads play as mentor to the beginning reference librarian, and offers that most dynamic aspect of interplay and learning.

And so it goes. If anything can be concluded about this issue, it is that continuing education is just that—continuing. And trying to find the best method of making that education program viable is an ongoing never-ending quest for perfection for as Sam Johnson said to insure for every librarian the granting of a wish "to appear con- siderable in his native place."

Bill Katz

I. AN OVERVIEW OF CONTINUING EDUCATION FOR THE REFERENCE LIBRARIAN

Current Trends in the Continuing Education and Training of Reference Staff

Dottie Hiebing

SUMMARY. Changes in the library's environment and in the expectations of its clientele are related to trends in reference training. Those changes include less time for reference managers to prepare training packages for staff; more initial library contact of clientele with paraprofessional staff; increased expectations of users that library service will be the same in rural areas as in urban areas; and an increased need for non-traditional approaches to reference continuing education and training. This article describes continuing education and training programs that help library staff adapt to these changes, such as the California Opportunities in Reference Excellence project, Maryland's reference training based on unobtrusive reference research, peer evaluation of reference staff in Minnesota, and several other programs specifically for training paraprofessionals in reference.

Dottie Hiebing is Director, Region V Library Cooperative, 55 Schanck Road, Freehold, NJ 07728.

5

Current trends in continuing education and training for reference staff reflect the changing scene in libraries. As the world changes and people's needs and expectations for information change, so must the provision of that information by libraries change. The training and education of those who lead people to the sources of information must also change in order to guarantee that the information provided is the right information at the right time.

Part of the changing scene in libraries affecting training is the lack of time reference supervisors have to prepare training packages for their staff. Another change is the increased recognition by supervisors and others that the first library contact people searching for information have is with para-professionals. The changing scene is also reflected in people's expectations that they will receive the same quality of service in answering their information needs in a rural area as they would in an urban area. The special needs of those requesting the information—whether they speak a different language from the person answering their question, whether they are young or old, or whether they have a physical disability—are also a concern to those training the information providers.

Those of us who are concerned with training reference staff are aware that the training needs in all types of library settings are similar if not the same. Graduate library and information science programs reflect this change through their "generic" education which requires graduates to learn the specifics of a type of library on the job or by returning to library school for specialized courses.

Finally, an increased need for non-traditional approaches to continuing education and training of reference staff is felt by supervisors, managers, and trainers alike. Continuing education no longer only means workshops. Increased research and experimentation by practitioners will be necessary to discover the formats and content of training which will assist libraries in providing staff trained to meet people's changing needs for information.

The following are examples of programs and techniques in training reference staff which are currently being used or are in various stages of development. The list is selective not exhaustive; for more information on any program, consult the resource list which follows this article.

TRAINING TECHNIQUES

Out of the numerous studies of unobtrusive reference tests by researchers Terence Crowley, Lowell Martin, F. Wilfred Lancaster, Thomas Childers, Terry Weech, Herbert Goldhor, Charles McClure, Peter Hernon, and others has come training of reference staff focusing primarily on the factors that contribute to providing correct answers.

Foremost in training resulting from this research is that carried out during the past few years by consultants at the Maryland State Department of Education in Baltimore: Sandy Stephan, Ralph Gers, Lillie Seward, Nancy Bolin and Jim Partridge. Based on a survey completed by an outside research firm, the team identified basic communication behaviors that contribute to improved reference performance and that are within the control of the reference staff. They then designed a workshop to teach the behaviors to staff who answer reference questions. Following those first training sessions, another study was carried out, and the results showed that those librarians who went through the training answered more than 77 per cent of the questions correctly, while those not attending the training answered 60 per cent of the questions correctly.[1]

The training involves clerical, paraprofessional, and professional staff and has been carried out in other states. It is highly participative and involves triad role-playing of the patron, the librarian, and an observer. Fundamental to this practice is non-threatening feedback provided by the observer.[2]

The training expectations are that the participants acquire two major sets of skills: the ability to use the model behaviors correctly, and the ability to give and receive technical feedback and positive reinforcement. The team also expects that transfer of training will occur once participants are back on the job, so strategies of peer coaching and "partnering" are used. Partners observe one another answering reference questions and help each other to use the desired behaviors. The program is designed to train reference managers, also, so that they can recognize and positively reinforce the participants when they are on the job.[3]

Research responding to the unobtrusive reference test results may eventually lead to additional training. Joan Durrance, Associate

Dean at the University of Michigan's School of Information and Library Studies, recently completed a study in which she came up with a different measure of reference success: the willingness of the inquirer to return to the same staff member at a later time.[4] As a result of her tests, Durrance concludes that reference librarians "must appear more interested in the questions they receive and make greater efforts to make their patrons feel more comfortable. They must also improve their interviewing skills and do a much better job of finding out what the patron really needs."[5]

Related to the peer coaching technique developed by the Maryland consultants is a program based on peer evaluation of reference staff which is used by the Ramsey County (Minnesota) Public Library. The staff, working with Geraldine King, Associate Director of the library, and Suzanne Mahmoodi, Continuing Education and Library Research Specialist at the Minnesota Office of Library Development and Services, developed a plan which combines self-assessment and peer evaluation.[6] A one-page self-assessment summary sheet is completed by each participant which lists reference librarian competencies (such as research skills, communication skills, knowledge of community, etc.) and factors affecting performance (such as personal, motivation, resources, work group, staffing, etc.). Staff members also list their job duties and responsibilities in priority order, and they prepare a draft list of their objectives for the next six months for consideration of the peer group.

Peer groups are established, and each group receives a self-assessment summary for each member of the peer group prior to the one-hour discussions. The discussions cover five areas: competency strengths and those needing improvement, factors affecting performance, previous objectives, future objectives, and job duties.[7] Discussions include clarification of the information, problem solving for new ways to accomplish tasks, and factors adversely affecting the individual's performance. Some guidance in group discussion in the peer evaluation process was provided.

An evaluation of the technique showed that the participants found the process beneficial and that the self-assessment was as helpful as the discussion. The process of relating competencies, which need to be and can be improved, to objectives for the following six months resulted in concrete self-development plans. The process was also valuable in team building, and the participants noted accurate and helpful feedback and a sense of support as results of the program.[8]

REFERENCE TRAINING
FOR PARAPROFESSIONAL STAFF

The first point of contact for people wanting information is more frequently a staff member without graduate library training. In certain parts of the United States, often in rural areas, all of the staff in the library are paraprofessional. Historically, state libraries with their access to federal funds have taken on the responsibility of training these staff members, and often the state libraries have provided funds to regional agencies to carry out the development and implementation of programs to train this group.

The most exciting and extensive reference training project currently underway is C.O.R.E. — California Opportunities for Reference Excellence. Funded since 1987 by the California State Library using Library Services and Construction Act funds, it is intended to improve the general quality of reference work in public libraries in California. Mary Layman directs the project, and the San Joaquin Library System in Fresno helps manage it. The project is targeted at reference staff with less than a bachelor's degree who work in California's approximately four hundred rural libraries.

In addition to training staff, the project supplies reference collections to branches and small public libraries with outdated volumes. A project curriculum committee made up of reference practitioners developed a core list of seventeen items to be provided to these libraries. During the first year, Spanish language materials were emphasized; Southeast Asian materials were the special focus the second year.

The curriculum committee started with a list of skills that reference staff need to use, and they supplied at least six different ways to teach each skill. Out of this work came a four-hour long basic introductory reference workshop. The first three hours are devoted to the reference "attitude" which includes such topics as reference communication skills, the ethics of reference and the reference process. The other hour is spent practising using six basic reference tools. A teacher's notebook was developed for the workshop as well student handouts. The workshop was designed so that it could be replicated.

During the first year, the workshop was offered seventy times and reached 1,000 staff members. Part of the development of the workshop was to train others who could lead the workshop during the coming years. The workshop is being evaluated now by Terence Crowley of San Jose State University and the results will be available in the fall of 1989.

Other products from the project are the following:

1. Reference correspondence course

The project is expanding a course that has been offered by the San Joaquin Library System for several years.

2. First day packets

These packets are for staff who come to work without ever working in a library before. The packets cover topics such as referring questions and patron confidentiality.

3. Mini-workshops

These topics are designed to reinforce skills that have been taught in the basic workshop.

4. Generic reference manual

The project staff is currently working on a manual that will include tips on how to do basic reference. It will focus on processes and not on policies and will use different types of reference questions.

5. Spanish language intake forms

These forms are intended to be used by non-Spanish-speaking staff when they are working with someone requesting information who speaks and writes Spanish. The form is a reference referral form.

6. List of helpful library phrases in Spanish

7. Specialized workshops

Workshops on reference work with special populations are now being developed. Brenda Dervin is preparing workshops for working with Spanish-speaking and Southeast Asians. Keith Wright is developing one on reference work with the physically handicapped. Each workshop will be presented five times in the state. Workshop manuals will accompany the workshops, and mini-workshops reinforcing certain points are planned.

8. Model reference behavior workshops

Ralph Gers and Nancy Bolin of the Transform Company will present five training sessions based on the Maryland training technique. Other trainers are also being trained so that the workshops can be duplicated.

According to Sharon Vandercook, who is Reference Coordinator at the San Joaquin Library System, the project will end in September, 1989.

Other trainers in other states are also developing courses to meet the training needs of those without the M.L.S. All of these courses include one or more components dealing with reference skills. Here is a list of some of the courses available now or about to become available:

1. Basic Skills Self-Study Course, Western Maryland Public Libraries.

Mary Mallory, Director of this system, is developing the ten-lesson correspondence course, several lessons of which involve reference materials or reference service. Each participant receives a kit, a descriptive worksheet for each lesson, and video tapes for some lessons. The worksheets ask the participants questions which they answer by using reference or other library materials.

The course has been used for two years, and over forty people have completed it. Ms. Mallory developed the course to meet the needs of those working in public libraries in the three-county system who do not have an M.L.S. There are long distances to travel in this part of Maryland, and many library staff were unable to attend workshops.

Planning is now taking place for a library assistant course which will include an advanced reference course covering geneology, health-related materials, and legal reference.

2. *Basic Library Management from a Services Point of View, University of Wisconsin-Madison, School of Library and Information Studies.*

This course has been taught for many years over Wisconsin's Educational Telephone Network (ETN) which links people at ETN sites all over the state with teachers in Madison. It is also a required course for Wisconsin's public librarian certification program. Darlene Weingand, a professor in the School of Library and Information Studies, reports that the course is now offered as a correspondence course. It includes two sessions on reference: reference materials and reference services. The course, which is made up of a syllabus and 13 audiotapes, is intended for those without an M.L.S. or an undergraduate degree.

3. *Rural Library Training Project, Washington State Library.*

Mary Moore of Washington State's Library Planning and Development has contracted with the Southern Alberta Institute of Technology to purchase this correspondence course. The course is composed of nine courses including one on reference and includes a telephone tutoring component. Ms. Moore is editing the course and will hire and train two telephone tutors. The tutors are selected for their ability to communicate well and their knowledge of libraries. Each participant will meet by phone with a tutor four times during the course.

Southern Alberta Institute of Technology has offered the course for four years to what are called "bush librarians" in Manitoba, Ontario, Newfoundland, and the Northwest Territories. Over 90% of those taking the course in Canada have completed it.

REFERENCE TRAINING
IN SCHOOLS AND INSTITUTIONS

Much of the reference training described so far is for people working in public libraries. Another continuing education trend in reference is the increased interest in this training for staff of other types of libraries. School media center staff, for example, are becoming more concerned about reference training, and in one state, institutional library staff are receiving special reference training.

Information Power; Guidelines for School Library Media Programs prepared by the American Library Association's American Association of School Librarians and by the Association for Educational Communications and Technology and published in 1988, clearly delineates the reference role of the information specialist:

> Students receive assistance in identifying, locating, and interpreting information housed in and outside the library media center.
>
> Library media specialists and teachers jointly plan, teach, and evaluate instruction in information access, use, and communication skills.
>
> Assistance is provided in the use of technology to access information outside the library media center.[9]

The guidelines also state the need in school library media centers for space and equipment that will encourage the accessing of information and the provision of reference service. "Increasingly, space is needed for the equipment and resources used to identify and access information outside the library media center and the school and for electronic distribution of media."[10]

Information Power also provides lists of competencies for various education levels of school library media specialists from initial preparation programs through continuing education and professional development activities. Some of these competencies relate to reference work: knowledge of information technology, systems management, and information policy; library and information programming and services and information needs and library services for special populations; information transfer by various media forms; and telecommunications systems and services, and computer systems and services.[11]

Sandy Stephan at Maryland's Division of Library Development and Services reports on the reference continuing education program carried out for the staff of the state's institutional libraries. Staff in these libraries often do not have graduate library degrees and may need training in basic library skills. The libraries in institutions also do not always have adequate reference collections.

The Maryland program assists the institutions' library staff in three ways:

1. by identifying reference tools they should have,
2. by training staff in using the tools they do have,
3. by providing back-up reference assistance through the University of Maryland's Law School Library.

It is encouraging to see that the reference continuing education and training programs for library staff are responding to the changing needs of library users and the changing environment in libraries. If the trends described in this article continue and if more research and development is carried out in this very important area of library education, the library community will have vital training programs available during the coming years.

REFERENCES

1. Sandy Stephan and others, "Reference Breakthrough in Maryland." *Public Libraries*, Winter 1988, p. 202.

2. Ibid., p. 203.

3. For more information on "peer coaching," see Ralph Gers and Lillie Seward, "'I Hear You Say. . . .' Peer Coaching for More Effective Reference Service," *The Reference Librarian*, XXII, 1988, pp. 245-259.

4. Joan C. Durrance, "Reference Success; Does the 55 Percent Rule Tell the Whole Story?" *Library Journal*, Vol. 114, No. 7 (April 15, 1989), p. 32.

5. Ibid., p. 36.

6. Suzanne Mahmoodi and Geraldine King, "Peer Evaluation of Reference Librarians in a Public Library," *Library Personnel News*, Vol. 1, No. 4 (Fall, 1987) p. 32.

7. Ibid.

8. Ibid.

9. American Association of School Librarians and Association for Educational Communications and Technology, *Information Power: Guidelines for School Library Media Programs* (Chicago: American Library Association, 1988), pp. 38-39.

10. Ibid., p. 88.

11. Ibid., p. 60.

RESOURCES

Geraldine King, Ransey County Library, 1910 West County Road B, Roseville, MN 55113, (612)636-6747.

Suzanne Mahmoodi, Office of Library Development and Services, 440 Capitol Square Building, 550 Cedar Street, St. Paul, MN 55101, (612)296-1452.

Mary Mallory, Western Maryland Public Libraries, 100 South Potomac Street, Hagerstown, MD 21740, (301)739-3250.

Mary Moore, Washington State Library, AJ 11, Olympia, WA 98504, (206)753-2114.

Stady Stephan, Maryland Division of Library Development and Services, 200 West Baltimore Street, Baltimore, MD 21201, (301)333-2113.

Sharon Vandercook, San Joaquin Library System, 2420 Mariposa Street, Fresno, CA 93721, (209)488-3229.

Darlene Weingand, University of Wisconsin-Madison, School of Library and Information Studies, CE Services, 600 North Park Street, Madison, WI 53706, (608)262-8952.

Continuing Education for ARL Librarians in Multi-Faceted Public Service Positions

Mary Ellen Collins

SUMMARY. Continuing education for the reference librarian, bibliographer and/or faculty member in an ARL library derives from every facet of the job. Certain functions, such as that of bibliographer, require formal orientation to the political climate of the teaching faculty. Other activities such as reference, online searching, and bibliographic instruction may involve prior experience but become more fully developed through the job itself. The role of faculty member necessitates publishing for promotion and tenure, which may include assistance from colleagues in critiquing papers intended for publication. Beyond diverse and demanding job requirements, however, the librarian needs intellectual and aesthetic development. A model used in the medical profession could serve librarianship well.

Continuing education for reference librarians must meet specific goals and objectives beyond the general goals of basic professional education (i.e., familiarization with the tenets of reference service and socialization into the profession). More specifically, continuing education should be integrated into any professional position assumed by reference librarians.

The literature affirms that librarianship is changing rapidly, a trend easily verified by on-the-job experience. The contents of a basic library school reference course must be constantly expanded to include new bibliographic and informational sources. Technology has created an urgent need for constant updating of knowledge

Mary Ellen Collins is Associate Professor/Reference Librarian, HSSE Library—Stewart Center, Purdue University Libraries, West Lafayette, IN 47907.

17

and skills. Margaret Steig affirms that any profession, especially librarianship, must include continuing education if it is to survive.[1]

Continuing education is of two kinds, as stated by Cyril Houle. These include first, deferred or extended preservice education; second, development of skills during the work years, after one is fully credentialed.[2] Continuing education should then embrace knowledge or skills that help a reference librarian to be a better professional and to perform reference related tasks more efficiently. The specific training may involve given tasks (i.e., online searching), the broadening of one's knowledge of a given field, or learning more about events in the world around us. While this paper specifically addresses the needs of reference librarians in academic libraries, it also incorporates the idea that reference librarians should be aware of current events and should read widely, beyond the professional literature.[3] The need for general knowledge becomes more acute as academic librarians seek to counterbalance involvement in a subject specialty.

Other components of continuing education for academic librarians may include any or all of the following: conference attendance and participation, as well as pre- and post-conference workshops and continuing education courses relevant to one's work, workshops on-site or off location for learning specific skills, the orientation process for a new reference librarian in an academic position, research and writing for publication and intellectual development.

AN ARL PUBLIC SERVICES REFERENCE POSITION

The position described in this paper is the norm in one large research university and is not unlike many others. It is that of a reference librarian who also serves a bibliographer in a subject discipline. The reference position described here is in a centralized library devoted primarily to the humanities and social sciences. The subject areas addressed in this library include communication, literature of English and other languages (Spanish, French, Russian, German, Japanese and Chinese, as well as the classics — Latin and Greek), history, political science, sociology, criminal justice, anthropology, audiology and speech pathology, art and design, music, philosophy, religion, ethnic studies (i.e., Black, Jewish) and education.

In addition to serving as a bibliographer, the incumbent has faculty rank, as do most public service librarians, which includes the aspects of teaching (public service), research and service (in associations and in university and departmental committees). Excellence in these areas is required for promotion and tenure. The three-pronged responsibilities of the reference librarian are traditional characteristics of higher education that have evolved over the past century. The librarian's responsibilities reflect this overall structure.

The incumbent in this position frequently has come from a smaller institution where no formal orientation was provided for the job: but rather a "jump in and swim" approach was used. Thus, the incumbent may bring considerable, though less highly structured experiences to the university job. Among prior experiences may have been the maintenance of vertical file materials, oversight of government documents, interlibrary loan, serials maintenance, work with microforms, user instruction, or online searching. Since the pace of reference in a smaller institution is less intense than in the university setting, adjustments in this respect are considerable.

The librarian emerging from such a background assumes new roles in the university setting. The job includes three areas of activity. First, the librarian has had presented to him/her details of the tenure/promotion process which outlines the areas of teaching, research and service in which performance is evaluated.[4] The faculty status model is applied to librarians at this institution with all of the rights and obligations that are usually implied. This means research and publication in refereed journals in the field of library and information science. The second component, excellence in librarianship, is analogous to teaching, and involves the bibliographic function, serving as liaison with departmental faculty in purchasing of monographs and serials to build the collection; regularly scheduled reference service; and assistance to the faculty with bibliographic lectures and research. This component also includes online searching relevant to the subject field as requested by a department's faculty and students.

The third component, service, includes activity in library department and university committees, as well as participation in associations at the national and state level. A librarian new to this situation must bring to the job sufficient reference experience (a minimum of two years), educational credentials, which may include a graduate degree in a subject field or a doctorate in library science or a more traditional subject discipline, and, perhaps, some research and writing experience, as well as association activity. Thus, he/she comes with the expectation of cultivating and serving successfully a specialized clientele, adding substantially to library collections, and achieving promotion and tenure in a period of five to seven years.

INTRODUCTION TO THE JOB

Much must be learned on the job. With a base to build from, the librarian is ready to assume the role of bibliographer — faculty member — reference librarian. This tripartite job necessitates various in-house and off site methods of continuing education. The head librarian (of this library, not the whole system) presents the new librarian with an itinerary — a schedule for meeting the various staff of the library system. Key people include the director, heads of school and departmental libraries and of special services such as interlibrary loan, computer services, and technical processes. Karen Stabler identifies several steps in the induction process including an introduction to the reference department and to the library's facilities and collections.[5] Dorothy Jones notes the importance of the political setting — going beyond the reference desk where the librarian works and seeing that library in the context of the library system and of the university.[6]

Along with the itinerary, the librarian is also introduced by the head librarian to the chairman of the department which he/she will serve as liaison. Additionally, the head librarian accompanies the new librarian to a meeting of that department's faculty, where he/she discusses the services and collections provided to members of that department. The head librarian likewise meets with each member of the reference staff at regularly scheduled meetings in which the new librarian receives more detailed orientation to the job, as well as a discussion of anticipated problems and questions. Jones regards this procedure as necessary in the development of the librarian even beyond the beginning stages of the appointment.[7]

THE REFERENCE DESK

Public service at the reference desk occupies much of the reference librarian's week. The average number of scheduled service hours per week of faculty member – bibliographer – reference librarians in this particular setting is about twelve, and may include evenings and weekends. This part of the job requires about 30 per cent of estimated work time.

The reference manual, combined with help from colleagues, becomes essential for learning standard operating procedures at the reference desk. Reference manuals may differ as to type and function. One type may be an orientation handbook for new staff, such as the manual from the McLennan Library of McGill University, specifically used for introducing new librarians to the basic functions and personnel of the reference staff.[8] It is now in its third edition, and it outlines procedures in the initial training program of librarians at the McLennan Library.[9] Another type of reference manual contains reference related details such as catalog information, schedules of the reference staff, organization of the library system and special services of the system, as well as circulation, reference, data gathering, or special collections of material. A third type may be a training manual. This type explains such items as forms used at the desk, floor layout of the library, personnel matters, or specific procedures for answering certain types of reference questions. One important characteristic of a training manual may be sample reference questions with lists of key resources arranged by subject field. A reference manual is an important tool in the job training of reference librarians, and as such, should accurately reflect the reference situation in a particular library.

The beginning librarian should study the manual, but also observe more seasoned colleagues. The observation process may involve following other reference librarians as they answer questions, to see the source used for the response. Other procedures involve perusing the reference collection, seeing familiar tools and many new ones.

Card and online catalogs contain features known to most practitioners. They also reflect the peculiarities of particular institutions. As noted previously, the card catalog in this library is a union catalog, reflecting the monograph holdings of each of the libraries in the decentralized system. Location changes did not keep pace with the reorganization of the libraries due to costs of technical processing staff; thus, locations are kept current in the main entry catalog only. The new reference librarian notes this as primary information, as well as the fact that separate catalogs exist for juvenile literature and serials. The reference staff constantly explains to patrons how the location system works.

The humanities and social sciences library houses the union card catalog. Augmenting it, however, is the online catalog, covering monographs, serials, government documents and the juvenile collection cataloged since 1976. Terminals for public use are few, and queues often result. The new librarian supplements the public terminals by accessing the online catalog with a microcomputer. Librarians use the online catalog whenever possible to answer telephone reference questions.

The reference staff works in a mutually helpful environment. Professional colleagues offer the benefit of their subject expertise when necessary. The staff at the desk consists of eight library faculty reference librarians as well as three full time support staff. Some support staff, responsible for the handling and filing of many reference materials, are able to assist a new librarian with their knowledge of these materials. Additionally, these support staff have been in service for many years and they form a vital, if informal, link in introducing new reference librarians into the peculiarities of this institution.

The new reference librarian may encounter collections and arrangements not part of his/her previous experience. Some that may be unfamiliar to a new reference librarian could include a large collection of government documents, problematic at this institution due to the scattering of holdings among several locations in conformance with the subject collections, and due to the changing organizational patterns of the library system itself over the years. The new librarian attempting to understand the collection, as well as the inadequacies of its bibliographic control, faces a daunting task, but is generally aided by colleagues' help. Bibliographic tools have changed and grown to provide access to a vast specialized literature. Collections such as Human Relations Area Files, Parliamentary Debates, the Early English Newspapers, and the ERIC Documents may require the new librarian to seek help.

Circulation is a separate function from reference, but, once again, certain practices are present that the new librarian must become acquainted with. These include in-library circulation for high demand reference books. Vertical file materials, and selected microforms are within the circulation responsibilities of this particular reference desk.

These details can be assimilated in the course of doing the job. No generally recognized time period exists for absorbing these localized procedures and practices. During periods when the library has been understaffed, a new librarian might serve at the desk within two weeks of arrival. Generally, evening and weekend hours were assigned later. Here again, procedures have been determined by tradition and practicality rather than formal planning. Stabler observed various types of staffing patterns that involved new librarians — the new librarian working alone, with help nearby, or with another experienced librarian.[10]

WORKSHOPS FOR ON-THE-JOB TRAINING

Workshops offered by colleagues in specific subject or bibliographic specialty areas assist, to some extent, the new librarian's acquaintance with special parts of the collection. In the humanities and social science library, a reference librarian must answer questions in a wide range of subjects and in varying degrees of complexity. Thus, taking advantage of subject expertise is one device that acquaints librarians with the collection. For example, a colleague offered a three-day workshop in government documents, the first covering the idiosyncrasies of arrangement and bibliographic control at this institution. Others treated legislation and law materials. Another colleague presented workshops on reference sources in children's literature, as well as an outline of the arrangement of the juvenile literature collection in the library. A workshop on governmental and nongovernmental statistical sources was useful to the entire reference department.

Workshops address the need of librarians to update reference skills, knowledge of sources, and local peculiarities. Staff members need to know a wide range of sources since the subject specialist is not always at hand. Obviously, one cannot predict when certain types of questions will be presented. Learning and adapting to this multi-faceted reference situation is a daunting responsibility.

IMPLICATIONS OF NEW TECHNOLOGY

The online environment has demanded a wide range of responses from librarians, including continuing education experiences. Librarians bring a variety of previous online searching experience to the reference situation. Some librarians search intensely, while others do not search at all. The level at which a librarian searches depends primarily on the nature of the comprehensive job assignment.

The increased use of CD-ROMs presents new challenges to members of the reference department. The new librarian will encounter CD-ROMs in ERIC, a heavily used education database, as well as CD-ROMs in a wide range of subjects. New staff members, along with the more seasoned colleagues, need to learn CD-ROM protocols. The heavy use that will naturally result due to the absence of enduser costs as well as browsing features, will bring about heavy demand on a librarian's time. David Taylor recently noted some of the implications of CD-ROMs as popularity, high demand creating frustration among users, changes in reference work — more demand on a librarian's time to assist with usage, more demand for other services in the library, and the need for publicity of the service.[11] The librarian bibliographers for education or for other disciplines in which CD-ROMs may be used extensively offer instruction in the special protocols.

PERSONAL ATTRIBUTES AT THE REFERENCE DESK

Perhaps no characteristic of academic reference librarians draws more praise from student users than all around approachability. Yet little or no attention is paid to developing these attributes in either the beginning librarian or in his/her more experienced colleagues. At this particular library, the notion of personal presence is discussed on occasion and is fully understood as essential to courteous service.

All the librarians in this department, since they function as bibliographers as well as reference librarians and faculty members, have made heavy commitments in other areas besides reference. Yet it is at this desk, with its nearly 100 hours per week of regularly scheduled service and its heavy use by faculty and students of a wide variety of disciplines as well as the public, that personal presence becomes a genuine necessity.

How can the aspect of approachability be developed? Some library schools give attention to the interpersonal aspects of public and/or reference service. Holland cites the University of Pittsburgh for offering courses that are behaviorally oriented, teaching future librarians skills in communication.[12] This is a trait which the new librarian with common sense and knowledge of the subject field should cultivate.

Conflicts arise when the librarian is alone at the desk with two telephones ringing and a line of patrons needing assistance. The rule of thumb expressed informally is to take patrons in person first, then answer telephone questions. Although no hard and fast rule exists at this library, it is generally felt "inperson patrons" deserve first consideration. The new librarian must grow accustomed to a very busy situation and develop skill at fielding questions both brief and complex.

What can be done to assist the new librarian who comes to a multi-faceted reference service in a research university? No workshops exist at this institution to help deal with especially hectic moments at the desk. It is a need that should be met. Holland suggests that self-instruction[13] is a viable method for learning interpersonal skills. Finding the time for this self-instruction when busy schedules demand other priorities is difficult.

OTHER ROLES OF THE LIBRARIAN

A reference librarian whose roles include subject bibliographer, faculty liaison, and faculty member with the attendant demands, soon discovers that the work is never finished. Reference service becomes a larger domain than the scheduled 12.25 hours actually spent at the desk. For persons acting as faculty liaison, calls come from faculty members needing research assistance. Requests come for online searches and bibliographic lectures. The need to fill faculty requests for library materials as well as to build the collection itself takes many hours of time. Attendance at departmental meetings and informal conversations with teaching faculty help the librarian to understand the politics and economics of a given department and are essential for library visibility. These roles constitute a subtle blend of strategy aimed at cementing departmental-library relationships.

The new librarian who brings some academic experience to this complex situation has a significant head start. Previous experiences undergird the working relationship of the new librarian with the head librarian. The head librarian assumes responsibility for mentoring and on-the-job guidance, part of a vital continuing education process, one that cannot be learned in library school. The head librarian should be a skilled politician who understands the tenor not only of the new librarians's department, but of every department with which this library must deal. This head librarian knows almost every faculty member personally, a feat accomplished by extensive outreach.

Collection development is a vital concern of the head librarian. In the regular meetings with the new librarian, the head librarian discusses this aspect of the job in some detail. Specifically, use of book and journal funds, dealing with rising serials costs, and management of the collection through deselection are emphasized. This library uses approval plans. These involve input from subject librarians in developing and monitoring the profile, as well as the inclusion of particular publishers. For this task, the new librarian must have recourse to the head bibliographer and the head librarian. The new librarian adds his/her own subject expertise to this process. The nitty-gritty of monitoring the approval slips and book titles is a process learned through interaction with the head bibliographer.

Serials constitute another important aspect of collection development for the subject librarian. In consultation with departmental teaching faculty and the head librarian, the new librarian builds the serials collection in his/her discipline. Weeding is the more difficult process. Since serials are such a dynamic part of any library's collection, weeding must be based on consultation with faculty who use journals in teaching and research. The head librarian guides the novice librarian through the political and bureaucratic maze. Use or nonuse by departmental faculty is not the sole indicator of a journal's worth for retention in or deletion from the collection.

The complex role of the bibliographer—reference librarian—faculty member continues into online searching. In some fields, this represents a heavy commitment of time and energy, as well as training in technique. Online searching assignments are determined by the job assignment, i.e., the discipline for which one serves as a bibliographer and performs bibliographic instruction. The number of requests rise and fall according to the academic calendar and depend, generally, on interaction with faculty and students in the course of giving bibliographic lectures.

What precisely is involved here is continuing education that has specific periods of inservice training. It is not the kind of subtle training imparted to the new librarian through interaction with the head librarian on matters of departmental faculty liaison. It is specific, skill oriented. It is the kind of skill that requires practice and study of specific techniques. These involve Boolean logic, recognition and use of protocols peculiar to databases offered by particular vendors, and billing procedures.

OFF SITE INSTRUCTION FOR ONLINE SEARCHING

Searching in a database heavily used by students and faculty becomes incumbent upon the new librarian in building the professional relationship and providing research assistance—an extension of reference service. Since funds for practice searching are not readily available, skills must be developed with the aid of the online search coordinator or other experienced searchers. The online coordinator provides direct search-by-search assistance, in-house workshops on institutional policy, arrangements for off site training, and enters into contracts, and establishes billing procedures.

Kathleen Gaul notes that searchers learn through a combination of methods,[14] most common of which are in-house training by an experienced searcher within the librarian's institution, training by vendors, or training by library networks such as INCOLSA of Indiana. These methods differ in the degree of effectiveness of the training, a function of the teaching methods used and the free time allotted for practice.

A problem in achieving proficiency in online searching arises because apart from occasional vendor offered time, funds are not available for practice. Proficiency is achieved mainly from working with more experienced colleagues, and by gaining experience. Requests for searches in seldom used databases require preparation on the part of the searcher in printed documentation on the specific database.

In-house training for a new reference librarian involves an introduction to the characteristics of particular institutions. Billing processes can involve considerable paperwork. Of course, general approaches to searching are taught in-house. Criticisms cited by Gaul, implying some ineffectiveness of training methods, reflect the style of the individual conducting the training sessions. The new librarian who comes without any knowledge or only a very small amount of introductory training would, with persistence, develop the skills necessary to serve the assigned constituency.

INCOLSA, in Indiana, is a library network that offers superior off site training programs in searching the databases offered by such vendors as DIALOG or BRS. Periodically, a calendar of INCOLSA's offerings is presented to the online searching coordinator who shares this with public service librarians. Workshops range from beginning to advanced and often deal with highly specialized scientific and business databases. These workshops offer an immediacy of instruction, adequacy of equipment, resources and personnel, hands-on experiences, and opportunity for questions. These sessions prove to be effective since they are commonly followed by searching on the job and guidance by the online coordinator.

Other off site instruction for the new public services librarian could include additional vendors as Wilsonline and Mead Data Central. The effectiveness of training in such specialized databases depends not only on hands-on experience at the site of the instruction, but also on the amount of use the public service librarian will make of it on the job. Frequently, due to the high cost of a database, or the lack of retrospective coverage, regular searching does not become feasible and whatever skills have been acquired are eventually lost.

INFORMAL AND CONTINUING EDUCATION

Bibliographic lectures are a necessity for the bibliographer — reference librarian; they may be regarded as essential to faculty liaison work. In bibliographic lectures the librarian teaches students and develops faculty and student relationships.

No in-service training exists for this kind of work. Effective performance depends on the librarian's previous experience with bibliographic instruction or with formal classroom teaching experience. On occasion, an incumbent may have left instruction material behind.

The lectures include instructions on how to use indexes, other key reference tools, online databases, CD-ROM products and bibliographies, as well as search strategies peculiar to each discipline. Tailoring bibliographies to specific classes is, of course, labor intensive.

Since writing for publication is necessary for tenure and promotion at this institution, research is performed under some degree of pressure. Each new librarian brings previous experience to this part of the job — some more than others. All come with full knowledge of this requirement. Appreciation for the amount of work involved varies among librarians depending on goal orientation combined with confidence built on previous experience.

Most librarians need a support system in this work. Colleagues, as well as supervisors, contribute significantly to the process of "vita building" in the area of writing for publication. These colleagues can referee a new librarian's papers, counsel on the choice of a topic, or provide editorial assistance. The head librarian may act in a consultative or counseling role in this area as well as others.

Subjects addressed in the writings of a new librarian may be those closest to the work he/she does every day. These subjects could include library or bibliographic applications of the librarian's subject specialty, or derive from reference services, online searching, bibliographic lectures, liaison work, or other activities involved in job performance.

The research involved in the development of a paper for publication can include a literature search only, or a literature search prefatory to empirical research into the reference process, the effects of the bibliographic lecture on student research, or hundreds of other topics. This exercise increases the librarian's awareness of the state of the art in these areas. The mentoring process, refereeing the paper in-house, constitutes a further dimension of continuing education. This facet of the librarian's work contributes the greatest direct growth to his/her knowledge and appreciation of the professional dimension of any in-service continuing education.

All of these roles of the bibliographer — reference librarian — faculty member described here, each accompanied by specific on-the-job training activities, form a complex picture of job performance accompanied by continuing education. The complexity of these functions (in combination) contributes substantially to the librarian's professional development, but only if the job does not become so overwhelming that it leads to frustration and burnout. The roles played away from the desk can serve to enrich the career of the librarian. Tenure achievement usually mitigates, but never eliminates, the pressure engendered by an active environment. However, career development demands a continuing commitment on the part of the librarian to education in the profession. Not to be overlooked, however, even at the beginning level, is the need for personal and aesthetic development, that dimension of life that makes reference service and bibliographic lectures meaningful in a broader sense.

WHAT IS NEEDED:
AESTHETIC AND INTELLECTUAL DEVELOPMENT

Norman Cousins points out that if one does not move beyond mere professional learning, the practice of a profession becomes impaired.[15] Any professional must grow beyond total immersion in his/her work.[16] A healthy intellectual interest in non-library issues enhances librarianship. Hobbies or intense interests outside the profession can stimulate enthusiasm for work; librarians can come to work refreshed, and can bring something of themselves to the task. A problem occurs in understaffed libraries, where the pressures of tenure and promotion combine with a type of professional interaction that results in a narrow work ethic, closing out other pursuits.

The need to develop the professional beyond the bounds of immediate work concerns has been discussed in a recent issue of the *Chronicle of Higher Education.* Mid-career professors need more support for personal and professional growth since the two are closely intertwined. Such concerns as retirement and financial planning are essential concerns of the professoriate, whether they be teaching faculty or library faculty.[17] Moreover, librarian attendance at meetings and workshops of professions outside librarianship has not become a trend, but could prove beneficial, i. e., an education bibliographer attending a meeting of the American Educational Research Association. Unfortunately, many librarians do not see this kind of interaction as important to their enterprise.[18] The major impetus for continuing eduction in many circles of librarianship has been developing technology. However the emphasis on technological knowledge as material for continuing education can lead to a concern with the technology itself, isolated from the humanity that developed it and whom it is intended to serve.[19]

In moving beyond the narrowness of practical workshops and conferences whose main thrust is technological expertise, one may consider a model which could serve as spring board to development of continuing education programs with a broader focus. This model, described in a journal aimed at medical professionals, can benefit librarians, especially public service librarians with multiple responsibilities.

Chester R. Burns, a physician, discusses the impact of a seminar he conducted on the lives of ten practicing doctors.[20] Sponsored by the National Endowment for the Humanities, the seminar dealt with the development of medical ethics in the larger context of American and world history. Material used in the four-week seminar came largely from assigned readings, two of which discussed American history and world respectively, while seven others concerned the history of medicine and medical ethics.

Prior to their participation in the seminar, each participant wrote an essay on the meaning of ethics in medicine. In the course of four weeks, reading was intensive, scheduled within a well planned program which involved outside speakers and the participant's own discussion. The program brought the physicians into contact with history, a subject not studied since college. The seminar further explored the professional ethical attitudes of the participants.

The seminar regarded history as a humanistic discipline which provided the underpinning for developing ideas and attitudes toward the profession of medicine. The seminar was planned by humanities professors and educational and medical professionals who helped make the vital connection to specific professional issues.

This model could be adapted for librarians. Any of the humanities disciplines—history, art, literature, music, religion studies or philosophy should be allowed to contribute substantially to continuing education. Such a program could help to bring librarians back to their roots, helping them to reexamine why they chose librarianship, and what they hope librarians will accomplish in the larger society. Professionals could address the problems of architecture in libraries, or, perhaps, pervasive issues of literacy and illiteracy. Broadly-based programs of this kind could offer librarians beleaguered by the problems of online searching and enduser searching, and all the other issues engendered by technology, a sense of the larger context of their profession—humanity and its wealth of ideas.

REFERENCES

1. Steig, Margaret F. "Continuing Education and the Reference Librarian in the Academic Library." *Library Journal* 105 (15 December 1980): 2547-2551.

2. Houle, Cyril O. "The Role of Continuing Education in Current Professional Development." *ALA Bulletin* 61 (March 1967): 259-267.

3. Steig, "Continuing Education and the Reference Librarian," 2551.

4. Jones, Dorothy E. " 'I'd Like You to Meet Our New Librarian': The Initiation of the Newly Appointed Librarian." *Journal of Academic Librarianship* 14 (September 1988): 221-224.

5. Stabler, Karen Y. "Introductory Training of Academic Reference Librarians: A Survey." *RQ* 26 (Spring 1987): 363-369.

6. Jones, "The Initiation of the Newly Appointed Librarian," 222.

7. Ibid., 224.

8. Young, William F. "Communicating With the New Reference Librarian: The Teaching Process." *The Reference Librarian* 16 (Winter 1986): 223-231.

9. McGill University. McLennan Library. Reference Department. *Training Program for Reference Desk Staff*. 3rd ed. Montreal, Canada: The Author, 1987.

10. Stabler, "Introductory Training," 367.

11. Taylor, David. "Reference ROMs: Six Implications for Libraries Building CD-ROM Database Services." *American Libraries* 20 (May 1989): 452-454.

12. Holland, Barron. "Updating Library Reference Services Through Training for Interpersonal Communications." *RQ* 17 (Spring 1978): 207-211.

13. Ibid., 208-209.

14. Gaul, Kathleen. "Learning to Search: How People Become Database Searchers." *Online Review* 10 (December 1986): 355-367.

15. Cousins, Norman. "The Importance of Continuing Education in the Humanities for the Health Practitioner." *Mobius: A Journal for Continuing Education Professionals in the Health Sciences* 2 (1982): 9-11.

16. Houle, "The Role of Continuing Education," 264.

17. Watkins, Beverly T. "Colleges Are Said to Offer Little Help to Senior Professors." *Chronicle of Higher Education* 35 (29 March 1989): A17.

18. Weingand, Darlene. "Continuing Education: No Professional Is An Island." *Journal of Education for Library and Information Science* 29 (Fall 1988): 143-144.

19. Weingand, Darlene. "Continuing Education: Horrocks on Houle." *Journal of Education for Library and Information Science* 28 (Spring 1988): 317-319.

20. Burns, Chester R. "Continuing Education in the Humanities for Practicing Health Care Professionals." *Mobius: A Journal for Continuing Education Professionals in the Health Sciences* 2 (1982): 122-132.

Educating Reference Librarians: A Basic Course

Louise S. Sherby

SUMMARY. A basic reference course for library school students needs to include more than information about specific reference sources. Employers expect graduates to bring flexibility and creativity to the solving of reference questions in a variety of library settings, many of which do not enjoy collections containing the titles the students memorized in class. Graduates also need skills in the evaluation and selection of reference tools, staff, and services; knowledge of the organization and administration of a reference department and how it relates to other departments; and facility in the application of current reference strategies and techniques. A sample course syllabus incorporating these concepts is suggested.

Educating reference librarians probably has been an area of concern for the field of librarianship since the establishment of the first full-time reference librarian position at the Boston Public Library in 1883.[1] Because educators and practitioners still have difficulty defining reference service, it is no wonder that the debate continues on how to train the professionals who will perform the function of reference service. If one scans job advertisements for reference librarians, the difficulties increase. Requirements often noted in these ads include things like "energetic," "creative," "people-oriented," "excellent oral/written communication skills," "teaching ability" (or bibliographic instruction), "general reference service," "online searching," "supervisory skills," and, of course,

Louise S. Sherby is Assistant Director for Public Services, University of Missouri-Kansas City, Miller Nichols Library, 5100 Rockhill Road, Kansas City, MO 64110-2499.

35

"experience." How does one teach all (or at least some) of these skills and abilities in one course of usually three credit hours? Can it be done at all? There does seem to be some discrepancy between what the library schools teach and what the employers of these students want. I would like to enter the fray based on my experience as a library school student, a reference practitioner of many years, a supervisor of reference librarians, and an adjunct professor teaching basic reference courses.

The literature indicates that reference traditionally has been taught in several ways. These methods include teaching specific reference titles, teaching genres or types of sources, using case studies, and using problems or question sets. Each approach has its proponents as well as its detractors. Another aspect of the argument is the relative weight of "theory vs. practice." No one method is sufficient to enhance the reference process in this age of increasing complexity of information resources and greater reliance on technology. But how to combine these various approaches and in what way to provide students with a meaningful educational experience that will enable them to approach their first professional position with a small degree of confidence?

As an employer one tries to establish job descriptions that accurately reflect the myriad duties of the reference librarian as well as allow for flexibility that will encourage the holder of any particular reference position the opportunity to bring his/her own individuality to the job. Yes, the employer would like to find a reference librarian who would exhibit all those characteristics mentioned above, but is that realistic? In addition, most of those requirements are really intangible personality traits that are very difficult to determine from a resume or in an interview. However, few job advertisements include the requirements that reflect how reference is most commonly taught with the exception of general desk duties. How do we reconcile all of these conflicting needs?

When designing a reference course, I first determine the reference sources and practices I want the students to learn in the course as well as providing some thought to those concepts I would like a beginning reference librarian on my staff to have at least a passing acquaintance with on his/her first day on the job. Basically that means thinking about what qualities are important for a reference librarian to have.

QUALITIES FOR REFERENCE WORK

The qualities most important for a reference librarian to have include a basic knowledge of the types of reference sources and what kinds of questions one can most often answer using each type. As a practitioner, I am not a proponent of the specific title approach. This approach usually requires large amounts of memorization of detail that is likely to change often and most assuredly will cause confusion and frustration on the part of the student in trying to keep the specific details of each source clear. It also usually involves the student having to learn details that can more efficiently be looked up in Sheehy's *Guide to Reference Books* or a similar guide to reference sources. It should be more important for the student to know the differences among almanacs, handbooks, and bibliographies than to know how many journals are indexed in the *Readers' Guide to Periodicals*, a figure that changes fairly often.

I also want my students to know what reference librarians actually do. This will in nearly every type of library, except perhaps the most specialized, include many more responsibilities than just answering reference questions at a reference or information desk. Therefore, it is important to at least discuss briefly the evaluation and selection of reference materials, interlibrary loan activities, library instruction, online searching, hiring, training and evaluation of staff, the organization and administration of a reference department, and the evaluation and measurement of reference service.

Additional qualities needed are the abilities to think, analyze, and communicate one's ideas orally and in writing. These are probably the most difficult to teach and are the skills that are the most discouraging to discover that graduate students, many with previous and current work experience, do not have. I require a great deal of written work during the course of the semester and I am always discouraged at how poorly students write and spell. In one of my classes, I was even asked if spelling and grammar would count on the final! Needless to say, the answer was most definitely yes.

PROBLEMS WITH CURRENT REFERENCE COURSES

The primary problem with current reference classes is that there is only one reference class required in most library schools. There is not enough time in one three hour course to cover all the essentials that need to be covered, even in a cursory fashion, regardless of the method used by the instructor. Many library schools require a basic cataloging class as well as an advanced class. Why is there not the equivalent requirement for reference service? Is this function seen as less important or requiring less skill? Every library school should offer and require students to take a basic reference class and an advanced reference class. In addition, those students planning to pursue reference work should also be required to take subject literature courses. Breadth and depth of knowledge is essential in translating a reference question into a question that can be answered using the sources available in one's library.

Another major concern is that many reference courses are taught from the point of view of the large research or academic library and not from that of the types of smaller to medium-sized libraries in which the majority of the students will actually work. Yes, it is important to provide a wide-ranging foundation of knowledge but it also is important to familiarize the student with the types of sources he/she is likely to find in the library in which the student will be working. Emphasis should be placed on flexibility and creativity in solving reference questions.

A third problem with educating reference librarians is that many faculty have not worked in a reference department in many years. It is essential that the faculty keep current with reference sources, the new technologies, and the trends and issues of concern to the working reference librarian. Dougherty believes that faculty keep up with the literature as opposed to keeping up with what is actually happening in libraries.[2] Keeping up with what is happening is not easy to do but is essential if the faculty are to maintain credibility with the students and with potential employers.

Another requirement should be a practicum or internship for all library school students. Nearly all professional schools require such a practical learning experience under the supervision of other professionals. These can vary from a few weeks to several years and are required in the fields of teaching, law, dentistry, medicine, and nursing. Such a requirement would provide the student with a "hands-on" learning experience that is invaluable. It is important that students be aware of what life is like in the "real" world of libraries. As much as possible students should be placed in a position similar to what they wish to pursue upon graduation, i.e., cataloger, reference librarian, media specialist, etc., in the type of library desired (academic, school, public, etc.). This is not an easy task and requires a great deal of effort on the part of the students, faculty, and the supervising librarians but will be worthwhile in terms of the advancement of the profession as a whole.

A PRACTITIONER'S REFERENCE COURSE

As mentioned earlier, I am a proponent of the genre method for teaching sources. This seems to be a method that works well in trying to train future reference librarians who will work in a variety of libraries. Lectures generally focus on the types of reference sources with certain titles used as specific examples. These types are reinforced by the use of problem sets. I usually assign eight sets of ten questions that are designed to point out specific characteristics of the genre using titles found in most libraries. At the same time, I use questions that I and my colleagues have been asked at a variety of reference desks. In this way I attempt to make the exercises reflect "reality" at least in a small way. I also do not believe in making the questions so obscure that the students merely get frustrated in their attempts to answer them. The use of such obscure questions does not truly reflect reality anyway since most reference librarians on the job will and do consult with each other when they have a question that cannot be answered with the obvious sources. Because students are expected to do their own work, the practice of "treasure hunting" merely serves to make them angry and negates the positive learning that can take place. In answering the questions, students are required to provide their search strategy in reaching the correct (or incorrect) answer. As a learning exercise, the search strategy is at least as important, if not more so, than the answer, and in reviewing the questions in class, the strategies are given equal attention. Due to lack of time in a three hour class, students are expected to do additional readings on each type of source outside of class in addition to the lectures in class.

Lectures on the reference genres and sources are allotted one half of the class time. The second half of the session is allocated to discussion of the reference process and its techniques. Topics covered in this part of the class include reference service, search strategy, communication, reference interviews, evaluation of reference sources, computer assisted reference including database searching, online catalogs, bibliographic utilities, CD-ROMs, etc., other responsibilities of reference departments, and the administration and supervision of staff, among others. In addition to class lectures and discussions, the students are assigned a variety of readings to supplement class activity. The reasons for using so many outside readings are to ensure that students do not hear only one point of view (mine) and to introduce them to the major journals and authors in the field of reference librarianship. It also makes class discussions much more lively.

THE USE OF WRITTEN ASSIGNMENTS

I also generally assign two additional written assignments with varying degrees of success from class to class. The first is the development of a pathfinder on a narrow topic. Because I believe that the ability to answer reference questions is largely influenced by the ability of the librarian to quickly develop an appropriate search strategy, I find such an assignment useful in reinforcing that skill. It also forces the student to look at a specific group of reference sources and evaluate them as to whether or not they should be included. Because the parameters are strictly drawn, the students have to think and use analytical skills in determining what the final product will include. If the pathfinder is well done, it also will provide the student with a concrete example of something he/she has done in the area of bibliographic instruction when interviewing for a reference job.

The other written assignment, the term project, challenges the student to bring together all the concepts previously discussed in class. The specific details vary with each class but the overall purpose remains the same. It requires the student to develop a "core" reference collection within the context of a particular community and type of library (e.g., a regional high school library in a rural area where agriculture is the major industry). The students have a choice of three scenarios that usually include a public library, an academic library, and a school library; I provide a few assumptions (such as cost is not a factor and all items are in print). The students may enhance the scenarios and the assumptions but they may not change them. The core collection is limited to no more than 75 items and they must justify the selection of each item within the context of the library and the community it serves. It is hoped that this brings together for the students the importance the community plays in the development of the reference collection as well as the principles of selection and evaluation. Because the scenarios include a choice of library, the students also can use the assignment to think about the type of library in which they wish to work and to become familiar with some of the specialized selection tools appropriate for that type of library.

A SAMPLE SYLLABUS

Based on my experience in my various roles, all of which influence the way in which I view library education, I would like to suggest the following syllabus for a basic reference class. It reflects the limitations of having only one class in which to include a little bit of everything and the limitations of a 14-week semester. I have found that I never have enough time to cover everything as completely as I would prefer (particularly when I encourage and expect class discussion), so if one has a 15 or 16-week semester, the syllabus can be adjusted easily.

A SYLLABUS FOR BASIC REFERENCE

Goals and Objectives of the Course: These should be clearly spelled out and attainable. Students should have a clear idea of the instructor's expectations from the first day of class. The goals and objectives also should be measurable so that the students and the instructor alike can measure the degree of success of the course.

Week 1:
  A. Organizational Matters/Class Expectations
  B. Introduction to Reference Service

Week 2:
  A. The Reference Collection
  B. Encyclopedias: Adult, Children's, Foreign, Subject

Week 3:
  A. The Reference Collection (cont'd)
  B. Dictionaries
     Reference Problem Set I Due

Week 4:
  A. Reference Service
  B. Almanacs and Yearbooks
     Reference Problem Set II Due

Week 5:
  A. Reference Service (cont'd)
  B. Current Information Sources & Directories
     Reference Problem Set III Due

Week 6:
  A. Reference Interview & Search Strategy
  B. Handbooks and Manuals
     Reference Problem Set IV Due

Week 7:
  A. Reference Interview & Search Strategy (cont'd)
  B. Bibliographies
     Reference Problem Set V Due

Week 8:
  A. Computer-Assisted Reference Service
  B. Bibliographies (cont'd)

Week 9:
  A. Computer-Assisted Reference Service (cont'd)
  B. Indexes & Abstracting Services
     Reference Problem Set VI Due

Week 10:
   A. Library Instruction
   B. Indexes & Abstracting Services (cont'd)
      Pathfinder Assignment Due

Week 11:
   A. Administration & Organization
   B. Biographical Sources
      Reference Problem Set VII Due

Week 12:
   A. Personnel Needs
   B. Geographical Sources
      Term Project Due

Week 13:
   A. Evaluation of Reference Services
   B. Government Documents
      Reference Problem Set VIII Due

Week 14:
   Final Exam

Assignments and Evaluation Criteria: These also should be clearly defined. I always include the description of the pathfinder and term project assignments as well as the requirements for the reference problem sets. I indicate the percentage of the grade that each course requirement will count toward the whole grade so that there are no surprises. The total grade is made up of class participation, reference problem sets, pathfinder, term project, and final exam.

CONCLUSION

Yes, the course is a lot of work and, yes, the students sometimes complain. However, this course is part of a graduate education program and is certainly well within the requirements of graduate courses in other disciplines. As I often tell my students, there is a lot of knowledge they need to acquire to become effective reference librarians and they will work hard—in school and on the job. Because I am a strong advocate of teaching more than just the books, I must find ways to include these other areas in a course that was originally designed just to teach sources. Such a course is a heavy load, but as an employer I am much more likely to hire a new reference librarian who can articulate in an interview the importance of the library community in collection development or the need for library instruction than one who can tell me the *Random House Dictionary of the English Language* contains over 260,000 entries.

REFERENCES

1. Allen Kent et al., eds. *Encyclopedia of Library and Information Science* (New York: Marcel Dekker, 1978), v. 25, "Reference Services and Libraries," by Thomas J. Galvin, p. 212.

2. Donald E. Riggs & Gordon A. Sabine, *Libraries in the '90s: What the Leaders Expect* (Phoenix, AZ: Oryx, 1988), p. 52.

Reference Ready Beyond the M.L.S.

Ruth E. Bauner

SUMMARY. Entry level reference librarians must make a rapid transition from the reference classroom to the scheduled service hours at the reference desk. A questionnaire was sent to academic and public librarians to ask them to list the most important items of information or abilities they find they need to teach the entry level librarian. This is a brief discussion of relevant literature and a report of the 72 per cent return on the questionnaire. Five "needs" surfaced as ranking high for each type of library with three listed in common. Some suggestions are given for developing in-service education programs for reference librarians.

INTRODUCTION

What is it that reference librarians need beyond the frequently advertised Masters degree in Library Science from a program accredited by the American Library Association? It was this question that motivated the author to send out a request for information. The request read "Please give me the benefit of your experience by listing the three most important items of information or abilities you find you need to teach an entry level reference librarian who has the appropriate M.L.S. degree." Two additional spaces were provided as "optional" in the event that someone wanted to list more items and/or abilities. A more detailed discussion of this request for information and the results will follow later.

Ruth E. Bauner is Head of the Education and Psychology Library, Morris Library, Southern Illinois University-Carbondale, Carbondale, IL 62901.

LITERATURE REVIEW; REFERENCE LIBRARIANS

Searching the literature posed questions. Where would information related to the needs of a new reference librarian be listed? What were shades of differences in meanings of key concepts? It was discovered that the former question had very few answers in the literature. Most of the material written gives the reader an overview of the activities involved in reference work[1] or tells how new librarians view the orientation they received on the job.[2] Or it is possible to find discussions of one particular activity needing emphasis in the reference department[3] or one particular method of teaching someone at the desk for the purpose of improvement.[4] It is also possible to find discussions of how educators in Graduate Schools of Library and Information Science teach students in reference courses. Shores[5] and Rothstein[6] discuss the relative importance of materials versus methodology in teaching such courses. Shores prefers "teaching reference as a course in literature," although he does not neglect philosophy and method. Rothstein writes "In some schools the basic reference course is no longer required. In a growing number of other schools, basic reference has become a part of a larger 'foundation' or 'integrated core' course."[7] Where basic reference does still exist, and where studying reference titles is important there is apparently little agreement on what should be studied, as reported by Summers.[8] He also concludes, of reference education, that there should be less emphasis on specific sources, greater emphasis upon group and interpersonal communication skills, and more emphasis upon subject knowledge. Discussed too are the merits of practice work or practicums as part of reference courses.

Nitechi identifies four skills needed by "public services librarians, particularly since the online technology has entered the world of libraries."[9] These skills are ability to communicate and conduct an effective interview, ability to analyze the information need, ability to retrieve information from sources of recorded data, and ability to give user instruction. In a different discussion of how to overcome what the authors believe to be only a 55 percent accuracy rate at the reference desk, the authors write that there are three important reference behaviors which need to be taught.[10] They are "verifying, which consists of paraphrasing or repeating the patron's question and asking if that is the specific question before trying to find the answer;'' asking a follow-up question; and drawing out the patron's specific question.

LITERATURE REVIEW; IN-SERVICE EDUCATION

But what of the librarian, recently graduated and ready to go to work? In-service education, on the job training, staff development, or continuing education? Do any of these concepts hold the key for new librarians faced with the demands of meeting patron requests at the reference desk? And if so, what are the abilities these professionals need to acquire?

First, it seems necessary to define and distinguish among the four terms which are all used in the literature for at least the past ten years. In-service education and on the job training seem to be interchangeable as do staff development and continuing education. In-service education is defined as "Courses or programs designed to provide employee/staff growth in job-related competencies or skills, often sponsored by employers, usually at the professional level."[11] On the job training is "Supervision and other supplemental instruction furnished to a learner while [the learner] is employed as a beginner or trainee in the regular duties of a position or job."[12] These are the two concepts then that relate to the transfer of skills to a new professional in order that the person function at the expected level. The other two concepts seem to relate to later experiences and perhaps at the volition of the individual. Staff development is "Employer-sponsored activities, or provisions such as release time and tuition grants, through which existing personnel renew or acquire skills, knowledge, and attitudes related to job or personal development."[13] According to the same source, continuing education is defined as "Educational programs and services, usually on the postsecondary level, designed to serve adults who seek particular learning experiences on a part-time or short term basis for personal, academic, or occupational development."[14] Therefore, for the purpose of this discussion, in-service education is considered.

What abilities should be included in in-service training and how should these abilities be taught? Shapiro believes that librarians are not familiar with basic publications, that they do not know how to conduct a reference interview, that they do not make referrals for information, and that they do not work well with the public.[15] Roberts reports that new reference librarians could use the same instruction designed for patrons: reference books and services, the card catalog, the computer search system, the structure of a discipline and the literature, and development of a search strategy.[16] The necessity for a reference librarian to learn teaching skills is an emphasis made by Clark.[17]

As varied as what the librarian needs to know are the ideas concerning how the person should be taught. Young defines in-service training for a reference librarian as "an in-depth and long term program of education for reference service suited to the specific needs and circumstances of a particular institution aimed at implementing the service goals established by that institution."[18] The recommended time to be spent on in-service training varies from a few days to several months. The more extensive programs are formalized, and the library usually has a professional staff person designated to plan and manage continued in-service training programs. A variety of methods have been suggested or employed: the study of a reference manual; tours and instruction periods; the study of actual reference questions and a hunt for the answers; videotaping at the reference desk; peer coaching and the buddy system. There is also a great difference of opinion about when the new reference librarian should begin to function at the reference desk. The opinions range from the day the person reports to work to six months of training before the librarian fields questions alone without the support of an experienced senior person. One might conclude from the literature that more planning should be done for assisting the new reference person, that more instruction needs to be given, and that a peer or buddy relationship should exist for some time to provide the feedback and support that is necessary at the reference desk. Specific libraries surfaced as having well planned in-service training programs: McGill University, University of Michigan, State University of New York at Albany, Brooklyn Public Library, and Dallas Public Library to name a few.

SURVEY

Questionnaires were sent to a total of 143 libraries, 92 university libraries and 51 public libraries. The university libraries were taken from the membership list of the Association of Research Libraries. Those eliminated from the list were research libraries with no university affiliation and university libraries outside of the United States. The latter were not included because it was not possible to send a postage paid envelope for the return of the questionnaire. The names of one large public library from each state and the District of Columbia were taken from *American Library Directory* (41st Edition). It was decided to include public libraries since their needs could differ from those of university institutions. Because the ranking of needs was not requested the fact that there were more university libraries than public libraries was considered to be unimportant to the study.

Letters were addressed to library directors with the request that the questionnaire be given to the "head reference librarian or another senior reference person." In most cases this was done; in a few cases the director chose to answer. From the 143 requests, 103 responses were received or 72 per cent. The break down for public libraries was 37 responses out of 51 questionnaires and for university libraries, 66 out of 92 letters sent. Actual numbers of responses cannot be reflected in the items tallied since some who answered offered more than one idea for each of the three abilities and also listed more than an itemized three. Some chose to use the additional two spaces that were optional, and a few went beyond that. Because the intent was to determine the "most important items of information or abilities" without asking for any rank order, all answers were accepted as being equally important. It is interesting to note that the percentage of returns from both categories of public and university institutions was essentially the same.

Some librarians wrote additional notes and offered materials, such as relevant published materials and information on in-service education programs. About four librarians indicated that as a policy they did not hire entry level reference persons or that for the last several years it had just happened that they had not. A few offered the information that they had formal "in-service education" programs for reference persons. Also a few indicated that they have an established position for a person to be in charge of their staff training programs and to be responsible for the accompanying manuals and training materials.

RESULTS

Because the questionnaire was open ended and not a check list, some answers were difficult to categorize. The author tried to put each item under the best choice of "information" or "ability." Another problem that appeared was that in some cases it seemed the respondent was sending a "wish list" rather than items of information or abilities that could actually be taught on the job. There was no attempt to exclude these, however, from the tally. The readers may determine for themselves the possibility for success in an in-service education program.

Information or abilities listed most often as needed in in-service education programs for entry level reference librarians and the number of times mentioned are:

1. Reference interview techniques — 53
2. Use of technology — 44
3. Policies, procedures, and philosophy of a specific library and reference department — 33
4. Interest in and ability to work with people (also coping with problem patrons) — 33
5. Reference sources — 25
6. Specialized frequently used reference sources — 20
7. Teaching skills — 20
8. Service oriented — 14
9. Search strategy skills (in finding answers to reference questions) — 14
10. Cataloging, classification, card catalogs, etc. — 13

It is clear that the overwhelming concerns are the first four with "how to get at the real heart of reference questions" leading the list. Second was the use of all the many technologies. On line searching, CD-ROMs, numerous network systems, and on line catalogs were all mentioned, as were older technologies such as using various microforms. Third were the practical working aspects of the libraries and reference departments—the policies, procedures, and philosophy of service. Fourth, when "interest in and ability to work with people" was combined with "coping with problem patrons," there was as much concern for in-service education as for the third item. It should be noted that if the fifth and sixth were combined into "the need to know reference sources" the total would be 45 placing it second on the list.

Furnished for the reader in Table 1 is the list of information and abilities libraries believe they need to teach entry level librarians through in-service education. "A" is used for academic or university libraries. In that column is the number of times the particular item was mentioned. "P" is used to indicate public libraries and "T" for the total number of times mentioned by both types of libraries. In this list the information or abilities appear in alphabetical order.

ACADEMIC AND PUBLIC LIBRARIES

When percentages of responses and item counts are calculated, it is readily apparent that librarians in university and public libraries expressed different needs for in-service reference education. The five highest needs for academic or university libraries are:

Use of technology	52%
Reference interview techniques	45%
General and specialized reference sources	42%
Policies, procedures, and philosophy of a specific library and reference department; unique features, collections, etc.	38%
Teaching skills	27%

TABLE 1. Information or Abilities Libraries Indicate They Need to Teach New Reference Librarians

	A	P	T
Ability for recall and mental retention	1	0	1
Ability to evaluate sources and use discernment (and individual judgement)	4	1	5
Approachability	0	1	1
Being a professional	3	1	4
Bibliographic verification	2	3	5
Cataloging, classification, card catalogs, etc.	9	4	13
Characteristics of local reference questions	2	1	3
Collection development and review media	3	5	8
Committee skills	1	0	1
Communication skills	6	5	11
Computer planning and programming	1	0	1
Foreign language reading ability	1	0	1
Government documents	5	3	8
Information about local area	0	2	2
Interest in and ability to work with people;	13	12	25
(also coping with problem patrons)	0	8	8
Interlibrary loan, library networks, and use of other local libraries	9	2	11
Knowledge of books and publishing	0	1	1
Knowledge of collections	0	2	2

TABLE 1 (continued)

	A	P	T
Knowledge of conducting research (to better understand questions)	3	0	3
Knowledge of subject areas	2	0	2
Liaison relationships with academic departments and faculty	3	0	3
Library committee participation	1	0	1
Life long learning (in liberal arts, general knowledge, and new reference sources)	4	2	6
Local directories and information	3	3	6
Management and/or supervisory skills	4	6	10
(Also financial management, budgeting, and statistics)	0	4	4
Microforms and other non book media	1	0	1
Organization of local reference collections	9	2	11
Organization of serials collections	2	0	2
Peer consultation	8	4	12
Policies, procedures, and philosophy of a specific library and reference department; unique features, holdings, etc.	25	8	33
Practicum or library work experience	0	1	1
Priority of work and time management	5	3	8

TABLE 1 (continued)

	A	P	T
Professional organization involvement	3	0	3
Public relations know how	0	2	2
Reference interview techniques	30	23	53
Reference sources	11	14	25
Research skills for personal research	1	0	1
Search strategy skills	8	6	14
Sense of humor	0	3	3
Service oriented	0	14	14
Specialized frequently used reference sources	17	3	20
Storytelling ability	0	1	1
Stress management in dealing with library users	4	5	9
Teaching and research emphasis of university	2	0	2
Teaching skills (individual and classroom levels)	18	2	20
Team concept	5	3	8
Telephone reference communication	0	2	2
Uncataloged collections	4	0	4
Understanding of bureaucracy and institution politics	5	3	8
Use of books rather than technology	0	2	2
Use of technology	34	10	44
Writing skills	1	0	1

Public librarians listed their highest needs as:

Reference interview techniques	62%
General and specialized reference sources	54%
Service oriented	38%
Interest in and ability to work with people; also coping with problem patrons	32%
Use of technology	27%

Space prohibits sharing with the reader some of the interesting comments made by both groups of librarians.

CONCLUSIONS AND RECOMMENDATIONS

There is relatively little literature on in-service education in libraries, and what there is seems to be in the early "how we do it" stage rather than to be reports of research that might provide help on methodologies and successes. However, it can be determined that some libraries have well developed formal programs using among other methods, printed materials, videotaping and peer tutoring; and extending from a few days to six months. Also some libraries have a position devoted to in-service education programs in their systems.

The fact that 72 per cent of the librarians chose to return the questionnaire would seem to indicate that there are needs among entry level reference librarians. Most of the needs can be addressed through in-service education, but not all of them. There are some common needs expressed by academic and public librarians. These are the need to learn reference interview techniques, the need to learn about general and specialized reference sources, and the need to learn to incorporate new technologies into reference work. In addition, academic librarians see a need to instruct new librarians in particular policies, procedures, philosophies, and collections of the library as well as teaching skills while public librarians indicate a need to teach a service orientation and a need to teach an interest in and ability to work with people including problem patrons.

Recommendations, to some extent become self evident:

1. Libraries and reference departments need written manuals for professional staff instead of relying entirely on one to one personal teaching. Written manuals could avoid inconsistency, fragmentation, and overload of information.
2. One person needs to be responsible for the teaching whether it is a full time staff person in the larger systems or the head of the library or reference department in smaller systems. Delegation of some of the teaching could occur in a planned and designated sequence. Part of the teaching process should also be regular feedback to the new librarian.
3. Since many libraries have a staff shortage and financial woes discourage adding a person to develop in-service education, perhaps a well written self instruction book related to at least the five most often listed needs would be beneficial. There could also be a list of trial reference questions for neophyte practice. This measure would, of course, not replace all one on one teaching, peer help, and supervision.
4. Finally, perhaps a professional organization such as a division of the American Library Association could make planning in-service education for the entry level reference librarian the focus of a continuing education program. Or the program might be provided on a state or regional level. The plan would be to assist those who are responsible for managing and/or teaching new reference librarians those items of information or abilities that they need to function successfully in their work.

REFERENCES

1. William A. Katz, *Introduction to Reference Work; Volume II, Reference Services and Reference Processes*, 5th ed. (New York: McGraw Hill, 1987).

2. Karen Y. Stabler, "Introductory Training of Academic Reference Librarians: A Survey," *RQ* 26 (Spring 1987) 363-69.

3. Alice S. Clark and Kay F. Jones, ed. *Teaching Librarians to Teach: On-the-Job Training for Bibliographic Instruction Librarians*. (Metuchen, NJ: Scarecrow Press, 1986).

4. Ralph Gers and Lillie J. Seward, "'I Heard You Say . . .' Peer Coaching for More Effective Reference Service," *Reference Librarian*, 22 (1988) 245-260.

5. Louis Shores, "We Who Teach Reference," *Journal of Education for Librarianship*, 5 (Spring 1965) 238-247.

6. Samuel Rothstein, "The Making of a Reference Librarian," *Library Trends*, 31 (Winter 1983) 375-399.

7. Ibid., 393.

8. F. William Summers, "Education for Reference Service" in *The Service Imperative for Libraries; Essays in Honor of Margaret E. Monroe*, ed. by Gail A. Schlachter. (Littleton, Colorado: Libraries Unlimited, 1982) 157-168.

9. Danuta A. Nitecki, "Competencies Required of Public Services Librarians to Use New Technologies," in *Professional Competencies – Technology and the Librarian*, ed. by Linda C. Smith. (Urbana, Illinois: University of Illinois Graduate School of Library and Information Science, 1983) 43-97.

10. Sandy Stephan and others, "Reference Breakthrough in Maryland," *Public Libraries* 27 (Winter 1988) 202-3.

11. James E. Houston, *Thesaurus of ERIC Descriptors*, 11th ed. (Phoenix, Arizona: Oryx Press) 1986, 118.

12. Carter V. Good, *Dictionary of Education* (New York: McGraw-Hill, 1973) 617.

13. Houston, 231.

14. Ibid., 49.

15. Beth J. Shapiro, "Ongoing Training and Innovative Structural Approaches," *Library Trends* 31 (May 1987) 75.

16. Anne F. Roberts, "Myth: Reference Librarians Can Perform at the Reference Desk Immediately Upon Receipt of MLS. Reality: They Need Training Like Other Professionals," in *Academic Libraries: Myths and Realities; Proceedings of the Third National Conference of the Association of College and Research Libraries*, ed. by Suzanne C. Dodson and Gary L. Menges. (Chicago: Association of College and Research Libraries, 1984) 403.

17. Clark, 32-44.

18. William F. Young, "Communicating with the New Reference Librarian: The Teaching Process," *Reference Librarian* 16 (Winter 1986) 224.

BIBLIOGRAPHY

Clark, Alice S. "In House Training: The Situation in ARL Libraries." In *Teaching Librarians to Teach: On-the-Job Training for Bibliographic Instruction Librarians*. Metuchen, New Jersey: Scarecrow Press, 1986, 32-44.

Creth, Sheila D. *Effective On-the-Job Training Developing Library Human Resources*. Chicago: American Library Association, 1986, 14-5, 107-10, 113-14.

Eichhorn, Karen. "Portable, Packaged Reference Training." *Public Libraries*, 22 (Spring 1983), 76-8.

Fetros, John C. "The Value of the Reference Questions in Training Programs." *California Librarian*, 33 (July 1972), 164-8.

Galvin, Thomas J. "The Education of the New Reference Librarian." *Library Journal*, 100 (April 15, 1976), 727-30.

Gers, Ralph and Lillie J. Seward. " 'Heard You Say . . .' Peer Coaching for More Effective Reference Service." *Reference Librarian*, 22 (1988), 245-60.

Isaacs, Julian M. "In-Service Training for Reference Work." *Library Association Record*, 71 (October 1969), 301-2.

Kolzina, Norma. "CE at the University of California, Berkeley." *College and Research Libraries News*, 43 (May 1982), 176-77.

Nitechi, Danuta A. "Competencies Required of Public Services Librarians to Use New Technologies." In *Professional Competencies – Technology and the Librarian*. Urbana, Illinois: University of Illinois. Graduate School of Library and Information Science, 1983, 43-97.

Rider, Lillian M. *Training Program for Reference Desk Staff*, 2nd ed. Arlington, Virginia: Educational Resources Information Center, ERIC Document ED 175 486, 1979.

Roberts, Anne F. "Myth: Reference Librarians Can Perform at the Reference Desk Immediately Upon Receipt of MLS. Reality: They Need Training Like Other Professionals." In *Academic Libraries: Myths and Realities; Proceedings of the Third National Conference of the Association of College and Research Libraries*. Chicago: Association of College and Research Libraries, 1984, 400-4.

Rolstad, Gary O. "Training Adult Services Librarians; Skills and Identity." *RQ*, 27 (Summer 1988), 474-7.

Rothstein, Samuel. "The Making of a Reference Librarian." *Library Trends*, 31 (Winter 1983), 375-99.

Shapiro, Beth J. "Ongoing Training and Innovative Structural Approaches." *Journal of Academic Librarianship*, 13 (May 1987), 75-6.

Shores, Louis. "We Who Teach Reference." *Journal of Education for Librarianship*, 5 (Spring 1965), 238-47.

Stabler, Karen Y. "Introductory Training of Academic Reference Librarians: A Survey." *RQ*, 26 (Spring 1987), 363-69.

Stephan, Sandy and others. "Reference Breakthrough in Maryland." *Public Libraries*, 27 (Winter 1988), 202-3.

Stieg, Margaret F. "Continuing Education and the Reference Librarian in the Academic and Research Library." *Library Journal*, 105 (December 15, 1980), 2547-51.

Summers, F. William. "Education for Reference Service." In *The Service Imperative for Libraries; Essays in Honor of Margaret E. Monroe*. Littleton, Colorado: Libraries Unlimited, 1982, 157-68.

Vink, C.M. *In-Service Training in South African Libraries*. Arlington, Virginia: Educational Resources Information Center, ERIC Document ED 267 820, 1979.

Young, William F. "Communicating with the New Reference Librarian: The Teaching Process." *Reference Librarian* 16 (Winter 1986), 223-31.

A Fast Track Over Rocky Roads: Continuing Education for Reference Librarians

Charlaine Ezell

SUMMARY. In order to keep pace with a sophisticated clientele who expect instantaneous delivery systems, reference service specialists who have typically looked at document delivery as their ultimate job function now need to look at satisfaction of patron needs. For reference librarianship to be successful, it has to be seen as a valuable and convenient commodity to the user, who comes to rely on the librarian and to trust in the necessity of the service as well as its availability.

Reference librarians, then, should look at broadening their services to reach individuals and specialized populations, not "the general public." They will revamp their present service programs to accomodate adult learners, small business owners, and communities with strong ethnic and cultural majorities.

Continuing education activities have to be offered in tandem with this transformation of the service itself so that librarians build on traditional reference skills by incorporating business administration, marketing, and adult learning as part of the total educational picture.

A friend of mine has always owned comfortable, four-door sedans. Then, one day, she went off to test drive a Porsche 911-Turbo. She returned both shaken and glowing from the trip.

"Are you really thinking of buying it?" I asked.

"I thought I was launching a rocket," she said, a little breathlessly. "In 5.8 seconds it accelerates to 60 miles per hour. And then it moves into second gear."

Ms. Ezell is the Continuing Education Specialist for the Library of Michigan, 717 West Allegan, Lansing, MI 48909.

It goes without saying that technology is changing the world, that life moves more quickly than it did years ago, that the number and frequency of demands made on our attention have increased for many beyond maximum stress levels. It is no surprise that my friend was both intrigued by the thought and overwhelmed by the speed.

What is seldom said is that technology has always made demands on the human psyche — from the days of pre-recorded history to the present. The rapid pace of technological changes is not the surprising new element, but rather the level of basic skills and competencies required of us to survive and grow in this world.

THE SPECIFIC, NOT THE GENERAL PUBLIC

This is certainly true of library science as a profession and for each specialization within it. Reference service librarians are beleaguered by a public whose number and frequency of demands for information have increased not only because of the population explosion, but also because that same public demands information without delays. They are also accustomed to the availability of information and swift gratification of their needs.

We are uncomfortable with the idea that we no longer serve "the general public," if indeed we ever did. We now, more than ever, serve specific publics — and we target many, many audiences. These publics are not homogeneous. Many of them do not recognize their own needs for information. Others are unable to take the initiative to search for it. Still other individuals — the functional illiterate person, the business owner, the representative of an ethnic group — require reference service specialists to extend traditional searches, to engage in perceptive reference interviews, and to reach beyond the bounds of traditional informational sources. These individuals are becoming the public reference librarians serve. In some cases, this has meant that the information these individuals require can be found, but is not always in a physical or environmental format that directly accomodates an individual's needs. For many, the reference tools needed to serve these people have not even been developed.

Reference librarians leave their colleges and universities, armed with their master's degrees, and are expected to move into overdrive their first day of employment. Reference librarianship is typically taught through formal academic degree programs that concentrate to two major areas: acquaintance with reference materials and components of the reference interview. Library science curriculums specialize in the treatment of such topics as the selection and use of various reference formats — encyclopedias, dictionaries, databases, etc. — but spent a smaller proportion of time developing the student's interpersonal skills required for a successful patron communication.

CONTEMPORARY REFERENCE EDUCATION

Once the degree program is completed, continuing education usually takes the form of on-the-job training, with coaching by colleagues and a supervisor, membership in professional organizations, mentoring, or structured continuing education such as workshops, internships, and the like. To develop interpersonal skills at the reference desk, one can find workshops on skill-building in perceptual development, questioning skills, and communication patterns. There are also many staff development activities, inservice programs, and vendor-sponsored workshops on mastering the various idiosyncrasies of different CD-ROMs and database searches.

These are really short-term solutions to the problem of providing continuing education for reference service specialists who will themselves be the primary providers of information and the custodians of channels of information in the future.

Little, if any, attention in today's continuing education offerings is given to the management of reference service — either in areas of demographic analysis, statistics, project planning and evaluation, or budgeting. These managerial skills are required of reference library practitioners moving into administrative positions, along with the responsibility for training and development of colleagues whom they supervise.

REFERENCE SERVICE FOR THE FUTURE

Eventually the accessibility of telecommunications and the sheer demand by the public for instantaneous service will require all libraries to supply information in technological formats. In the future, users of reference services will have no face-to-face contact with their reference librarian—their demands for information will be transmitted by satellite, fiber-optics, cable, microwave. There will be no eye contact, no opportunity for practicing open and inviting verbal and non-verbal communication, but a much greater need to literally read the patron's mind, as it is reflected in a request for information via non-human channels. And there will be less continuing education devoted to the mastery of various idiosyncratic database and CD-ROM packages, since compatibility and uniformity of all software and hardware will be the norm.

Similarly, the ways that continuing education is presently offered will undergo transformation. Today, the costs of providing such training—workshop formats, conferences in distant parts of a state or country, group or teams or task forces—and the unique kinds of planning and time necessary to sponsor workshops that demand the physical presence of people at any given time will preclude their sponsorship. In their place will be self-paced, learner-centered education, a personalized career development pattern that is supervised by trained coaches and mentors. In the future, reference librarians will want to find training that allows them to learn how to learn, and continuing education becomes at once a much broader and much more specific activity than it is now.

FUTURE FORCES

In 1983, the American Society for Training and Development in Washington, D.C., cited thirty-four "future forces" that would change the way we live and work. Of these, four were explicit in the ways that adults learn:

There will be more knowledge available about human learning and motivation. There will be an increase in technologies that facilitate learning. There will be an increased need for expanded thinking models to organize vast amounts of information. There will be an increase in the dominance of information processing as the major learning model.[1]

To a reference library specialist, the ASTD study emphasizes the need to understand how people learn and why. This will radically change the quantity and quality of reference services offered. No longer will the librarian be "the bridge" between the library collection and the user. The librarian will be an interface. The users will look to the librarians to process requests and to screen out or read into the request what the users themselves would — in short, to make decisions on the value and usefulness of materials, by placing the librarian in the role of the user. Users will expect the reference librarian not only to organize and retrieve documents but also to process the information into a format of value to the user.

Already many public librarians are requested to provide medical and legal information to patrons who unassumingly expect the librarian to "give them information." Basic competencies for reference librarians will move beyond document delivery, beyond information delivery, to problem analysis, data research and reduction, decision making, presentation skills, and problem solving.

This type of reference service implies a high level of trust and mutual understanding, and far less disinterestedness between the user and the librarian than is considered appropriate now.

A RELATIONSHIP BASED ON TRUST

It erodes the trust relationship if the reference service is not available when the user needs it. When businesses and industries can operate within minutes to span a globe with information that can be updated within microseconds, is it unreasonable to believe that libraries will also be expected to respond equally quickly? We already know that the time factor is so crucial for many people that they will pay for the service in order to have it on time. A client waiting several days or weeks for the results of a database search or an interlibrary loan request will be understandably frustrated and look elsewhere to satisfy his or her information needs. More libraries will want to follow the lead of Memphis/Shelby County Public Library which opened a QUIC information center that answers phone questions in five minutes or less.[2] We are looking at the need to provide reference service that is available 24 hours a day, 365 days a year.

Once the trust relationship has been developed, it will require nurturing. An Opinion Research Corporation study shows that "while most Americans are generally happy with the service they receive from businesses, at least one-third of them believe businesses are performing unsatisfactorily in four crucial areas: providing prompt attention with little waiting time, providing solutions to problems that come up with the product or services sold, providing clear, detailed information, providing personalized attention to meet special needs."[3]

CUSTOMIZING REFERENCE SERVICE

Libraries are public service businesses and the same criticisms of the private sector may be true of us. We know we should customize our reference services not only to the general public, which has for years meant the white, employed or educated walk-in traffic, but to each and every individual user. But the minority populations are now the majority in some parts of the country: 46% in Texas, 43% in California, and 32% in New York State. California is one state which took the initiative in sponsoring such programs as the 1989 CORE program, which has as one of its two major goals, the improvement of the ability of libraries to do reference work with special populations, specifically Asian and Hispanic patrons and physically handicapped clients.[4]

For some libraries, this means revamping the entire reference collection simply because it is geared to a predominantly English-speaking public with traditional tastes, learning styles, and reading preferences. In tandem with this is the need to provide multi-lingual reference staffs, tools, wayfinding systems, brochures and public events in the first language of the clientele we serve. Many libraries now have educational information centers for the unemployed or the uneducated. Many have TTDs for the deaf, reference service for the homebound, reference and government contract information for business owners, and materials in various literacy levels and physical formats, but not every library can provide all these services to all the specialized populations completely.

In a provocative report for the State-National Information Network for Independent Higher Education, Dr. Harold Hodgkinson notes that

> Higher education will have to get used to a smaller contingent of white, middle-class students from suburban backgrounds in their entering classes, and will have to provide new programs in order to attract minorities, older adults, and programs offered in conjunction with industry, the military, and other users of educational services.[5]

There is another implication in the Hodgkinson report for libraries: the need to develop cooperative networks of service between educational systems and themselves; between the public and private sectors. Continuing education will be necessary in order to show librarians how to predict, plan and implement such networks.

MARKETING THE BENEFITS

Another way to establish this trust relationship is to clearly market the benefits of use to the proper clientele. Again libraries have tried to advertise "reading" and "information" as ends in themselves instead of the benefits that accrue from reading and accessing information. We could learn from Charles Revson, founder of Revlon Cosmetics, who understood exactly what the customer wanted. "On the factory floors, " he said, "our product is cosmetics, but in the department stores, we sell hope."[6]

Librarians typically look at their profession in broad, comprehensive terms. Far better would it be to look at it narrowly, specifically, on a one-to-one basis. What reference librarians should be aggressively marketing is not books or information, but advantages that appeal to the consumer: service which is "fast" or "free" or "accurate." Our consumers are interested in making good grades, upgrading their businesses, finding a safe place to stash a child after school, looking for a comfortable spot to relax, saving time, saving work, being more attractive, improving themselves, and making money. Our reference policies often discourage the use of the library by the parents of latchkey children, the classroom of students simultaneously needing a single piece of information, the contest participants.

Another obstacle that must be overcome is the persistence of reference librarians to become so enamored of the comprehensive nature of information that they give the user too broad and general an array of material. Many times the users do not want a book; they want an answer. And they do not want to know how the answer was obtained; they simply want the librarian to find it for them.

LEARNING FROM THE PRIVATE SECTOR

Regretfully, not every reference librarian sees the development of interpersonal communication skills as an integral part of quality reference service. Nor do they see marketing, targeting specific audiences, identifying service needs, or developing new styles of service as more important than the time they spend serving the public they have come to serve well already. One of the major goals of continuing education for reference librarians, therefore, has to be the determination of those skills which allow librarians to identify, package, and promote new reference services in such a way that they reach the user for whom they are intended.

Business and industry have a history of analyzing the demographics and sifting consumer needs; libraries are only beginning to do this. Businesses take it for granted that a certain percentage of their research and development budgets will be applied to the development of new products, market surveys, and analysis of consumer needs as well as for the promotion of existing products. If this education is given to librarians at all, it is given to administrators, not the reference specialist.

Continuing education today builds on formal education programs in library schools. We should require of these that they become active providers not only of traditional course offerings, but also that they enter into partnerships with colleges of business administration (including public administration, marketing, and public relations) and less so with colleges of education to offer coursework on the administration of a public service agency. Reference librarians themselves should also take advantage of opportunities in other fields for learning to serve users with specialized information needs — adult learners, literacy education, career development and counseling. Many have only recently been established as formalized academic programs, such as degree programs in adult and continuing education.

CE THAT IS TWO STEPS AHEAD

For those looking to advance degrees in librarianship, the declining number of accredited programs is a serious obstacle. However, in the matter of continuing education, there is an extensive array available — much of it not found within traditional library continuing education parameters.

Too often we limit our field of vision to classes or workshops, or to membership in professional organizations. However, an individual's potential is broadened by exposure to continuing education *that may relate indirectly to future job functions*, not only the current one. In this way, exposure to fresh ideas, particularly through working relationships with non-librarians, provides a stimulant to improved performance in the present job and often leads to others.

The proliferation of non-library related networks, organizations, volunteer associations, etc., obviates the need for a reference librarian to feel limited, even in small rural communities, to a narrow range of continuing education interests. Certainly for many individuals, committee work, chairing and participating in meetings of any organization will be a major source of continuing education in leadership skills, management of budgets, laws of organizational governance and group dynamics. This will inevitably contribute to personal career development. Equally, it not only helps librarians to stay abreast of what happens in a community, it allows those librarians to contribute to and bring about those changes.

It is hoped that the business and corporate community will illustrate to the public sector how essential it is to provide inservice training, both for the management as well as for the support staff, under the supervision of skilled trainers and human resource development specialists. It is the norm for executives, especially middle managers, to undergo extensive training upon promotion to a new position. The costs of such training are cheerfully paid; the benefits to the corporation or company are manifold. The average *monthly* payoff for training for managers is over $10,000.[7]

THE WILLINGNESS TO TAKE RISKS

Although many librarians will undertake responsibility for their own continuing education, they must have the support of their supervisors and governing bodies in terms of financial support and administrative leaves of absence. More importantly, it requires that the administrators be willing to listen, support and implement the new ideas a librarian returning from a workshop, training session, or conference activity brings back to the workplace. Unfortunately for many reference librarians, regular and frequent attendance at functions designed to further continuing education is not always seen as either necessary or newsworthy. Even more rarely does participation in such functions result in an upgraded salary, increased benefits, or promotion.

Many state libraries, library associations, consortiums, and vendors of reference products have set up structured continuing education programs. Many library systems, too, are employing personnel trained in human resource development, just as they employ fundraisers, grant-writers, and automation specialists. Training coordinators within a library are responsible for providing opportunities for staff development based on identified needs. Their background is in adult learning theory — and they are uniquely suited to develop inhouse programs that insure that maximum learning occurs. One such program developed which allowed trainers and reference service specialists to join forces was the "Improving Reference Skills Workshop"[8] sponsored in Maryland. Here the emphasis was on learning desirable reference skills and ensuring that they would be practiced once the librarian returned to the workplace. Every continuing education program should be planned with just such learning transfer in mind. Through the use of peer coaching, action plans, learning contracts, group reinforcement, and sympathetic mentors, the reference librarian can broaden and deepen any learning experience.

A HEAD START FOR OURSELVES

Reference librarians interested in planning their continuing education often have to take responsibility themselves to select from the offerings available. Sometimes continuing education is where you find it. Some of our most valuable resources will have to be fashioned out of the materials and opportunities at our disposal, in the style of Robinson Crusoe. Librarianship, unlike other professions, gives individuals a head start: we are able to investigate through our own agencies many of the print and non-print resources on any subject. Because of the range of interests housed within libraries, we can pursue any topic of interest to us. As for future trends in librarianship, simply scanning the want ads for open positions will indicate the skills and qualifications that are desirable: the ability to manage, to handle specialized collections, to organize information within technological parameters, to work with special populations. The writer and journalist, Shana Alexander, once said that we should plan our careers by knowing where we want to be two jobs from now. Worthwhile advice, but for many of us, our careers in the future have not even been conceived of yet. This is the hallmark of an information age.

Continuing education involves more than just commitment. It involves risk. Like any change, learning new skills is resisted. Only by rewarding attempts by individuals and library staffs for trying new services, even if they result in occasional failures, will we encourage the creation and spread of better reference services. We are engaged in the never-ending, ever-changing process of providing service to a population that is itself ever-changing. We must base all our decisions about reference service on our experiences in the past, yet our decisions will bring about the future.

Like my friend who searches for the car that fills her speed-demon dreams, we will assume some risks, and find ourselves in a world where the pace is incredibly accelerated but the roads are by no means paved.

REFERENCES

1. "Future Forces Affecting the T & D Field," a pre-study questionaire developed by the American Society of Training and Development, Washington, D.C., 1983.

2. Card, Judy, "Staff Development at Memphis/Shelby County Public Library and Information Center," *Public Libraries*, Summer, 1988, pp. 103-105.

3. "New Study Shows Consumers 'Dissatisfied with Service,'" *Sales and Marketing Executive Report*, April 26, 1989, p. 1.

4. *California State Library Newsletter*, December, 1988, No. 96, p. 9.

5. Hodgkinson, Dr. Harold, "Guess Who's Coming to College: Your Students in 1990." A Research Report from the State-National Information Network for Independent Higher Education. Published by the National Institute of Independent Colleges and Universities, January, 1983.

6. Von Oech, Roger, *A Kick In the Seat of the Pants*, Harper & Row, 1986, p. 129.

7. _____, *A Whack on the Side of the Head*, Warner Books, 1983, p. 28.

8. Gers, Ralph, and Seward, Lillie J., "Improving Reference Performance: Results of a Statewide Study," Maryland State Department of Education, division of Library Development and Services, Baltimore.

The Reference Librarian's Critical Skill: Critical Thinking and Professional Service

Threasa L. Wesley

SUMMARY. What is the most critical ability that a new librarian should cultivate in preparation for a reference career? Some would claim communication skills are vital; some would advise concentration on extensive knowledge of reference sources; others might state a case for computer literacy skills. This article argues that the single most important skill for a reference librarian to possess is the ability to think critically about the use of reference materials. Illustrations are given to demonstrate the primacy of this proficiency in all areas of reference responsibility and suggestions are made concerning the need for increased focus on critical thinking in education and training programs.

What is a reference librarian's most critical skill? A great variety of proficiencies are presented in library schools and in library science journals. Students in graduate programs encounter courses designed to teach competence in areas such as management techniques, online searching, use of specialized reference tools, and communication skills. Skimming through library journals one finds articles on fund raising efforts, policy writing procedures, staff supervision issues, resource sharing goals, and literally hundreds of other activities that a reference librarian will probably encounter while working in the field. Indeed, in a career requiring abilities in so many diverse areas, how can one prepare adequately to enter the profession? Must one divide the brief time in a graduate program into small fragments to gain instruction in the many responsibilities tied to reference work? Or is it possible to establish a core of pri-

Threasa L. Wesley is Coordinator of Instructional Services, Steely Library, Northern Kentucky University, Highland Heights, KY 41076.

mary skills which will form a more integrated preparation? If it is possible to determine a focused nucleus, these critical skills must be defined clearly in order to prepare these new professionals for successful careers.

THE REFERENCE LIBRARIAN'S RESPONSIBILITY

Perhaps the nature of these core skills can be defined best by stepping back from the surface perspective of the individual responsibilities a reference librarian holds — reference assistance, collection development, bibliographic instruction, public relations, etc. — to get a broader view. This broader examination helps to clarify the role that a reference librarian is attempting to fulfill through these multitudinous activities. That professional role is to serve his or her community as an information-use consultant. Explicitly, this means that, on behalf of library patrons, the librarian should make informed choices among information sources based on analysis of individual needs and a critical knowledge of reference sources. Some theorists argue strongly against this interventionist view of the librarian's role in information use, claiming that the patrons should have full freedom to select information sources for themselves. If this philosophy is followed, the librarian's role is then limited to a directional one, merely facilitating access to the full range of information available. However, when evaluating the contribution that reference librarians can make to society, the emphasis rightly belongs on the verb "choose." The responsibility each reference librarian faces at the reference desk, whether in a public, school, special or academic library is to assist patrons to choose the best sources of information for their particular information need. As professionals, librarians cannot justify being passive channels of information. James Rice wrote in "The Hidden Role of Librarians," that one would not go to a doctor with an ailment and expect to be offered a list of drugs that could possibly be taken for the problem. Patients expect the physician to use his or her professional knowledge to make a selection.[1] Similarly, in our information producing culture, each patron has a wide variety of information sources "to take" for an information need. Rarely will a library user be faced with difficulty in locating citations for information on a topic. This is particularly true with the ever growing numbers of computer-produced access tools covering increasingly greater numbers of information sources. Even in smaller libraries with traditionally limited sources, such as school and special libraries, reference staffs are finding that with computer access they can affordably offer their patrons large databases of information through online commercial products and shared union catalogs. In all but the career-long research endeavors, the volume of cited information on almost any subject can no longer be digested and effectively used by a single individual.

A second difficulty has developed for users trying to use libraries independently. Perhaps also as a result of the development of computer-assisted bibliographic techniques, producers of research guides are favoring the development of all-encompassing indexes and bibliographies rather than selective, critical listings. Obviously, users require more active research assistance to select source materials from these extensive, non-evaluative listings.

With this understanding of current research materials and practices, reference librarians have a professional responsibility to use their expertise and act as information consultants, providing a critical selection of sources, making evaluations and choices for the patron, and assisting the patron in making connections between the sources and his or her individual information requirements.

PREPARATION FOR A PROFESSIONAL ROLE

With the role of expert consultant defined for the reference librarian, it becomes clear that the most valuable skill a reference librarian can cultivate is an ability to think critically about the use of information sources. This analytical thought is the one thread that runs through all quality reference services, connecting efforts to form the best information service for library patrons. A reference librarian's ability in the critical use of reference materials will have obvious implications for all of his or her functions—in-person reference assistance, teaching library use skills to patrons, collection development, online searching, etc. For more than a decade educators in all academic fields have been actively studying the part critical thinking skills can play in preparation for a career. Attributes of graduates who have acquired these conceptual, evaluative skills include the ability to think creatively, adapt to new environments, integrate broad ranges of experiences into problem solving, develop innovative approaches to problem solving, recognize long-term effects of one's actions and have a sense of social responsibility. Certainly, a list of qualities such as these seems tailor-made for a successful reference career. Librarians are needed who can analyze the information problems of our field and create solutions. These problems include those presented by individual reference questions as well as more complex situations such as a lack of adequate information sources in an area of research, the need to choose for purchase among competing publications, or the expressed need for new or improved reference services. The decisions and choices involved in all these areas of reference service require just these thoughtful, analytical, evaluative approaches to the use of reference materials.

ESTABLISHED EXPERIENCES WITH CRITICAL THINKING IN REFERENCE WORK

Perhaps the one area where the need for critical, evaluative thinking about reference sources is most explicitly recognized in library science education and training programs is reference collection development. Certainly, discussions take place concerning the need for effective decision-making and selection as well as the criteria for these decisions such as relevancy, accuracy, perspective, and bias. Library science students learn to use evaluative tools such as reviewing sources and critical bibliographies. Hopefully they are also encouraged to evaluate the reviewers as they become more proficient critical users of information.

Since collection development work has a long history founded on critical decision-making, perhaps a more appropriate model for the development of a philosophy of critical thinking in all areas of reference work can be seen in the specific field of bibliographic instruction. In the early stages, efforts to instruct library users were concentrated on facility tours and the mechanics of using specific reference sources, i.e., citation guides, descriptions of indexes in an encyclopedia set, discussions of how call numbers are assigned, etc. This instructional approach corresponds directly to the librarian who limits his or her assistance at the reference desk to giving "tours" of how to use certain reference books. Later, concern in the instructional field turned to concentrating on research strategies in presentations to users. The strategies were standard, intended to be applicable to all subjects. This stage in the development of bibliographic instruction theory can be seen as analogous to the approach of reference librarians who make some suggestions concerning the types of reference materials that could serve a particular information request. However, most librarians stop short of recommending specific titles. Recognition of the need to individualize research methods began to be considered in this type of instruction as researchers were asked to select specific reference materials to plug into each step of the research plan. Nevertheless, the strategies often appeared to students as straight-forward, simplistic processes. The true intellectual demands and complexities of library research were not adequately conveyed. Today, bibliographic instructional librarians are teaching researchers the critical thinking skills necessary for them to effectively devise individualized research strategies through analysis of their own information needs. Moreover, librarians are now teaching the evaluation and selection of sources which fulfill those strategies, asking patrons to question the authority, bias, and perspective of the information they read and hear before choosing sources.[2]

Reference librarians should be using these same critical thinking techniques as they evaluate and use their reference collections in service to their patrons. Truly, librarians engaged in bibliographic instruction have progressed from serving simply as guides to buildings to being teachers of critical research skills. Isn't it time this professional approach was extended to the mainstay of reference work — individual reference assistance? The following description of the critical use of reference materials in the standard practices of reference assistance will demonstrate how an evolution similar to that which has taken place in bibliographic instruction could significantly improve general reference assistance.

COLLECTION ANALYSIS

The process of recommending information sources to patrons in reference service begins with an evaluative examination of materials available in the current collection. Although critical examination of potential purchases for a reference collection is often practiced, the critical analysis of owned sources is less frequently undertaken. Basic questions concerning scope, purpose, and quality need to be considered to evaluate the potential relevance of the source. Is this information source selective or comprehensive for the field? What were the criteria for any selections made by the editor? Is this work intended to support advanced or elementary research? Is this a summary, factual source or a representation of the varying viewpoints in this field? What biases — political, social, temporal, etc. — are evident? Is the research still timely? Is the source successful in presenting the information as it claims? This type of examination which relates directly to the content of the source carries far greater import for reference service than does any preparation concentrating on the mechanics of using a source, i.e., interpreting citation format, locating indexes, etc. Phyllis Reich wrote that the tools of library research, i.e., reference materials, are "much like a piece of laboratory equipment whose operation requires some special skills and knowledge, but is incidental to the main purpose."[3] While the *Science Citation Index* appears unconquerable to a new reference librarian, manipulation of any "equipment" comes rather easily with time. The librarian's time spent learning reference sources would be best spent evaluating the appropriateness of the source's content.

DIRECT REFERENCE ASSISTANCE

The critical thinking librarian then uses this foundation of an in-depth knowledge of his or her collection's strengths to build a specific search strategy and choose relevant sources in response to individual requests for reference assistance. Appropriate sources are thoughtfully selected. The individual who asks for *Readers' Guide* is not merely asked if he or she "understands how the index works." Rather, the critical thinking librarian discusses with the patron the subject of the research to determine if this or other sources should be used. Nor should the patron who requests information on gun control be bombarded with every general news report found through a newspaper index, from liberal editorial pieces to legal treatises on the constitutionality of these laws. This approach constitutes a limited service and is a non-professional approach. Rather the critical thinking librarian spends time in the reference interview gathering details about the patron's intended use for the material and the patron's level of experience with the topic. Is he or she gathering varying perspectives for making a voting decision? Is the patron writing the text for a speech to a support group for bereaved individuals who have lost family members through violence involving guns? Is this a student who has already decided to oppose gun control because of one book he/she has read, but needs at least ten sources for a class project? Does this patron have the experience to effectively use a comprehensive, uncritical bibliography? Would a highly selective source serve better?

Armed with these details about the patron and the intended use of the information, the critical thinking librarian can then outline a strategy for retrieving appropriate information. The parameters of the subject focus and the level of investigation planned combine with the librarian's experience with his or her resources to form a specific research plan. Relevant sources are chosen and effective access points are discovered. In addition, the critical thinking librarian estimates the quantity and level of information required. In some cases, suggestions are even made to encourage use of sources that present information or concerns that the patron may be overlooking. Indeed, the responsibility to choose, select and advise patrons regarding appropriate information sources should never be taken as a license to censor points of view at odds with the librarian's values.

It is in consulting services such as these that the reference librarian plays a truly professional role. As the critical expert on information sources, the librarian is the person who can and should contribute knowledge concerning a source's bias, determine the most appropriate subject headings, and have the perspective necessary to anticipate the variety of information needed for the research.

WHY REFERENCE LIBRARIANS ARE NOT UNDERTAKING THIS RESPONSIBILITY

Few would disagree that the previous discussion illustrates the value of the critical use of information sources in reference desk assistance. This is but one example of the impact this working focus can make in the professional activities of reference librarians. Novices in the field should be prepared to undertake the full range of critical decision-making and thus serve their community effectively as information consultants. Many library educators claim that this thoughtful analytical approach to reference service is exactly what they are teaching in their graduate programs. If true, this educational background is not always translated into practice. Why do we see articles in professional journals recommending sources such as *InfoTrac* CD indexes based solely upon the popularity of its mechanical aspects while ignoring the questionable quality of the indexing in the source?[4] How else can we explain the habitual responses of reference librarians who simply tell a patron that a requested source is not owned rather than discussing the subject of the request that might be covered by other sources? How many times is someone led to *World Book* without first investigating the information needed? Why do bibliographic instruction handouts offer exhaustive listings of sources often too long and tangential for the intended audience to absorb? Why aren't the reviews written by librarians more evaluative than descriptive?[5] With so much of this non-evaluative work going on in our field, library educators and reference supervisors must re-evaluate the focus of their work with new librarians. Obviously, a stronger, more explicit emphasis needs to be stated in the education and training programs. Indeed, the nucleus of these efforts should be the critical use of reference materials in all phases of reference work.

HOW WE CAN ENCOURAGE REFERENCE LIBRARIANS TO OFFER CRITICAL SERVICE

All members of the library profession's community bear responsibility for encouraging librarians to think critically. As a starting point, library science students and professionals need to be regularly confronted, through course work and library science literature, with the requirements of professional reference services. A clear, explicit emphasis on critical thinking skills sensitizes librarians to their full role as information consultants. Beyond this philosophical grounding in their critical role, library science students need practice in making qualitative decisions and choices regarding reference sources and services. Course content should emphasize communication, learning, and behavioral theories as an appropriate base for these future decisions rather than presenting mechanical skills such as A-V production as a foundation. Emphasis should be placed on the many resources we have for critically judging reference materials — evaluative bibliographies, reviewing sources, ranking of journals, guides to subject area literatures, etc.

Library science courses, as is true with any academic study, can suffer from over-abstraction. Students should have opportunities to apply theories and struggle over real-life decisions realizing that one standard policy does not fit all situations. Critical decision-making activities should be a major portion of each course. For example, students in reference courses could be asked to review and select certain sources for study rather than merely following a pre-scribed list from the instructor. Assignments could help students analyze various levels of service in different types of libraries and for patrons with differing levels of experience. Investigations should be undertaken into the effects differing communication styles can have on the success of instructional presentations for specific types of audiences. In short, the focus of all coursework should be that individual decisions, requiring critical thinking on the part of the librarian, need to be made in each aspect of reference work. Perhaps potential library science students should even be encouraged to take electives or concentrate their undergraduate work in liberal studies where thinking/decision-making skills can be polished.

Once librarians are working in a reference position, they need conditions supportive of the time required to fulfill their role as information-use consultants. Library administrators need to recognize the labor-intensive nature of this type of professional work. Staffing and procedures need to be developed to allow adequate time for in-depth analysis of reference sources and extensive contact with patrons in reference interviews.

Reference librarians, themselves, can pave the way for acceptance of their role as information-use advisors by working with target groups of patrons prior to the actual requests for information. For example, an academic librarian can set up informational programs for faculty on designing assignments that REQUIRE critical use of information sources. Business librarians can alert patrons to new evaluative bibliographies in specific areas of interest. Public librarians can send recommendations to their business patrons concerning end-user sources most valuable for their work. In this way the librarian is actually moving beyond his or her primary goal of critically selecting information for specific requests to a larger societal role of educating members of the community concerning the importance of being critical consumers of information themselves.

CONCLUSION

Reference librarians daily face a complex challenge in choosing among a vast array of information sources for very specific, individual information needs. The best preparation new professionals in the field can receive to prepare for this challenge is to obtain a sound grounding in the primacy of this evaluative role as a selector/consultant and have opportunities to develop the critical thinking skills required to make these evaluations. Those in our field responsible for education and training will serve these new librarians well by focusing their efforts on developing these critical thinking abilities, preparing them to both accept and succeed in their role as information-use consultants.

REFERENCES

1. Rice, James. "The Hidden Role of Librarians," *Library Journal* (January 1989) 114(1):58-59.

2. A brief list of leaders in this development includes Jon Lindgren, Mona McCormick, Mary Reichel, Topsy Smalley, Harold Tuckett and Carla Stoffle. Others are also making significant contributions.

3. Reich, Phyllis. "Choosing a Topic in a Research Methods-Oriented Library Instructional Program," *Research Strategies* (Fall 1986) 4(4):186.

4. Reese, Carol. "Manual Indexes Versus Computer-Aided Indexes: Comparing the Readers' Guide to Periodical Literature to InfoTrac II," *RQ* (Spring 1988) 27(3):384-89 and Guyonneau, Christine H. "Magazine Index Plus or Academic Index?" *College & Research Library News* (July 1988) 49(7):430-34 are representative of the few articles examining the reference value of the InfoTrac indexes. A significantly larger number of articles deal exclusively with the popularity of the printing capabilities, convenience, and speed of use of these indexes. Examples of these numerous user popularity studies include Flynn, Ellen P. "User Reactions to InfoTrac in an Undergraduate Library," *College & Research*

Library News (January 1989) 50(1):14-16; Van Arsdale, William O. and Ostrye, Anne T. "InfoTrac: A Second Opinion," *American Libraries* (July/August, 1986) 17(7):514-15; *Choice* review (October 1987):292; Stephens, Kent. "Info-Trac: Laserdisc Technology Enters Mainstream," *American Libraries* (April 1986) 17(4):252.

    5. James Rettig accurately states that "a number of reviewers . . . produce slipshod, superficial evaluations." "The Reference Reviewer's Responsibilities," *The Reference Librarian* (Fall 1986) 15:22. He attributes this failing, in part, to the fact that "Nobody teaches would-be reference book reviewers how to review reference books." Ibid:21.

Library User Instruction
in the Curriculum:
Background and Status Update

Charles D. Patterson

SUMMARY. Teaching patrons to use library resources unaided has long been recognized as highly desirable, yet the education of reference librarians to do this important instruction has been scattered and haphazard. Slow to develop and emerge as a separate course in library school curricula, this article reports that the situation has now changed, due primarily to the organized efforts and perseverance of practitioners and library and information science educators.

HISTORICAL PERSPECTIVE

Those familiar with the history of library education in America know the significance of the study undertaken in 1920-1921 by Charles C. Williamson which thoroughly examined the then existing fifteen programs which prepared men and women for careers in library work. The results of that investigation are documented in the landmark publication *Training for Library Service* which appeared in 1923. It is beyond the scope of this paper to detail the extensiveness of that study or to cite its major recommendations for the improvement of library training, evolving as it had from its beginning in 1887, to its status, as perceived by Williamson, near the end of the first quarter of this century. It is important, however, to emphasize that common in and central to the curricula of all library schools visited by Williamson, was the study of reference work.

Charles D. Patterson is Professor, School of Library and Information Science, Louisiana State University, 267 Coates Hall, Baton Rouge, LA 70803.

Quoting the Williamson report, the study of reference work included the following:

> A study of the standard works of reference, general and special encyclopedias, dictionaries, annuals, indexes to periodicals, ready reference manuals of every kind, special bibliographies, and the more important newspapers and periodicals. Works of similar scope are compared, and the limitations of each pointed out. Lists of questions made up from practical experience are given, and the method of finding the answers discussed in the class. Problems in selection of reference books, especially for the small library, are assigned and talked over. The aim of this course is not only to promote familiarity with a considerable number of well-known reference works, but also to give the student some idea of the method in the handling of books, to familiarize him with the use of indexes, tables of contents, and varying forms of arrangement, and, finally, to suggest some method of comparison and evaluation.

> Lectures and problems from the standpoint of college and university libraries, large reference libraries or departments. Principal topics: interlibrary loan coordination and cooperation in reference work; organization of reference material; law libraries and law books; care and use of manuscripts; medical libraries; patents publications; legislative reference; local history and genealogy; publications of learned societies; dissertations; indexes to foreign periodicals; trade and professional journals.[1]

In the Williamson report, of the eleven schools indicating the number of hours devoted to classroom instruction in the major and more important subjects in the curriculum, the number of hours devoted to reference work ranged from 30-69 hours, with the average being 48 hours. Only the study of cataloging (60 hours average) and book selection (50 hours average) ranked respectively first and second above the study of reference work. Reference work was secure within library science curricula of 1923.

CHANGE AND PROGRESS IN TEACHING REFERENCE

Although the study of reference work remains an essential part of all library school programs, there have been significant changes in content and in how reference work is taught since Williamson conducted his study, as library school curricula have adjusted to meet the mercurial demands of an information society. Three observable changes, or phenomena, deserve mention, all of which have evolved to major prominence in the four decades following the end of World War II.

First, in examining the quotation above, not only are the aim and course content specified, but also the methodology used in teaching the student to acquire an understanding of the way in which the beginning librarian learns to identify sources and locate information in the library, i.e., "Lists of questions made up from practical experience are given, and the method of finding the answers discussed in class."[2] Although discarded as archaic and useless by some library educators, this method of teaching reference is still widely used. Also emerging and gaining popularity in the 1960s was the "case study" method of teaching reference work which has, as its central objective, the study and analysis of a situation and the conclusions drawn as a result of detailed examination of that situation. An approach now often combined with the traditional question and answer format, the "case study" method is a widely accepted vehicle for teaching reference concepts and functions, and its advocates stand firm in proclaiming its effectiveness.

The second, and more dramatic change in reference work and its teaching, has been the introduction of the computer and its rapid and direct application to library operations, a phenomenon that has affected how we gather, store and disseminate data, and one that is now integral and fundamental to our information society as we move more toward the brink of an electronic revolution. Information specialists, as reference librarians are now frequently called, complete their professional education with a knowledge and understanding of the computer, its application to reference work, and the many reference sources available in CD-ROM and other formats.

The third phenomenon provides the focus of this paper. This change has been the resurgence of interest in and the increasing need and desirability for the library patron, particularly those in the academic setting, to unaided locate information in the library. Evolving under various nomenclature as bibliographic instruction (BI), library user education, and instruction in library use, the concept of teaching the patron how to use the library developed very early. In his article "Origins of Bibliographic Instruction in Academic Libraries," John Mark Tucker writes, "The birth and early years of bibliographic instruction in academic libraries took place in the 1876 to 1914 period," and that "many of the major issues that now demand our attention were articulated in this period."[3] The immediacy of this latter statement is as true today as it was when Tucker made his observation in 1978.

Of particular interest in Tucker's identifying the origins of bibliographic instruction in academic libraries in the period 1876 to 1914 is the realization that none of the library schools included in the Williamson study mention the training of the reference librarian for teaching use of the library. This is entirely plausible for as Williamson points out, in writing about the teaching qualifications of library school faculty of that time, "It is not at all surprising that among library school instructors special skill in teaching is not conspicuous. Only 7 per cent of the instructors have had any kind of training in the science or art of teaching. It seems safe to assume that none at all has had the slightest instruction in the methodology of the teaching of library subjects."[4] And further that "only 20 per cent, of library school teachers bring to the library school any experience in teaching. The outstanding successes on the faculties are found almost entirely within the 20 per cent, who had behind them good teaching experiences in school or college before taking up library school instruction."[5] Library school faculty ill-prepared in teaching methodology would, understandably, not attempt to instruct others in what they themselves were lacking.

ORIGINS OF A BI PROGRAM

At Louisiana State University, the origin of attempts to educate the library user date from the 1930s when Ella V. Aldrich, a graduate of Columbia University School of Library Service, established the Department of Books and Libraries. *Books and Libraries*, by

Aldrich, first appeared in 1936 and it was used as a textbook for the one-credit course required for all freshmen at the university. Aldrich modified later editions for general use by other academic libraries, and for more than thirty years her book was adopted as a text for similar courses taught throughout America, making it one of the first of its kind. Although the Department of Books and Libraries no longer exists at LSU a one-credit course, not now a general requirement, is taught by university reference librarians and is available to all students and it is required by some departments in the university.

REFERENCE LIBRARIANS ARE TEACHING LIBRARIANS

By the 1950s there was general concern among academic librarians regarding students' knowledge of the library as a resource to aid them in achieving success in the work. Some of the progressive institutions of that era offered a course designed to improve library competency and several tests were developed to administer to incoming freshmen. If a student did well on the test, the student was exempt from taking the course.[6] Who taught the course and who administered the test? Invariably it was the librarians, members of the reference staff, who assumed this instructional responsibility. Were these librarians prepared to teach? Where and in what manner did they acquire the knowledge and skills that would make them effective in the classroom? Although some librarians had had previous teaching experience, those who did not were faced with problems in adjusting to the role of teacher. This situation exists today, This is a task for which many librarians are ill equipped, and it is one for which their formal library education has not prepared them. Teaching use of the library has not been a part of the reference course taken by most librarians while in library school, and such preparation was unknown in the study of reference at the time Williamson made his report.

By the 1960s the academic reference librarian had become a teaching librarian, but the preparation of the teaching aspects of the reference librarians' job had not assimilated into the reference curricula of our library schools. In short, the full potential of the third change was not being met.

BI LIBRARIANS ORGANIZE

Confronted with what then had become a common and prevalent situation, academic librarians within the American Library Association (ALA) "in 1967 formed the Committee on Instruction in Library Use. In 1971, the Bibliographic Instruction task force, which became the Bibliographic Section (BIS) in 1977, was created within the Association of Colleges and Research Libraries (ACRL). In 1977 ACRL published its *Guidelines for Bibliographic Instruction in Academic Libraries* and the Library Instruction Round Table (LIRT) was organized within ALA. Project LOEX (Library Orientation and Instruction Exchange) was established in 1972, with the primary objective of collection, organizing, and disseminating bibliographic instruction materials. LOEX, ACRL/BIS, and LIRT have been the prime movers in advocating the cause for library user education."[7] In a 1980 article "Training and Education of Library Instruction Librarians" Sharon Hogan states:

> The thrust of the BI education effort over the past decade had been in the area of continuing education, as evidenced by an ever-increasing number of programs, reinforced by other responses as well: library association committees devoted solely to education; clearinghouses established to exchange materials and ideas; continuing education seminars offered by library schools; a wealth of writing and publishing on techniques, methodology and local implementation; and most recently, a move toward in-service training programs by individual libraries.[8]

Much of what Hogan states in the above quotation has become reality. Diligent library leaders, extensively involved in BI activities, have been successful in planning and mounting workshops and conference programs devoted to bibliographic instruction. LOEX continues to do a brisk business as a BI national clearinghouse, and director Teresa Mensching reports that statistics and activities have increased during recent years. She states that "at the end of 1988, the LOEX Clearinghouse had 565 college, public, school and special libraries as paid members, the highest number in five years. The number of sample instructional materials loaned to member and non-member contracts also increased.. In 1988, 9,827 items circulated, the largest number since 1983. Reporting on a 1987 LOEX National BI Survey,[9] Mensching states that "of 1826 academic U.S. libraries which were sent a copy of the questionnaire, 834 (45.7%) returned completed forms. Three hundred seventy-seven (72.9%) of the member libraries that were sent questionnaires responded, while four hundred fifty-seven (34.9%) of the non-member libraries returned forms. I think this is a good indication of sustained interest and activity in bibliographic instruction." Finally, as Mensching points out, "the annual LOEX National Library Instruction Conference held each May usually 'sells out' with over 150 participants."[10] The LOEX Clearinghouse is fulfilling its role as a national center for dissemination of information and materials as BI activities accelerate and expand.

GROWTH IN BI LITERATURE

There also has been an unprecedented increase in journal articles, bibliographies and monographs devoted to BI published recently. Barbara Wittkopf, in her fine summary article on bibliographic instruction in the 1988 *ALA Yearbook*, the first of its kind in this publication, declared that "1987 was a banner year for bibliographic instruction."[11] In addition to documenting the many activities, accomplishments and publications, she notes also that 1987 marked the tenth anniversary of the founding of the ACRL Bibliographic Instruction Section (BIS) and the Library Instruction Round Table (LIRT), a decade of achievement of which all BI workers can be proud. Although these activities have done a great deal to promote the cause of library user education, the question of how best the formal education of the bibliographic instruction librarian is achieved remains unanswered. It is a fact that the majority of advertised reference positions now specify user instruction as a part of job requirements and many reference librarians accept these positions knowing little about teaching.[12] Librarians have been aware, for many years, of the advantages of library user instruction, yet the formal education of the individuals who do this instruction has been neglected. The responsibility of their education rests properly with the programs of library and information science education.

Cognizant of obligations to satisfy needs of those charged with teaching library users, librarians and library and information science educators have provided a substantial and steadily growing volume of literature devoted to instruction in library use. Surprisingly, very little of that literature reveals that library schools have taken the necessary steps to incorporate library user instruction into existing reference courses, much less devote an entire course to this important instruction. Not until the 1970s was there evidence of programs of library education assuming responsibility in providing education for teaching use of the library. A 1975 study by Sue Galloway surveyed fifty-five library education programs accredited by the ALA. Of the 47 schools responding to that survey, only four offered courses devoted specifically to library user instruction. Galloway states that "Librarian instruction received only superficial attention; [and that there is only] a cursory mention in the curricula of less than half of the schools . . . thus, library schools have responded poorly to meet this genuine need."[13]

Other studies relating the development of BI in library school curricula have been reported in the *Journal of Education for Librarianship* and its successor, the *Journal of Education for Library and Information Science*. Writing in 1978, Esther Dyer stated, "Library schools have been slow to respond to this need [for courses in BI] and interest; however, several schools are planning to include library instruction in the curriculum . . . Library schools are failing in their obligation to their students if they do not assume an increasing role in teaching librarians how to teach."[14] In 1980, Maureen Pastine and Karen Seibert reported "that the status of bibliographic instruction [in library schools] has not improved substantially," but that 11 of the reporting schools had a "distinct course on the subject."[15] Although this reflects a much improved situation from that reported by Dyer, Pastine and Seibert advise caution stating that "Library school deans and directors feel they are addressing the issue of training for bibliographic instruction through other courses and/or by providing opportunities for practical experience."[16] These authors report further that feedback from recent library school graduates indicates that this form of instruction is not adequate. A 1985 article by Robert Brundin provides a survey and overview of education for bibliographic instruction and in his concluding remarks he places the onus of responsibility with the schools of library and information science. Brundin states that "There is, thus, a definite role for library schools in the preparation of library educators. However, library schools cannot produce good teachers any more than can faculties of education. What the schools can do is provide for students an understanding of the importance and complexity of the teaching function, and a means for developing those teaching skills which they possess."[17] From the foregoing it can be concluded that although segments of some courses offered in library schools consider the matter of teaching library user instruction, only a few schools have an entire course devoted to the education of those who will provide this important library service.

1989 STUDY DOCUMENTS PROGRESS

Fortunately, this situation has now changed for the better as more schools of library and information science are providing a course devoted solely to library user instruction. From a recent informal questionnaire survey of accredited library and information science programs in the U.S. and Canada, and also of those schools holding associate membership in the Association for Library and Information Science Education, it was determined that the number of schools having a separate course on library user instruction has increased dramatically and that there are now twenty schools offering a course designed specifically for those planning to teach use of the library. Thus, there has been great progress in closing the gap between the supply and demand for well qualified bibliographic instruction librarians.

The following Table summarizes data from those schools that responded to the questionnaire survey. (See Table 1.)

An alternative to the separate course is the Certificate of Professional Development like that offered by the University of Wisconsin, Madison. This is a noncredit program that provides Continuing Education Units (CEUs) in five core areas, one of which is biblio-

Table 1

Institution Contacted - 77 Responded - 68	Separate BI Course	Covered in Reference	Offered under Special Topics	School Media Offered Through Education	Offered as C.E.	Designing a Course
Buffalo*	X					
California St.	X			X		
Central Arkansas	X			X		
Dalhousie*	X					
Hawaii*	X					
Indiana*		X				
Kent*						X
Kentucky*	X	Offered first time 1989-1990				
Kutztown U	X					
Louisiana*	X					
Mankato	X			X		

92

School				
Michigan*	X			
Missouri*	X			
Montreal*	X			
N. Illinois*		X		
Oklahoma*	X			
Peabody/Vander	X		X	
Pratt*	X			
Puerto Rico*	X			X
Rutgers*				X
San Jose*	X	Course in curriculum – not taught for some time		
Simmons*	X			
S. Connecticut*	X	Course in curriculum–not taught for some time		
Washington*	X			
Wisconsin*		X		X

* = ALA Accredited Program

graphic instruction. This certificate program, open to those individuals holding the first professional degree, has been immensely popular and draws participants from across the nation. This popularity, according to program director Darlene Weingand, is due in part to the fact that most BI librarians were unable to have (or did not take advantage of) this necessary education as a part of their professional degree programs but that in their present positions, find that it is a part of their employment responsibilities.

THE LSU LIBRARY USER INSTRUCTION COURSE

Since its inception at Louisiana State University in 1985, the course Library User Instruction has been offered during four separate semesters with a combined enrollment of 38 students. Of this total, 21 were women and 17 were men. This course, taught in the seminar format, allows for the greatest possible flexibility, including student involvement and participation, guest lecturers, and a variety of teaching methods, techniques, and presentations. Seminar participants have the opportunity to read and investigate from a range of suggested topics germane to library user instruction, and to present findings before the group. A second major component of the class is that in which each member defines the group as a specific audience and then teaches a simulated class which, understandably, can vary greatly in both subject and content. Students completing the Library User Instruction course are further given the opportunity to earn additional academic credit, applicable to their degree program, by teaching a series of actual BI classes to university students, monitored under the watchful eye of an experienced member of the library reference staff. Letters from former students who completed the course and who are now employed as reference librarians, attest to its success and usefulness in preparing the prospective BI librarian.

CONCLUSION

Although Tucker identified the origins of bibliographic instruction in academic libraries in the period 1876 to 1914, the education of reference librarians to perform this function was not a part of the library science curriculum when Williamson did his survey that was published in 1923. Slow to develop, it was not until more than forty years later that the ALA groups were organized, and that LOEX was formed. The status of the current situation is now very encouraging as more schools have made library user instruction an integral part of their curricula. The education of the teacher of library user instruction has at last found its rightful place and with an increased level of effort and educational intensity, the profession is now being well served in this important area of academic library service.

REFERENCES

1. Charles L. Williamson, *Training for Library Service: A Report Prepared for the Carnegie Corporation of New York.* (New York), 1923.

2. Ibid., 14.

3. John Mark Tucker, "The Origins of Bibliographic Instruction in Academic Libraries, 1876-1914." In: *New Horizons for Academic Libraries*, (New York: K.G. Sauer, 1979), 268. See also Tucker's "User Education in Academic Libraries: A Century in Retrospect." *Library Trends*, v. 29 (Summer 1980) 9-27.

4. Williamson, 36.

5. Ibid., 37.

6. See: "Library Skills Tests" In: *Evaluating Bibliographic Instruction, A Handbook.* Bibliographic Instruction Section. Association of College and Research Libraries. American Library Association. 1983. 63-65.

7. Charles D. Patterson, "Librarians As Teachers: A Component of the Educational Process," *Journal of Education for Library and Information Science*, v.28, no.1 (Summer 1987) 3.

8. Sharon A. Hogan, "Training and Education of Library Instruction Librarians," *Library Trends*, v.29 (Summer 1980) 105.

9. Teresa B. Menching, "Trends in Bibliographic Instruction in the 1980s: A Comparison of Data from Two Surveys." In: *Research Strategies*, v. 7, no. 1 (Winter 1989) 4-13.

10. Letter to the author dated February 21, 1989.

11. Barbara Wittkopf, "Bibliographic Instruction" *The ALA Yearbook of Library and Information Service* v. 13 Chicago, IL, American Library Association, 68-69.

12. C. Van Fleet, and D. Watson: "Analysis of Academic Reference Librarian Positions as Revealed in Professional Publications." Unpublished report comp. at Louisiana State University School of Library and Information Science, Research Annex, Feb. 1987. Of the 262 reference positions listed in *College & Research Libraries* and *LJ Hotline* in 1986, 78.6+ percent specified BI as a job responsibility.

13. Sue Galloway, "Nobody Is Teaching the Teachers," *Bootlegger*, v.3, no.13, 29.

14. Esther Dyer, "Formal Library Science Courses on Library Instruction," *Journal of Education for Librarianship*, v.18, no.4 (Spring 1978) 359-361.

15. Maureen Pastine and Karen Seibert. "Update on the Status of Bibliographic Instruction in Library School Programs," *Journal of Education for Librarianship*, v.21, no.2 (Fall 1980) 169-171.

16. Ibid. 169.

17. Robert Brundin. "Education for Instructional Librarians: Development and Overview," *Journal of Education for Library and Information Science*, v.25, no.3 (Winter 1985) 177-188.

Connecting to the Electronic Library: A Paradigm Shift in Training Reference Librarians

Mary Ellen Larson

SUMMARY. The technology of the electronic library, because of its reliance on remotely accessed databases, has created an environment where the user can autonomously control information flow and content. This environment forces reference librarians to redefine their relationship with the user community, shifting their role from a mediator of preestablished information sources to a partner in the creation of individual databases. This shift in paradigm requires that reference librarian training shift its focus from a source-orientation to a process-orientation.

A great deal has been written about the "electronic library," much of it focused on how technology will alter the way librarians perceive and interact with their patrons. It is obvious that technological advances have created an environment that is radically different from anything librarians have experienced. The development of integrated circuit technology has made the personal computer an affordable consumer product. Parallel developments in communications technology make it possible to access a central information source from any point in the world.[1] Information access, once a tightly centralized and controlled process, has become a less constrained, almost autonomous activity whose boundaries are limited only by the financial resources and creativity of the consumer.

This shift in the control of the information access process dramatically affects how libraries organize and disseminate information. The traditional paradigm of the self-contained library "unit" is giv-

Ms. Larson is an Instructional Specialist with the Penn State University Libraries, E308D Pattee Library, Penn State University, University Park, PA 16802.

ing way to the "library without walls" where users may be scattered across the continent, each accessing a central database from their personal workstation. Indeed, one writer has described an electronic "branch library" that combines online access to files, document delivery via telefacsimile, and telephone assistance to create an environment where the patron no longer goes to the library to find information—information finds him.[2] This structure is far removed from the traditional notion of a library where patrons travel to the library to find the information that they need.

Technological change has occurred so rapidly in the past few decades that libraries have been hard-pressed to effectively integrate hardware advances into the daily workflow, much less theorize about how these hardware changes affect their relationships with users. By default, it seems that we have merely translated our existing paradigms (the methods we use to conduct reference interviews, the content of our bibliographic instruction classes, for example) into electronic terms. The prevailing philosophy seems to be "Do what has to be done but do it electronically."[3] We have yet to develop a new paradigm to guide our relationship with our "electronic users."

The traditional locus of interaction between the library and its users is the reference area, so it is logical that any reexamination of library/user relationships should begin here. How well does the traditional role of the reference librarian respond to the challenges of an increasingly autonomous information environment? If this role needs to be redefined, how can information science curricula support the development of a "new" reference librarian? This paper explores these questions by: (1) explaining the impact of electronic information access on the librarian/patron relationship (2) outlining the traditional model of reference librarianship and suggesting ways in which it can be enhanced to include the "electronic library" (3) suggesting ways in which library schools can optimize the training of reference librarians in this new environment.

THE ELECTRONIC LIBRARY

The development of technological innovation in libraries not surprisingly parallels similar development in the private sector. The hallmark of business management information systems is the perception that the institution, not the individual, is responsible for designing and managing information access. The overall expectation is that information systems allow management to achieve more timely, complete control over the organization.⁴ Therefore, the structure and design of an information system must correspond with the institution's needs rather than the individual's.

In much the same way, technological innovation in libraries is driven by the information needs of the institution. Electronic databases, such as those vended by Dialog and BRS, initially responded to the publisher's need to archive large amounts of data in an easily retrievable form. Similarly, online catalogs were initially an attempt to create a central database that could be amended easily and cost-effectively. Although "user-friendliness" is an attribute to which online catalogs and databases aspire, the impetus for development came from the needs of the institution not the individual.

The architect of the organization-specific management information system is the "chief information officer," someone who provides directional leadership for system-wide information gathering and dissemination.⁵ Usually a technologist, this person defines hardware and software applications within a well-defined context of institutional goals and objectives, chief among which is cost-effectiveness. Libraries have often operated under a similar system; a central "computer czar" (who often directs the computing activities of the library's parent organization as well) plans and implements the development of library automation. This individual is a technologist (and sometimes a librarian) and much of the architecture of a library's online system may reflect his vision and that of his staff.

Yet the paradigm of centralized information control is breaking down, largely because the personal computer has encouraged the creation of "private" software environments that only slightly resemble those of the institution. Communications technology allows the creation of peer groups through electronic conferencing and these groups cooperatively create new applications whose impact ranges far beyond the productivity-driven designs of the chief information officer. The end-user is able to perform an "end-run" around the organization's information structure.

Similarly, the personal computer, coupled with a modem, has effectively removed the user from the confines of the library's walls. Information that was previously available only by personally consulting a librarian can be had for the price of a phone call and a royalty fee. This autonomy exists within the library walls, as well. Online catalog terminals and CD-ROM units located at remote sites within the library have effectively removed the library patron from the (physical, at least) sphere of the reference librarian.

As Joanne Euster points out, this autonomous environment changes the access relationship between the library user and his information resources. First, physical and geographic barriers have collapsed. The personal computer/modem combination has made the physical structure of the library irrelevant – the library is now as close as the nearest telephone line. Telefacsimile has made it possible to acquire a copy of a journal article from anywhere in the world, and universally available online databases make it possible to create and maintain global bibliographies in a matter of minutes. Second, users themselves have changed. The ubiquity of the personal computer has encouraged users to expect that information will be delivered quickly and conveniently in a variety of formats. For example, it is often difficult for students to understand why libraries with finite budgets can not afford to attach printers to every online catalog terminal. Finally, because information in our society is now a consumer good, information, time and money are perceived as interchangeable concepts. People are willing to pay for using computers and receiving computerized database searches, thus giving economic value to a commodity that was once viewed as "free." Information has become a commodity, like iron or tin.[6]

DEFINING AN APPROPRIATE ROLE MODEL

How well does the traditional client-centered reference librarian model address the demands of this new environment? Does the new paradigm of the electronic library demand an equally new paradigm for reference librarianship? The answers to these questions are clear if one considers the basis of the reference librarian model.

The traditional reference librarian model rests on the primacy of the "core professional task" that gives our profession its unique identity – the one-on-one interview at the reference desk.[7] In this situation, the reference librarian acts as an intermediary between the user and the information source, predigesting and interpreting information to suit individual needs. In the performance of this function, the librarian interacts with the user in a manner similar to that of the doctor with his patient. He dispenses "special" information to a clientele that perceives him as all-knowing. This role has a powerful appeal to many in librarianship because it strengthens a perceived tenuous claim to professional status.

As Brian Nielson points out, the foundation of the traditional reference model is a limited, controlled service distribution point.[8] Yet, as we have seen, the electronic library renders the static service point essentially useless, since users are no longer required to come to the library to access information sources. If the foundation of the traditional paradigm no longer exists, then its usefulness in dealing with the "electronic patron" is also suspect. A paradigm shift in the reference librarian model, one that retains the best features of the traditional model, is then necessary.

Perhaps the roots of a new model lie in the work of Ivan Illich, who suggests that experts need to "deprofessionalize" their relationships with their clients and work toward a sharing of knowledge.[9] The autonomy of the electronic environment is forcing a new definition of the traditional "helping" mode. Because geographic barriers to information access have ceased to exist, because users are seeing themselves in a more commercial relationship with information providers (who may or may not be librarians), librarians can no longer control the information environment exclusively. Rather, they must share control of the environment with the user.

The development of Local Area Networks (LANs) provides a technology where control of the information environment can be shared by the institution (in this case, the librarian is the representative of the institution) and the user. This is the perfect atmosphere for the development of a mutually supportive model of reference assistance, where the librarian shares knowledge with the user, acting as a teacher and advisor (much like the first reference librarians of a century ago) rather than a purveyor of books or information.[10] The development of such a model would also enhance the librarian's position with the patron community. By helping users to become more information self-sufficient, librarians have the opportunity to empower users.[11] Those who are perceived as "empowering" are often viewed as powerful in their own right, and this power may do more to strengthen the status of the profession over time than claims of professionalization.

A PARADIGM SHIFT IN TRAINING

Will the traditional reference curriculum support the performance of the reference librarian in the electronic environment? The traditional reference course is "source-oriented," focused on learning about specific representatives of reference genres, with topics like bibliographic instruction and online information added as "special topics." This emphasis is entirely appropriate when the primary function of the reference librarian is to answer questions at the reference desk. But if one accepts the concept of the collaborative reference librarian outlined earlier, there are certain advisory and consulting functions in that model that the curriculum should address. These functions do not preclude the exercise of the traditional question-answering activities. Rather they cast them in a different light, blending them with other skills that are part of total "reference librarian" package.

Rather than structure a basic reference course according to genres (for example, Unit 1:Bibliographies, Unit 2:Almanacs and Yearbooks), it may be more functional to organize content by process, including all the activities in which reference librarians could be expected to participate: question negotiation and resolution, user education, collection development, online information retrieval, individual/group project planning and implementation. The objectives of such a course would focus on the skills that are needed to perform these processes properly: (1) communication skills — interpersonal, oral and written (2) question formulation and refinement skills — negotiating a reference interview and resolving it with a mutually satisfactory answer (3) organizational skills — the implementation of a formal strategic planning process and its function in encouraging small group development (4) interpretation skills — identifying learning tasks in training users and staff, analyzing these tasks within the framework of various learning theories, and implementing instructional programs (5) database organization — understanding how databases are structured and maintained.

These skills are supported by a "cognitive framework," a body of knowledge that is the "meat" of the reference librarian's message. This framework consists of the traditional reference curriculum (identification of individual sources within genres) combined with an understanding of the literature organization of specific disciplines. The purpose of this framework is not to teach "sources" in isolation but to provide comprehensive literature structures that suggest relationships among these sources. An understanding of these relationships also enhances an understanding of database structures. It is this corpus of knowledge that offers substantial support for the processes of question negotiation, bibliographic instruction, online retrieval and project planning outlined above.

It can be argued that the remainder of the information science curriculum deals with precisely the topics suggested here. Yet the virtue of including these topics in a reference course is that discussion can focus on their immediate application to the reference process. The purpose of including these topics is not to treat them "in-depth," but to demonstrate how they combine to form a complete picture of reference activity. If the relationship between the patron becomes more symbiotic and global with technological innovation, then the reference curriculum should strive to reflect this change with an inclusive curriculum.

The electronic library, with its ability to create an autonomous user community, offers many possibilities for creating a new relationship between the librarian and the patron. The model which has traditionally defined this relationship is giving way to an enhanced model which places the librarian and user in mutually supportive, rather than subservient, roles. The reference curriculum can reflect this paradigm shift by changing its focus from "source" to "process" and by providing a cognitive framework that uses literature structure to organize relationships among sources. Such a curriculum will prepare a reference librarian to engage in an empowering, rather than dependent, relationship with their user community.

REFERENCES

1. Bacon, Glenn. "Forces Shaping the New Information Paradigm." *In Libraries and Information Science in the Electronic Age*. Hendrik Edelman, ed. Philadelphia: ISI Press, 1986, 154-165.

2. Brown, Doris R. "Three terminals, a telefax, and one dictionary." *College and Research Libraries News* 46 (November, 1985), 536-38.

3. King, David and Baker, Betsy. "Human Aspects of Library Technology: Implications for Academic Library User Education." In *Bibliographic Instruction: The Second Generation*. Constance Mellon, ed. Littleton, Co.: Libraries Unlimited, 1987, 85-107.

4. Bacon, p. 156.

5. Bacon, p. 157.

6. Euster, Joanne. "Technology and Instruction," in *Bibliographic Instruction: The Second Generation*, 53-59.

7. Nielson, Brian. "Alternative Professional Models in the Information Age." In *Bibliographic Instruction: The Second Generation*, p. 24-37.

8. Nielson, p. 30.

9. Illich, Ivan. *Toward a History of Needs*. New York: Pantheon, 1978.

10. Hopkins, Frances L. "A Century of Bibliographic Instruction: The Historical Claim to Professional and Academic Legitimacy." *College and Research Libraries* 43 (May, 1982):192-98.

11. Euster, p. 55.

Continuing Education for Librarians— Training for Online Searching

Anne Page Mosby
Glenda Hughes

SUMMARY. Rapidly developing technology has changed the environment in libraries so that some degree of computer search ability is required now in order to give standard, non-obsolete reference service. New library school graduates regularly receive a basic understanding of DIALOG, BRS, and other database utilities, but some feel more inclined toward working with computers than others. At the same time, seasoned librarians are faced with new learning requirements for computer searching. How do librarians in the "transition generation" handle the change required by professional technological development? A wide range of responses—from enthusiastic to reluctant—requires flexibility and variety in training and continuing education methods.

This paper will address the human factor in some issues of broad technological change. The authors will offer some observations about how we as a profession are adapting to the new environment of computer-enhanced information. A case study of one library's experience with training and continuing education for online searching will illustrate a response to this changing library environment.

Be aware always that all things change, and become accustomed to the thought that the nature of the Universe delights above all in changing the things which are, and making new things like them. Everything that exists contains the seed of what shall come from it.

—Marcus Aurelius, *Meditations*
Book IV, Section 36

Anne Page Mosby is Reference Librarian/Associate Professor and Glenda Hughes is Maps Librarian/Assistant Professor at Georgia State University, Pullen Library, 100 Decatur Street, Atlanta, GA 30303.

105

THE ENVIRONMENT OF TECHNOLOGICAL CHANGE

As we approach the 21st century, the pace of technological innovation continues to accelerate. Any detailed work that must be done in an exact manner and done repeatedly is a candidate for automation. Even though a job has been automated once, it will continue to change, so that, to remain employable, people must be prepared to upgrade and adapt their vocational or professional skills continually. Some jobs and professions are disappearing altogether. Moreover, there are larger demographic factors which affect the American job market, including increased competition in the global marketplace, the relative decline of the economic position of the middle class, world population pressures, increase in the U.S. median age, and a rising retirement age in the United States. Nevertheless, some people who find themselves in this transition to a rapidly changing environment—the "transition generation"—are developing enjoyable and meaningful work lives which include the survival behaviors of continuing education and training.

We exist in a dynamic environment, but changing conditions can be managed. When people perceive the larger context of technological change and imagine their position within it, they may find their own responses and attitudes altered. From this broad perspective they can commit themselves to the risk of learning new behaviors. They may even find the process fun and exciting. Ideally, workplace organizations seek humane and unselfish solutions to these challenges and employees develop a shared vision, so that everyone can work together in implementing goals. In an environment which supports and even encourages change, employees will keep pace by growing and changing, while continuing to offer their unique personal contributions.

EXPERIENCED EMPLOYEES
IN CONTINUING EDUCATION PROGRAMS

Professional workers who understand the implications of technological momentum are engaged in the ongoing process of knowledge building and creative activities. Continuing education, retraining, and life-long learning are not limited to any one segment of the population. These mechanisms allow employees to remain active participants in the workforce. They are necessary techniques, and they can be structured in such a way that the possibilities are exciting and non-threatening. Adults have the capacity to continue to learn throughout their lives, mastering new responses for changing conditions. But the scale and momentum of change in today's workplace means that accelerated, augmented, or structured educational programs are required.

Although a major goal of continuing education is to integrate new staff into an organization, another primary goal must be to retrain people in needed skills areas so that experienced employees with valued accomplishments are retained. The fear of being "over-the-hill" can be eliminated when the organization acknowledges that employees are valued and offers them the opportunity to add new skills to established abilities. In order to succeed in a learning situation, however, the continuing student must acknowledge the need for regular updating and training in areas of interest, making this his or her intentional choice. Reassuring experienced employees of their value while at the same time helping them to perceive the need for further training may be difficult. But institutions must give this reassurance, and the trainer must re-enforce it in order to achieve the desired results.

When older, experienced employees enter training, there are different challenges for the trainer. These trainees may have some knowledge and experience exceeding that of the trainer and the other trainees. Because of their knowledge, experience, and status, older employees may be uneasy about the training experience. Mature people, long out of classroom situations, may sometimes find it difficult to grasp large amounts of information in such a setting. The competitiveness that allowed mature employees to achieve successfully in the past may make it difficult for them to admit problems or expose their error. Older people may learn best through lecture and the written word, while younger people may interact best with graphics or multi-media training material. Some older employees may have physical limitations. Reading a terminal screen through bifocal or trifocal lenses is a common handicap that few unaffected people take into consideration. Other physical and psychological restrictions may add an extra dimension of complexity to training situations for any age group. Attempting to allow for individual differences is part of the challenge for trainers and training programs.

Developing team training as the learning method may help to integrate a mixture of characteristics into an environment where real learning can take place. There are benefits to a shared learning experience. Teamwork and understanding can carry over to the workplace where the entire organization will profit from an emphasis on achieving through cooperation. "The advantage of team-building efforts is that once changes are accepted by the group, group members themselves can reinforce the new patterns of behavior. A team that has developed sufficient levels of trust will be able to work on whatever problems arise in a self-correcting way that allows for changes in structure or technology as well as changes in member behavior" (Cohen, p. 377).

TECHNOLOGY AND THE CHANGING LIBRARY ENVIRONMENT

Libraries are not immune to the continuing education and training requirements for currency in new technology. In fact, the impact on libraries may be greater than in other arenas because the information world (including libraries) has fueled so many technological innovations. Hyatt reviews at least five important developments in library automation: (1) machine-readable bibliographic files; (2) computer library networks, such as OCLC and RLIN, permitting the sharing of machine-readable cataloging; (3) changes in organizational structures and staffing patterns due to automation of certain key library functions in cataloging and bibliographic control, interlibrary loan, acquisitions, and circulation; (4) development of online public access catalogs; and (5) creation of local area computer networks (LANs), permitting library users to access library information without having to be physically present in the library. With these major trends, people who were originally drawn to librarianship because of its relative non-competitiveness and stability may have a difficult time reassessing their options and opportunities in the new environment. However, they should not lose sight of the benefits available to them through the collegial mindset promoted by many libraries.

Reference librarians are often thought of as generalists who may develop a number of specialties or areas of expertise during their careers. Regardless of their background or interests, their work at the public service desk requires them to respond appropriately to questions in any area while working in concert with their colleagues. A question on treasury bill rates may be followed by one on tropisms in plants, followed by requests for information on eating disorders, and so on. Anyone who has worked at a reference desk has a healthy respect for the power of the question, since the way a "best question" is phrased leads to "the best answer." Every reference desk worker has had the experience of communicating with the library user to learn the "real" question. The seed of the answer is within the question, and librarians play a special role—empathetic communication, knowledge of information sources and how to access them, and the ability to teach users some of the information searching procedure. Successful reference librarians are always in the process of developing their communication skills and must be flexible enough to have open minds to explore new directions. Librarians who possess these kinds of generalists' skills may use them to their own benefit when faced with nearly overwhelming technological change. One of the most charming characteristics of the library profession is the great variety and diversity of people drawn to it. This rich array of colleagues is our greatest resource for the period of the computer revolution.

New technology has changed forever the way librarians give reference service. It is hard to conceive of any library—academic, special, public, or school—still functioning without automated processes of some kind. Changes in technology are happening in the library world almost everyday—new databases, new equipment, new software, new protocols, and enhancements to search strategy. How people adapt to such change is an important question in this technological environment. Some librarians in this transition generation are delighted and some are disquieted. Each of us has a personal threshold of tolerance for absorbing new technology.

Our images of reference service have changed greatly over the years. It was a different world in the days before photocopy machines and word processors, when scholars actually read articles or books in libraries for hours at a time and made extensive written notes on index cards. The days before the information explosion and widespread use of computer databases in libraries—about 1975—now seem like a distant historical era, when reference questions were attacked and conquered "the old-fashioned way" through knowledge of reference sources on the shelf or through laborious searching in card catalogs, indexes and bibliographies.

As fast as we have been able to adapt to the new technological opportunities, new trends have become standard modes of service, for example, the current widespread acceptance of CD-ROM databases. And if the recent past has produced such great change, what does the future hold for us as new technology allows us to enhance the way people acquire and interact with information, knowledge, and wisdom? Even those with an active interest in technology may find it difficult to visualize the changes awaiting them. For example, increasing instances of numeric and fulltext databases will require more data-handling expertise from librarians. Hypertext will offer possibilities for accessing and absorbing information in new ways. Online catalogs will be enhanced with additional online indexes and files, increased off-site access, and expert systems. Librarians will be doing online ready reference through bulletin boards and real-time conferencing.

How do ordinary people respond to this rapidly evolving library environment? How do they handle the professional responsibilities which have been altered by technological changes? F.W. Lancaster summarizes the plan of action:

> The developments occurring in technology and their application in innovative approaches to communication make it imperative that librarians continue their education throughout their professional careers. Continuing education is becoming increasingly important in all branches of human activity. Universities, national libraries, professional societies, and international organizations have the responsibility to develop courses, workshops, seminars, and congresses to ensure that the librarian understands and applies appropriate new techniques, instead of continuing to rely on the traditional methods

of the past. Librarians themselves must accept some responsibility in this area by convincing the appropriate organizations that such continuing education courses are necessary and by identifying their own specific needs for further education and training. (Lancaster, p. 179)

ONLINE SEARCHING FOR NEW AND EXPERIENCED LIBRARIANS

Librarians' collective training and continuing education experience in online searching serves as a concrete example of what we have learned in the past two decades of rapidly developing library technology. Potential online searchers are individuals who may be described as either "technologically reluctant," or "technologically absorbent," depending on their computer experiences acquired on-the-job, or through formal curricula. The two groups have different degrees of familiarity with and facility with computers. Yet, experience and exposure do not entirely explain the continuing reluctance to embrace online searching which some librarians exhibit. Some may feel the pressure of an unfamiliar search style, which is a very different personal style from the traditional way they answer reference questions. They may be overwhelmed by a complicated framework of unfamiliar hardware and a seemingly endless choice of software, and mystified by the way a computer "thinks." For others there may be the unresolved issue of paying for information. They may have a dread of spending someone else's money in a fee-based service, or a fear of "wasting" the library's limited budget. Still another cause of reluctance to use and promote online databases is the conviction that library users will get the wrong impression and think everything they may need is magically covered by the online search.

Recent library school graduates enter the profession with basic database training and probably with repeated personal experiences of using database searching to do their own research and writing for classes. Therefore, new graduates coming to their first library jobs, may already be comfortable with computers. What the new professional needs is a thorough orientation to the procedures and policies of the new employer. For example, what type of question at the desk might generate a ready reference search? What kind of logging information does the searcher record in order for the library to pay the vendor's invoice? What is the fee structure for online searching service? Thus, an early assessment of the individual's online training needs is necessary to generate an adequate training plan. Both the individual and the online trainer must assess the current situation together and agree on the objectives for new training. This may mean that the library send the librarian to a vendor workshop, followed by a phasing-in period for actually doing online searching. A very important component of this process is that the online policy of the library is explained clearly.

Training and retraining for online searching skills is a fact of life for both new and experienced librarians as the technology develops. Those transition generation librarians who came into the profession before the mid-1970s have especially been exposed to a variety of technological changes in that period, and have experienced a multiplicity of training experiences for online searching. Both new and experienced librarians continue to define for themselves and for their specific library environments how to respond to computer age challenges. One response reflected in the professional literature has been the extensive discussion about how to integrate online searching into reference departments rather than make them separate services. Such integration may work for one reference department but not for another. In this context what can reference librarians — even the reluctant ones — do about acquiring and updating online skills?

ONE LIBRARY'S RESPONSE

Experimenting with a variety of approaches to online training has allowed the authors' library colleagues to recognize and include all kinds of learning styles. This experience has involved an effort to set a tone for personalizing online training which is geared to individual interests and needs. It is acknowledged that every reference librarian will find his or her own niche in the computer search function, and that not all will develop the same degree of online activity. Vendor workshop fees are underwritten by the library administration for various online training sessions. There is latitude for doing practice searches so that the new searcher has enough search encounters to remember protocols and to develop search strategy. Even with a tight budget, the library has permitted leeway to allow for beginner's inexperience or mistakes. The consistent message from the library administration has been one of support for new learning and personal expansion. The DIALOG system's ONTAP files offer inexpensive practice as do their monthly free files, and all searchers are encouraged to use these for preliminary searching or experimentation. Since we have multiple passwords we have come up with a sign-up system for taking advantage of any monthly free files, a great benefit for new searchers seeking practice. Flexibility of scheduling searches, and integrating ready reference searching more fully into the options available at the reference desk provide the framework for new searchers to accept searches. Additionally, all of the reference staff who make search appointments are asked to focus on the new searcher's need for receiving search questions. Moreover, cross-over learning has proven to be very powerful. A pattern established in one set of circumstances, – e.g., searching in paper indexes, online catalogs or CD-ROMs – will transfer to another situation, – e.g., interactive searching with one of the online systems.

Other online training techniques have been used to develop autonomous searchers as personal situations demanded. Refresher or specialized courses offered by most vendors are available as a librarian's search experience builds. The aim of becoming an accomplished searcher fits well into the goals-based evaluation procedure, so that a person may choose to focus on a manageable online training goal during a specific timeframe. A training plan is key to helping a beginning searcher move at his or her own pace. For several years an outline of training was used by the trainer to monitor the trainee's progress through the basic training steps. In recent months we have also used a vendor-produced videotape to augment local training. The elementary language and explanations of the video tended to actually reinforce trainees' self-confidence that they do, indeed, know what they are doing! The library has also been generous in supporting librarians' attendance at national online conferences, in addition to vendor or systems workshops. Regular meetings have been held to discuss and communicate online issues and to share search strategies or new learning, at first just for all searchers, then as agenda items in the scheduled reference department gatherings two or three times a month. Copying and posting pertinent articles has been another way of keeping current with online professional literature.

An important method of leveraging the formal search training of experienced librarians was to use a team approach for learning the hardware, telecommunications software, question strategy, file selection, and actual searching. The team was made up of a coach who was an experienced searcher, two reference librarians with from 15 to 20 years professional experience each, who were reluctant to add responsibilities to already full assignments, and a mid-career map librarian new to the library, who was concerned about adding yet another skill to a full list of specialized responsibilities. The team met on a regular basis to insure exposure to and eventual familiarity with online routines by doing searches together and gradually building up an understanding of file specific techniques. One accomplished reference librarian whose "second home" was the reference collection decided that she wanted to develop a level of comfort for ready reference searching equal to that of her ability to quickly query OCLC. She also set as a goal learning more about database options in order to advise library users at the reference desk. The interlibrary loan librarian wanted to be able to do simple searches for ready reference and for ILL verification, and to be updated on the online jargon and procedures in order to feel more comfortable in the computer environment. While these two highly valued, seasoned librarians may never want to specialize in online searching, they will have developed their own online objectives. Together, with group support, it became easier for all of them to take the online plunge. The map librarian's experience is illustrative of the results of this method of training.

ONE LIBRARIAN'S RESPONSE

"I have always relished change, and, in fact, sought it out. But in spite of my curious nature, in ten years of library service, I had never had a job in which online searching was required of me. I had been trained to use DIALOG and BRS, but had never used either one regularly. Naturally, I was eager but somewhat anxious when my new job allowed me the opportunity to become a 'real' online searcher.

"Opportunity, training, and encouragement came together with my own desire to tackle new challenges. My feeling that librarians should be current in all aspects of information processing helped me overcome my anxiety, so that I was able to succeed with the process. I had several rational arguments for my commitment to learning online searching:

1. I had used Boolean logic in my college mathematics classes, and had a satisfactory understanding of it.
2. The library has seven compact disc or laser disc indexes in the reference area. I felt the searching concepts and strategies would be transferable from the CD products to online and vice versa. The library's users were searching on these products as well as doing dial-up searching of the online catalog.
3. While it is often true that reference librarians cannot achieve the subject expertise of their patrons, it seems important to me that we should try to achieve significant expertise in information handling.
4. People are often lined up for our first-come-first-served CD sources and signed up days and occasionally weeks in advance for our scheduled CD databases. To help our clients use these products more efficiently, we need to help them assimilate search strategies and concepts rapidly.
5. And lastly, because of the proliferation of homebased personal computers among our users, I have felt for a long while that I was not keeping up with technology and that my clients might doubt my competence in other areas if I were not more knowledgeable about automated information handling and, particularly, online searching.

"It seemed to me that going through this training process with two other librarians in somewhat similar circumstances, i.e., older, experienced and somewhat reluctant about the process, would be beneficial to each of us. I thought we could encourage each other and reinforce each other in our training. I hoped we could meet regularly after our training to discuss our progress, search strategies, and results.

"I was afraid there would not be enough searches for all of us to become as proficient as we wanted to be. And continuing to work together would help us over the long haul to retain our skills and to gain more expertise. All the CD-ROM products in our reference area have reduced the demand for online searches though the demand seems to ebb and flow, and at peak times, those searchers already trained were almost overwhelmed by searches. So there was, and is, a need for trained searchers. I am a subject specialist (map librarian) with a joint appointment in the reference and cataloging departments. I hope to develop a specialized clientele in geography, earth sciences, urban planning, and related areas.

"I think I was realistic in my expectations of the training and my abilities. I have completed only a half dozen solo searches. But I believe they have been successful. Before each search I have had enough time to consult the appropriate documentation and experienced searchers, if I thought it appropriate, so that I have planned my searches carefully. And I have been pleased with the results. Because of my late start, it is possible that I am somewhat more uneasy about the process than a younger librarian would be. But I am a longtime, personal computer owner and user, so it is not the computer itself that makes me feel uneasy. Perhaps it is being a child of the depression and a believer in the now somewhat tarnished 'free services for all' theory of librarianship that adds to my unease.

"I have continued to practice with the other librarians with whom I trained, and will probably do so until I have done many more searches. My greatest remaining anxiety is departmental online searching policy and procedures. Still, I plan to persevere until I can internalize these, because the excitement is here."

CONCLUSION

It is hoped that other libraries and other reluctant searchers can benefit from one library's experience in training and continuing education for online searching. New information handling technologies make it necessary for librarians to become lifelong learners on a scale much greater than at any time in the past. This will continue to be the case and the pace may even accelerate. As in other professions, continual training will remain an inevitable part of librarians' work lives. It is important for reference department heads and online coordinators to acknowledge individual learning styles of the adult learner. Training in online searching should involve experimentation with different models, such as, one-on-one handholding sessions, working within a training team, transferring learning from one situation to another. Using different combinations and permutations, the online trainer can offer a variety of approaches to learning online searching, as we all develop within the rapidly changing library environment of the computer revolution.

BIBLIOGRAPHY

Arms, William Y. and Lisa D. Holzhauser. "Mercury: An Electronic Library," *OCLC Newsletter* No. 175 (September/October 1988) 15-18.

Broadbent, Marianne and Kerry Grosser. "Continuing Professional Development of Special Library and Information Center Managers," *Journal of Education for Library and Information Science* 28 (Fall 1987) 99-115.

Brookfield, Stephen D. *Understanding and Facilitating Adult Learning.* San Francisco: Jossey-Bass, 1986.

Byles, Torrey. "Academic Computing Comes of Age," *Wilson Library Bulletin* 63 (February 1989) 21-28.

Crampon, Jean E. "Training Backup Searchers . . ." *Online* 4 (October 1980) 25-29.

Creth, Sheila. "National Adult and Continuing Education Week," *College and Research Libraries News* 47 (November 1986) 657-658.

Designing and Delivering Cost-Effective Training—and Measuring the Results, compiled and edited by Ron Zemke, Linda Standke, and Philip Jones. Minneapolis: Lakewood Pubs., 1981.

Dickinson, Dennis W. "Demythologizing Continuing Education," in *Academic Libraries: Myths and Realities: proceedings of the Third National Conference of the Association of College and Research Libraries,* edited by Suzanne C. Dodson, Gary L. Menges. Chicago: ACRL, 1984.

Fine, Sara F. "Technological Innovation, Diffusion and Resistance: An Historical Perspective," *Journal of Library Administration* 7 (Spring 1986) 83-108.

Ford, J. Kevin. "Self-Assessed Training Needs: The Effects of Attitudes Toward Training, Managerial Level, and Function," *Personnel Psychology* 40 (Spring 1987) 39-53.

"The Future of Reference Service: A Panel Discussion Held at the University of

Texas at Austin, Spring 1988," *College and Research Libraries News* 49 (October 1988) 578-589.

Glogoff, Stuart and James P. Flynn. "Developing a Systematic In-house Training Program for Integrated Library Systems," *College and Research Libraries* 48 (November 1987) 528-536.

Hyatt, James A. and Aurora A. Santiago. *University Libraries in Transition.* Washington, D.C.: National Association of College and University Business Offices, 1987.

"Human Response to Library Automation," *Library Trends* (Spring 1989). Special issue in press.

Lancaster, F. W. *Libraries and librarians in an age of electronics.* Arlington, Va.: Information Resources Press, 1982.

Leonhardt, Thomas W. "Toward a Global Information Culture: Education, Libraries, and Technology," *Library Acquisitions: Practice & Theory* 12 (1988) 333-339.

Mancall, Jacqueline C. "Teaching Online Searching: A Review of Recent Research and Some Recommendations for School Media Specialists," *School Library Media Quarterly* 13 (Summer 1985) 215-220.

Mark, Linda. "Putting the Pieces Together in Boston," *Wilson Library Bulletin*, 63 (January 1989) 72-73.

McManis, Gerald L. and Michael S. Leibman. "Management Development: A Lifetime Commitment," *Personnel Administrator* 33 (September 1988) 53-58.

Mintz, Florence. "Retraining: The Graying of the Training Room," *Personnel* 63 (October 1986) 69-71.

Phillips, Louis E. "Certifiably Educated," *Association Management* 39 (September 1987) 73-76.

Quint, Barbara. "Connect Time," *Wilson Library Bulletin* 63 (November 1988) 88-89.

RASD/MARS Education and Training of Search Analysts Committee. "Continuing Education for Search Analysts," *RQ* 26 (Spring 1987) 284-290.

Shapiro, Beth J. "Ongoing Training and Innovative Structural Approaches," *The Journal of Academic Librarianship* 13 (May 1987) 75-76.

Smith, N. J. "Humanizing the Computer for the Older Adult," *Ohio Library Association Bulletin* 56 (April 1986) 25-26.

Tenopir, Carol. "An In-House Training Program for Online Searchers," *Online* 6 (May 1982) 20-26.

Weingand, Darlene E. "Continuing Education Programs and Activities," in *Education for Professional Librarians*, edited by Herbert S. White. White Plains, N.Y.: Knowledge Industry Publications, 1986.

Wagel, William H. "Building Excellence Through Training," *Personnel* 63 (September 1986) 5-10.

Online Searcher Education and Training: Options and Opportunities

Linda Friend

SUMMARY. Reference librarians face an increasingly complex work environment, with much of the complexity driven by the rapid expansion of electronic technologies. Staff development and continuing education must be considered a high priority as databases change and proliferate in online, CD-ROM, and other forms. This article discusses the common types of online training currently available, outlines some things to include or think about when developing in-house programs, and covers some special elements to consider when end users are the potential trainees.

INTRODUCTION

By the end of this decade, most reference librarians (and many other public services staff members) will also be database searchers in one form or another. Some librarians have been able to withstand the pressures to subscribe to database services, but CD-ROM and online catalogs are great levelers and few reference areas now remain outside the influence of automation. A recent issue of *Database*[1] describes a survey by Martha Williams' research firm which found that after only four years of marketing, about 80% of university libraries now had CD-ROM installations, with an average of three titles per location, and almost half of 257 major organizations surveyed also had purchased this technology; public and special libraries are also becoming active in acquiring CD-ROMs. The headline reads, "Survey Shows CD-ROM Posing First Threat To the Online Industry," but as an educator and information consumer I prefer a more positive view: there are now even more ways to

Linda Friend is Search Service Coordinator, Pennsylvania State University Libraries, University Park, PA 16802.

match a user with a source of needed information in a timely and generally cost-effective manner. Such rapid advances in technology, however, have profound implications for the education, training, and continuing development of librarians and other users. This article will review the types of training currently available (focusing on traditional online searching which has the most variety), discuss some of the things to think about when designing a training program, and consider the increasing presence of the end user in library database operations.

DEFINITIONS

Both education and training are necessary in order for a practitioner to develop a thorough understanding of the online industry and to be able to access information electronically. For professional librarians, education generally takes place first in the library school curriculum, where students are introduced to the theoretical concepts of information science, the information channels operating in various subject disciplines, overall concepts of information policy in the U.S. and abroad, theoretical details about how command languages operate, general concepts such as controlled vocabulary, indexing, and boolean logic, and the innate advantages and limitations of database searching. Training has a more practical focus, whether it takes place in formal course work or alternate delivery methods, and should provide potential users with detail: the in-depth acquisition of the intellectual and possible mechanical skills needed to manipulate a search system effectively.

Training Environments

Nearly every advertisement for a reference librarian now lists online searching skills as a qualification (either required or desirable), and there are numerous opportunities to acquire this knowledge, including formal degree programs, seminars and workshops, continuing education and staff development programs, and self-study.

LIBRARY SCHOOLS

Most library school graduates have been exposed to the theoretical background of online information retrieval as well as gained some practical, often system-specific knowledge. Krieger surveyed the course catalogs of 61 schools of library and information science and found that all of them included database searching instruction in some form within the curriculum.[2] Harter and Fenichel tried to answer questions about the place of online searching in the curriculum; the single online course was identified as the most popular approach, while a few schools offered an integrated program or introduced searching as part of another course.[3] The debate continues about whether it is actually appropriate for library schools to be teaching "skills" simply because of demand from the marketplace: White feels that such training should really occur on the job as staff development, or in continuing education programs, since offering courses in searching means that students will fail to take other (possibly more valuable) electives.[4] In spite of such criticisms, it seems certain that online information retrieval will continue to have a legitimate place in library school curricula.

CONTINUING EDUCATION

Once on the job, a searcher has a number of options for learning about various aspects of database searching. In such a volatile area, "the overwhelming magnitude of database creation and change makes systematic updating a necessity rather than a luxury, whether the library's use of online services is modest or extensive."[5] Training is a very useful element to include as part of the daily work flow: a service will succeed or fail depending on the expertise of the people involved. Continuing education can take place through the use of outside agencies, in-house programs, or self-education.

Outside agencies tend most often to mean programs offered by vendors or producers, although other organizations such as user groups, networks and consortia, independent trainers, and library schools may offer such opportunities. Originally conceived as a marketing device to help sell their systems, vendor and producer training is a well-established and increasingly elaborate part of the training scene (in contrast to CD-ROM producers, where educational programs in the use of the systems are almost non-existent). Vendor training tends to emphasize manipulation of the system itself, with much time spent on unique features and the most efficient means of retrieving particular types of information. DIALOG, for example, offers a basic system course as well as about 15 other seminars in popular subject areas (agriculture, chemistry, patents, social sciences/humanities, business) and on special topics (quick reference, updates, refreshers). BRS has seven training courses ranging from introductory and advanced sessions to subject seminars in full text, biomedical, business, and other topics. Vendors generally charge a fee for most sessions, but attendees often get free online time during and after training, either in the full system or in practice databases. Many database producers also offer training to stimulate use and teach efficient searching techniques. The National Library of Medicine and Chemical Abstracts Service have extensive training programs (they are, of course, vendors as well as producers), but many other producers also offer detailed sessions about their offerings, often at no cost to attendees. Networks and consortia may have their own staff to provide training in specific systems, or may act as brokers to bring in outside training talent for the membership. To help a potential attendee decide among such options, an ALA committee produced a comprehensive set of guidelines to continuing education seminars, stressing what should be included in a training session offered by a vendor, producer or independent trainer.[6] The advantages of vendor training are many: attendees receive the most up-to-date information available about a particular system, from experts who know tips and techniques for the most efficient searching. Vendors often have very elaborate training materials that can be a gold mine of useful ideas for passing on knowledge to others at the local library. In terms of disadvantages, vendor training may not be offered in a location convenient for the trainee, may be too expensive to take advantage of often or allow multiple people to attend, and vendors tend (understandably) to emphasize the databases and system specifics and it is up to the trainee to integrate this new knowledge with what he/she already knows about other systems, print sources, etc. Also, the instructor is not at hand after the session to answer questions as they come up (although customer assistance desks are generally quite responsive and helpful).

LOCAL TRAINING

In-house programs take place in one form or another in all but the smallest libraries. If someone goes to a vendor training session, it is usually their responsibility to pass on the recently acquired information to others. Some libraries take advantage of media: for example, BRS has a three-part videotape/workbook training course to teach basic commands, search strategy formulation, and special features, and Learned Information offers a general video overview of database searching called *Going Online: an Introduction to the World of Online Information*. Vendors often have well designed, generally inexpensive printed user aids for the full system as well as for any end user options. Many also provide online training files and classroom use discount programs for online access.

In-house programs generally carry the responsibility for educating staff at all levels of the organization. The search service manager (or comparable committee or group responsible in a particular library) needs to keep the administration informed for policy and financial reasons; fellow searchers can educate each other in their particular areas of expertise; non-searchers who work on public services desks need to have enough general knowledge to field basic questions intelligently and make effective referrals; staff in various areas need background information to judge whether the capabilities of online searching may be important to integrate into their jobs (interlibrary loan verification, online options for ordering full text of documents, collection development uses). Some libraries are large enough to have online user groups which can offer refresher sessions on categories of databases, discuss new or expanded system features, help in producing in-house user aids, or discuss search strategies and searching techniques in an informal, supportive atmosphere. It can also be a useful forum for news and issues: copyright, fee structure, library searching policies, online vs. print vs. CD-ROM choices, news from the online industry, etc. In-house training and education becomes considerably more complex when a library has access to several different database systems and/or CD-

ROM's, but keeping staff up-to-date is even more crucial in this type of environment where delivery of a new update of CD-ROM software or a change in an online system's command structure may signal an immediate and sweeping change in how some element of a search is performed.

In a useful model, Carol Tenopir suggested a multi-phased approach to in-house training used at the University of Hawaii.[7] Basic introductory sessions, offered about once a year, were for librarians new to the system. In the course of four half-days, new searchers had an opportunity to learn the history and development of database searching, boolean logic, DIALOG commands, the specifics of several popular databases, development of search strategies, etc. Refresher sessions, offered about six months later, gave an opportunity to emphasize special features, answer questions and discuss search approaches in more detail. An advanced strategy session gave experienced users a chance to lead discussion of challenging topics and share experiences. Other in-house options for sharing knowledge included a monthly searchers meeting, as well as occasional information sessions for staff outside reference.

In-house sessions are valuable because the trainer is generally a staff member and available to answer questions as they come up. In addition, local training can be consciously tailored to the needs of the attendees. However, there must be individuals with teaching ability on the staff, and the administration needs to be willing to support the not inconsiderable time and materials costs for developing in-house training.

SELF-EDUCATION

Self-instruction is certainly possible, but offers some problems for the novice searcher since uncorrected mistakes tend to be self-perpetuating and may lead to inefficient, costly searches. The educational, theoretical aspects of online searching can appropriately be attained through self-study, but system-specific information is much better learned from one of the training sources previously mentioned. There are a number of good online textbooks currently in print; users need to check edition dates and be aware that the most accurate information about a system or database will be in the vendor documentation rather than in a book.

Self-instruction tends to be a regular part of the activities of more experienced searchers, although they may not recognize it as such. Professional journals can be a rich source of information about systems and techniques, particularly information retrieval-oriented titles such as *Online*, *Database*, *Computers in Libraries*, *CD-ROM Librarian*, and *Online Review*. Vendor documentation, newsletters, and other publications offer definitive information about a system. Some products are augmented by online help or tutorials, particularly CD-ROM's and online end user systems such as Knowledge Index and Colleague. Customer assistance desks are good sources of continuing education in the form of search help on specific problems or more general needs.

DEVELOPING IN-HOUSE TRAINING: SOME PRACTICAL SUGGESTIONS

In-house training can cover a whole spectrum of formal and informal training experiences. A good place to start when attempting to determine training needs is with the concepts provided in "An Introduction to Online Searching: a Suggested Outline."[8] This is a very comprehensive introductory workshop outline; indeed, to cover all the elements mentioned, even briefly, would take many hours. However, a trainer can use the outline as a checklist and choose the most useful and necessary items for his/her audience (some sessions could be broad-based, others might deal primarily with the mechanics of a new search vendor or CD-ROM product). Seventeen topics are suggested, all of which fall within one of six general areas: Financial/funding considerations; vendors and producers; search mechanics; advantages and limitations; impact on the library's operations; the searcher interface. For further background information, Byerly's *Online Searching: a Dictionary and Bibliographic Guide*[9] continues to be useful for its brief definitions and as a sourcebook to over 700 annotated journal articles and other references covering the full range of online topics published through about 1982. Thirty-two subject areas are included in the general overview (promotion and marketing, searching skills, training and education, etc.), with a second section covering specific subject areas such as science and technology and the law; this bibliography is an extremely useful resource for trainers who are looking for one convenient source of theoretical articles and practical techniques.

Suggestions

The following list of suggestions is subjective (and probably unscientific) but is the result of personal experience in planning and developing training sessions of many types and for many levels of users for accessing online databases, CD-ROMs and OPACs.

1. Before doing any planning in detail, it is really important to develop a list of training objectives. These may be revised somewhat as training progresses, but objectives provide a necessary focus right from the beginning.
2. A schedule of activities is also useful, if only to make the designer(s) estimate how much time each step in the development process will take, as well as the eventual training. Make sure that the trainer has time for adequate preparation: some experts in instructional methodology estimate that at least ten hours of preparation time are necessary to develop one hour of instruction.
3. Even when training people you see every day, it is useful to consider the trainee population: for example, what is the level of understanding about the hardware/software in use, what areas of subject expertise are represented, what levels of prior learning can you build on?
4. Overcome the temptation to give too much detail or cover too many topics in a single session.
5. Try to take into account the different learning styles that may be present in the group. Some individuals learn best from printed materials, others respond well to hands-on practice, still others benefit from question and answer sessions or demonstrations.
6. Think about the time of day to schedule a session. If you

have a choice, most people seem to be fresher during the midmorning hours.

7. When developing any type of training, try to plan the session so that trainees have ample time to absorb the information.

8. Pacing is important. Lectures on complex topics should be given in relatively short sections and combined with more active learning techniques such as discussion, demonstrations or exercises.

9. Explain at the beginning what advantages there are to learning the information to be presented; providing motivation is very important since all the trainer can really do is cover a topic and present a bridge. Each attendee must take the information and make this potential knowledge his own by spending the time to practice and learn.

10. Make sure to define any new or potentially unfamiliar concepts as you go along.

11. Make sure to give attendees some printed materials to follow during training, even if they consist of only the objectives and a session outline.

12. The trainer should try to be approachable and even be willing to stray a bit from the session outline if conditions warrant it. Questions should be encouraged: if one person doesn't understand a concept, probably others are equally mystified.

13. Practice time, preferably supervised, should be used whenever finances and facilities allow it. Users will retain more if they can put their new knowledge to work right away. A set of planned exercises are particularly helpful since the trainer can then make sure that the class uses specific techniques.

14. Try to make it easy for further learning to take place, maybe by scheduling a follow-up session three or four weeks later. All the time you spend in training will be worthless if users fail to use the system frequently enough for skill development and memory to take hold.

15. Try to get some formal or informal evaluation of the session. Comments often provide ideas for improvement of the training package.

TRAINING END USERS

Over the past 10 years, more and more information consumers have also become searchers, and CD-ROM technology is now hastening the process. A large body of literature already exists on the topic, including a recently published annotated bibliography of over 500 citations (about 160 of these are *primarily* about end users).[10] Planning an end user service of any kind is a time-consuming process with many decision points. An excellent overview of all aspects of the process, including training, management, funding, and system choice is available as a new monograph edited by Kesselman and Watstein.[11]

Vendors are finding that more of their workshop attendees are non-librarians, but in practice most end user training is probably happening in libraries that have developed various programs to meet the demand. Although many researchers continue to use intermediaries, there is certainly a trend toward self-service and direct use of systems. Why is this so? At least in terms of online searching, some are seeking to expand uses of a home or office computer. There is also more vendor/producer advertising aimed toward potential end users: the library market is pretty well saturated and they are looking for new clients by advertising in specialty and computer magazines, exhibiting at conferences of researchers, etc. Some end users may actually be non-users of libraries, or live at a geographic distance. There is also the urge for immediate gratification: some feel they need information faster than hard-pressed library staff members can provide it, and they like personal access for the same reasons that shoppers gravitate to a self-service shoe store or researchers appreciate a library collection with open stacks. The systems themselves are becoming more user friendly (at least on the surface through menus, help screens and tutorials), so less detailed system knowledge is necessary to begin.

Advantages for the end user include the timeliness of the information, the ability in most cases to choose output (hard copy or disk), and the satisfaction of being in control. In addition, I believe that end user searchers are becoming better library users as a result: by learning to phrase a question effectively for online retrieval, they are in effect setting specific objectives for what they want to gain from the process. The result seems to be a carryover in making end user searchers more competent and efficient library researchers in general.

There are, of course, obvious limitations to end user searching that must be addressed when thinking about training. Some are system-dependent:

- online systems, including CD-ROM, are really not user friendly enough for the novice or infrequent user.
- each online system or CD-ROM interface is different, with few common features or commands to help a user transfer training from one to another.
- thus far, there are limited databases available through systems specifically designed for end users, although the situation is improving.
- new users have potential problems to overcome with hardware, software, and sometimes telecommunications. Many new searchers become frustrated just trying to log on.

Other limitations are user-dependent:

- users may be uncomfortable with electronic technologies (although this is changing).
- users may not be willing or able to invest the time to become competent searchers. Or, in the case of CD-ROM, the long lines or appointment sheets may discourage use.
- they may not search frequently enough to develop and retain a minimum skill level.
- they probably will lack (or likely will not read) any kind of paper documentation beyond something fairly simple. For the home or office user, manuals and thesauri are expensive, and even people with easy access to search aids will only use them in desperation.
- users commonly experience problems in their choice of terminology. Novices will try to enter sentences instead of phrases or keywords, and they seldom think about concepts like synonyms, variant spellings, stopwords, or plurals.

—many novice end users lack a really clear understanding of boolean logic or ideas to make a search more precise.

With all these negatives, library trainers must develop efficient ways to put end users together with the information they need. The basics are often sufficient: without considerable time expenditure for coaching and one-to-one consultations, most end users will search simplistically compared to a trained intermediary, but will generally produce results adequate to their needs. From my experience, end users need to know:

- that learning a system will take a time commitment but is generally worth the effort.
- about available systems/databases/CD-ROM's and what they include.
- the equipment needed for searching.
- advantages and limitations of searching.
- how to put together an adequate search strategy in language the system will understand.
- enough about the mechanics of searching to log on and off, enter a strategy (including boolean and positional operators), and print, display or capture records to diskette.
- enough techniques to be able to come up with ideas to revise a strategy if too many, too few, or totally irrelevant results are retrieved.
- about any costs involved or other limitations (e.g., page charges for CD-ROM prints, online connect time, per-citation display charges, etc.).

Suggestions

Another ALA committee has written an excellent set of learning objectives for end user training that covers: (1) Under-standing the system; (2) planning the search strategy; (3) operating the system; (4) interpreting search results.[12] For formal training sessions, my fifteen suggestions in the previous section still apply, with particular attention to pacing the session and choosing very judiciously the topics to be covered. In addition:

- Keep things as simple as possible.
- Emphasize the importance of pre-search planning.
- Make sure to cover the basics.
- Give examples of search topics that work or don't work and explain why.
- Provide information in several formats, if possible (e.g., a "quick reference" list of commands with examples as well as a more detailed training packet).

CONCLUSION

Librarians and other reference staff are being challenged as never before to develop and maintain levels of expertise in an increasing number and variety of computerized reference systems. The challenge is growing: we are being asked to interpret and pass on knowledge of systems and databases to an increasingly literate and demanding population of researchers. With CD-ROMs in many reference areas, staff must have a high level of understanding of each system, but users now expect, rightly or wrongly, an equally good level of microcomputer knowledge. If a user downloads citations from an online database or CD-ROM at the library, and then has trouble manipulating the information using his/her own word processing software, the library staff member can be a likely target of a request for assistance — no matter that there are many word processing packages now in use and no individual could be expected to be familiar with them all.

In addition, the proliferation of systems adds to the complexity of reference service. In 1980, Bourne and Robinson predicted that "it seems likely that the search systems and databases will grow toward greater compatibility and standardization."[13] Thus far the likelihood is remote, but it will be interesting to see if the proposed NISO standard for a common command language has any effect. One thing is certain: the work of a reference librarian in the 1990s should be unusually stimulating, sometimes stressful, and always changing as technology advances. Training will continue to have a crucial role in all online-related activities.

REFERENCES .

1. "Survey Shows CD-ROM Posing First Threat To Online Industry," (In SDI: the Database News Section). *Database* 12 (3) (June 1989):11.

2. Tillie Krieger, "Online Searching and Its Place in the Library School Curriculum." *The Reference Librarian* 18 (Summer 1987): 239-253.

3. Stephen P. Harter and Carol H. Fenichel, "Online Searching in Library Education." *Journal of Education for Librarianship* 23 (Summer 1982): 3-22.

4. Herbert S. White, "Defining Basic Competencies." *American Libraries* 14 (8) (September 1983): 519-525.

5. American Library Association, Reference and Adult Services Division, Machine-Assisted Reference Section, Education and Training of Search Analysts Committee, "Continuing Education for Search Analysts." *RQ* 26 (3) (Spring 1987): 285.

6. American Library Association, Reference and Adult Services Division, Machine Assisted Reference Section, Education and Training of Search Analysts Committee, "Online Training Sessions: Suggested Guidelines." *RQ* 20 (4) (Summer 1981): 353-357.

7. Carol Tenopir, "An In-House Training Program for Online Searchers." *Online* 6 (3) (May 1982): 20-26.

8. "An Introduction to Online Searching: a Suggested Outline," In James J. Maloney, *Online Searching, Technique and Management.* (Chicago: American Library Association, 1983): 173-179.

9. Greg Byerly, *Online Searching: a Dictionary and Bibliographic Guide.* (Littleton, Co: Libraries Unlimited, 1983).

10. Fred Batt, *Online Searching for End Users: an Information Sourcebook.* (Phoenix: Oryx Press, 1988).

11. Martin Kesselman and Sarah B. Watstein, *End-User Searching: Services and Providers.* (Chicago: American Library Association, 1988).

12. American Library Association, Reference and Adult Services Division, Machine-Assisted Reference Section, Direct Patron Access to Computer-Based Reference Systems Committee, "Library Users and Online Systems: Suggested Objectives for Library Instruction." *RQ* 25 (2) (Winter 1985): 195-197.

13. Charles P. Bourne and Jo Robinson, "Education and Training for Computer-Based Reference Services: Review of Training Efforts to Date." *Journal of the American Society for Information Science* 31 (1) (January 1980): 34.

II. EDUCATION AND TRAINING VIEWS

The Dynamics of Reference Librarianship

Karen Y. Stabler

SUMMARY. The reference environment is constantly changing and hence there is a growing concern for improving the quality of service. Job specific training is an important and viable option for improving these services. This training should be organized and continuing. Basic steps for such a program include (1) providing a positive environment for learning, (2) initiating a good orientation program, (3) undertaking a needs assessment, (4) selecting appropriate training methods, (5) selecting trainers, (6) selecting those to be trained, and (7) continuously evaluating the results of the program. Examples of topics for training include traditional reference sources. However, the tremendous impact of computer technology on librarianship has necessitated the need for technical training on a multitude of computer systems.

There is renewed interest in the importance of training in the business world. This is particularly true as our society moves from an industrial economy to an information-based economy. Many businesses today understand the importance of training for services and have developed innovative programs to enhance their position by improving quality over their competitors. John Naisbitt and Pa-

Karen Y. Stabler is Head of Information Services, New Mexico State University Library, P.O. Box 30006, Las Cruces, NM 88003.

tricia Aburdene write "the recognition that people are a company's critical resource – and its greatest storehouse of knowledge – is creating a boom in corporate training and education. Corporations are finally willing to invest in people and their skills through training and education to the degree that they have always invested in equipment."[1]

Although there are differences between libraries as service organizations and businesses as profit organizations, they both must be competitive to remain viable institutions. In the past, it appears that librarians stood aloof behaving as though they had a monopoly on information and knowledge. Today, it is clear that there are many competing information-based services. To name a few would include university computing centers competing with university libraries, end-users directly connecting with remote online vendors such as BRS and DIALOG thus bypassing the library, and users ordering materials directly from a service rather than using interlibrary loan.

REFERENCE ENVIRONMENT

The realm in which reference librarians work is rapidly changing. Reference librarians have added other duties beyond the traditional reference desk duty. Such duties and responsibilities may include participation in bibliographic instruction, online searching, collection development, committee work, and publications. Besides the above, reference work is becoming more complex. Not only are more and more reference books becoming available but the books are more complex. Technology is making its impact on reference services creating a sense of technostress among its members. Librarians may do remote online searching, search one or more bibliographic utilities, search locally mounted databases, learn the protocol for several CD-ROM products, partake in electronic mail, and teach users to use the online public catalog. Users needs are not only satisfied with information that is available locally but improved access to information makes the reference librarian work in a universal environment. Thus, in order for librarians to be effective and competitive it is essential that dynamic training programs be established to enhance the quality of service.

At the same time that the quantity of service is increasing, there are real questions about the quality of service provided. There have been several obtrusive and unobtrusive studies questioning the caliber of service provided both in public and academic libraries. In summarizing twenty studies evaluating the quality of reference service conducted in the last two decades, Hernon and McClure suggest the following:

1. provide "half-right" answers to factual and bibliographic questions; they may answer correctly 50 to 62% of these questions
2. spend, on average, no more than five minutes per reference question
3. experience problems in conducting reference interviews, in negotiating "typical" questions, and in implementing effective search strategies to resolve the information needs
4. fail to provide referral to questions when they "don't know" or cannot find an answer[2]

CURRENT STATUS OF EDUCATION AND TRAINING

The minimum education for librarians is an accredited ALA masters degree; however, there are an increasing number of librarians who are earning a second subject masters. A few libraries have internships for librarians such as those sponsored by the Library of Congress, the University of Illinois at Chicago Circle, and the Council on Library Resources. Internships imply training and are usually applied to beginning librarians or librarians who are planning for a mid-career change to management. Internships do not address the continuing training needs for a career in reference. When searching for articles on training in *Library Literature*, the subject heading is "in-service training" with related subject headings of "continuing education" and "institutes and workshops." Conroy defines continuing education as focusing on the individual and that individual is to translate and apply the learning to the work situation.[3] Often continuing education takes place off-site. This training appears to fall in three categories: conferences and institutes, workshops particularly for new technology, and continuing education courses. The library professional and library-related organizations schedule numerous conferences each year. Librarians may attend or read summaries of the conferences which are often provided in the library literature. For learning about new technology, there are numerous opportunities. Examples would include workshops provided by vendors such as BRS, DIALOG, ORBIT, and others, by database producers, by the bibliographic utilities such as OCLC, RLG, and WLN, and by vendors of online catalogs. Finally organizations such as the American Library Association, the Association of College and Research Libraries, and the Public Library Association provide several continuing education courses. All of these programs are excellent and should be encouraged and supported. However, the programs are not directly aimed at the needs of each particular library, and the decision to attend often seems to depend on the motivation of each librarian and not by a systematic approach of the library. Other limitations of continuing education courses are that the times of the programs do not necessarily coincide with the needs of the librarians at a particular location. Programs also lack follow-up, and the courses are long and concentrated.

The primary objective of training, according to Creth, is "to bring about a change — an increase in knowledge, the acquisition of a skill, or the development of confidence and good judgement. Job training is not successful unless the person can do something new or different or demonstrate a change in behavior."[4] This type of training often takes place in-house. There is limited library training literature and that literature which is directly related to training generally is for cataloging, for new technology, and for classified staff. In-house training can offer substantial benefits. It can be customized to the needs of the particular institution, cost effective, and be directly job-related. Topics can be taught when there is a need, and when done correctly follow-up reinforces the transfer of learning. Training sessions do not have to be long and involved, but can be short and relevant. Lawson states "training should be given at a time when it is the most helpful to the employee. Experience has

shown that if one does not use new skills within a week, after training, one loses them. Therefore a training program is most effective
if the participant begins using the new skills within 24 hours after
the training is completed."[5]

STEPS FOR DEVELOPING TRAINING

The environment must be appropriate for good training to take
place. A positive cooperative setting should be established so that
there is no punishment for not knowing, but rather reward for asking questions and learning. In addition, training is important in developing the corporate culture which Miller defines as broadly accepted and usually deep-seated beliefs, attitudes, and expectations
among members on how the people in an organization will act in
different circumstances.[6] Developing this culture is important because it reinforces the standards for reference. For example, should
the librarian provide instruction on the use of tools or should the
librarian provide the answer? Should librarians be satisfied with a
quick answer or should a complete answer be given even if it requires several hours or days to complete? Are all users treated the
same or do some users receive special assistance and some receive
very little?

A well run Reference Department should develop a good orientation program. Advantages of such a program include having the
supervisor set the standard for the Department, making the new
employee feel at ease, begin explaining the policies and procedures
of the particular institution, and stressing the behavior expectations.
Unfortunately, the result of a current survey on introductory training demonstrates that new employees are not satisfied with the
training provided in the majority of libraries surveyed.[7]

Initial steps in developing training for reference are to determine
the current and future continuing directions of the Department.
From this information, the supervisor determines the goals and objectives. After these have been established, a needs assessment
should be made. For example, if a major objective is to improve the
percentage of correct responses, one needs to examine the skills of
the librarians, their attitudes, behavior, interviewing skills, and the
collection. The following are examples of different ways of gather-

ing information. One, the staff in reference departments should keep lists of recurring and difficult questions. From these questions, the staff should be made aware of the particular research needs and interests of its users, and if needed, in depth discussion should follow — particularly in regard to difficult or highly used reference materials. Two, a survey should be taken to get the reference librarians perceptions of where training is needed. Jeffrey Hallett writing about training needs in business points out that training should be in response to providing better quality to the customers and thus many needed programs will come from the ideas of employees rather than the training officers.[8] Three, the strengths and weaknesses of the staff should be assessed. The supervisor should examine the education, experience, interests, and abilities of each member of the staff. Four, the collection should be reviewed to see that the best and most up-to-date materials are available for the most likely asked questions. Five, the supervisor should observe as well as receive feedback from users on attitudes, behaviors and skills such as the reference interview. And six, a good supervisor should be able to determine the troublesome areas and focus on them.

After determining the training needs of the particular Reference Department, the supervisor should determine the best training methods. Creth points out that coaching and acting as a role model are two good examples of training methods for supervisors.[9] Margaret Magnus writes that one learns better through experience and in the context of work.[10] This current way of thinking helps support mentoring which is a popular method of training today. Another common way is the lecture method. One of its major advantages is that a large number of people can be trained at once. On the other hand, it can be a passive activity for the learner. The introduction of new technology is often presented by demonstrations. This method has the advantage of visual reinforcement; however, demonstrations sometimes tend to be marketing sessions providing only all the advantages of the new system or equipment. The important concept to remember with demonstrations is to provide hands on experience for the trainee. The purpose is not to show what the trainer knows, but rather to teach the skills to the trainee. Discussions and role playing are particularly good methods for improving techniques of the reference interview or how to handle a problem patron. There are good commercial products such as video cassettes that can assist training for attitudes and behavior. Training can take place during part of the time devoted to reference meetings, in a mini reference series, or brown bag lunch series can be instituted where particular topics can be discussed.

The selection of who should be chosen as a trainer is critical. Supervisors have several alternatives from which to choose. The designated trainer can not possibly be the expert on all topics nor would they have the time to provide all the training in such a changing environment. Librarians on the staff who have developed expertise in a particular topic or index can become trainers. In fact Naisbitt and Aburdene state that "the top-down authoritarian management style is yielding to a networking style of management, where people learn from one another horizontally, where everyone is a resource for everyone else, and where each person gets support and assistance from many different directions."[11] There are several benefits in using one's own staff. It provides an opportunity for librarians to show their expertise to their peers. Working at a particular locale helps make the instruction more individualized to the needs of the library's users, and finally, teaching reinforces and enhances one's own knowledge about a particular subject tool.

Selecting those to be trained is also extremely important. Not all librarians have to be present at every session. However, just because one has several years of experience does not mean that librarians do not need training.

Constant evaluation and feedback are essential for good training. As Creth states "training should be seen as a change agent."[12] If training does not create a change or improvement of a skill or behavior then training has failed and a new approach must be developed.

EXAMPLES OF TRAINING
FOR TRADITIONAL REFERENCE

Some examples of training sessions have been listed. My experience involves working in three different academic reference departments. Although there are many similarities there are significant differences in emphasis requiring expertise in different subject areas. In depth knowledge of typical types of questions or highly used reference books more quickly improves the quality of service and reduces the trial and error approach and consequently losing face before the user. For example, at a large land grant university library, there are numerous questions in the fields of agriculture, science, and technology. In depth knowledge of reference sources in those fields as well as the ability to understand scientific terminology are essential. On the other hand, at a private liberal arts university library, the librarian must have in depth knowledge of authors, philosophers, literary periods and reference works related to these areas. Although most librarians are familiar with the basic tools and what they do, the level of skills in using these same books may vary greatly depending on the reference environment.

Reference books are continuously changing. For example, *Sociological Abstracts* has changed considerably since its first mimeographed 50 cent issue in 1953 containing fifty-two abstracts and elementary indexing. An issue today contains over 2,000 abstracts to journal articles, citations to book reviews, book abstracts, conference proceedings and papers as well as information to order if not available locally. In addition the indexing is much more sophisticated providing both the independent and dependent variables of the study, population group studied, and methodology.

New reference materials are continually published. Although libraries often display these books, reference librarians do not necessarily take the time to review them. Therefore, time should be used discussing new books. The discussion should indicate how the new book compares with traditional books, what information is included, and how the information is organized.

From time to time, difficult and seldom used tools need to be reviewed. Some examples may include how to use the *Human Relations Area Files*, *United Nations Documents Index*, legal materials, or locating British parliamentary papers. Just because it was known at one time how to find the information, it does not mean that these reference sources should not be reviewed, particularly if the needs of a certain library do not require frequent use of them.

Discussing unique collections in a particular library is very profitable. This not only allows the librarians to know what is available but they can also promote the collections. Of course, reference librarians should be well informed about Special Collections and Archives. Microform collections are often neglected and should also be discussed. In addition indexing of some microforms collections are exceedingly difficult to understand.

Another area where training can supplement the collection are sessions on other library and/or information services provided in the community or university. Knowing the limitations of ones own collection or expertise and knowing the strengths of others can prove to be very helpful. The emphasis should not be in making a referral but rather to complement the information already available at the local library.

TRAINING FOR TECHNOLOGY

There seems to be more concern for training for technology than training for traditional reference sources. This fact is particularly true when the technology is very new. The need to train library staff seems more urgent, not only because technology is new, but because it is not always obvious what is in each database and how to search it. However, one of the major problems in training for technology is that the technology is coming faster than the training. Many of those who are knowledgeable about the technology may not have the time or in some cases may not have the ability to be a good trainer. Documentation is often inadequate and the sales representatives are not always informed. Thus, there is a real training dilemma with technology which is further exacerbated by the stress it puts on librarians having to learn a number of different systems which have been added to an already busy schedule.

Remote online searching was one of the first areas where there was training for reference technology. Vendors and database producers have been particularly aggressive in providing training. This training often takes place off-site and although often well done has some drawbacks. It is very concentrated thus difficult to digest, lacks follow-up, is not necessarily timely, i.e., one takes the training when it is available. Furthermore, the examples for searching are always perfect and do not necessarily represent the real world of searching. For the training to be really effective, the individual library needs to develop follow-up to reinforce the training session.

An in-house example of training for technology may include a session on improving searching conference proceedings on OCLC. Describing the MARC record and the relevant OCLC fields, i.e., 110, 111, 411, 511, and 670 are a good beginning. The next step would be to provide examples of searching the Name-Authority file so that one could find a list of cross references. From these entries, one can more quickly search the bibliographic record through the Corporate Author Search. The session can be further strengthened by demonstrating several examples and then giving each attendee examples to search.

Currently training in reference technology encompasses a variety of systems such as microcomputers and their operating systems, CD-ROM, public online catalogs, and electronic mail. My experience for the best programs follow the same pattern. There are several short sessions, e.g., half an hour to an hour which take place over a short period of time. The first session provides information about the database or system. The second and third sessions are highly interactive providing ample time for the trainees to have hands on experience. After limited time the trainer should offer a follow-up session to evaluate the progress of the trainees and to evaluate the program for possible improvements.

CONCLUSION

Since a major resource in every library is its librarians, they must receive effective training to be competitive. The reference librarians are those who work most directly with the users for they are the persons who have the primary responsibility for providing information or locating materials to satisfy the needs of the users. If the users needs are not met the library fails its mission and becomes merely a custodian of materials.

Today's work environment is rapidly changing and in order to keep current librarians must be trained and retrained. For reference librarians this means not only keeping current with reference materials and technology but also in methods of delivering the best service. "Training is not a cure all, but it does provide positive, relevant learning experience and can be a very favorable impact on employee morale."[13] Training should not only improve the quality of service but should place emphasis not on working harder but rather on working more intelligently.

It is management's responsibility to see that there has been proper training. However it is the responsibility of the employees to learn. Both management and employees must actively participate in training or the program will not be successful.

REFERENCES

1. Naisbitt, John and Patricia Aburdene, *Re-inventing the Corporation: Transforming Your Job and Your Company for the New Information Society* (New York: Warner Books, 1985) p. 165.

2. Hernon, Peter and Charles R. McClure, *Unobtrusive Testing and Library Reference Services* (Norwood, NJ: Ablex Publishing, 1987) p. 3-4.

3. Conroy, Barbara, *Library Staff Development and Continuing Education: Principles and Practices* (Littleton, CO: Libraries Unlimited, 1978) p. xv.

4. Creth, Sheila D., *Effective On-The-Job Training: Developing Library Human Resources* (Chicago, American Library Association, 1986). p. 3.

5. Lawson, Karen E., "Effective Employee Training Must Go Beyond Education," *Bottomline* 3:22 (Dec. 1986).

6. Miller, Ernest C., "Planning: Strategic Planning Pays" *Personnel Journal* 68:129 (Apr. 1989).

7. Stabler, Karen Y., "Introductory Training of Academic Librarians: a Survey," *RQ* 26:363-369 (Spring 1987).

8. Hallett, Jeffrey J., "Training: Another Look at an Old Friend," *Personnel Administrator* 32:39 (Oct. 1987).

9. Creth, *Effective On-The-Job Training* p. 86.

10. Magnus, Margaret, ed., "Training Futures," *Personnel Journal* 65:69 (May 1986).

11. Naisbitt and Aburdene, *Re-inventing the Corporation* p. 62.

12. Creth, *Effective On-The-Job Training* p. 5.

13. Young, Marlene B. "Organizational Training: Benefit or Obligation?" *Personnel Administrator* 32:30 (Oct. 1987).

Origins and Attitudes: Training Reference Librarians for a Pluralistic World

Phoebe Janes
Ellen Meltzer

SUMMARY. A critically important component for all new and continuing reference librarian training is the rapidly changing demographic climate at academic library reference desks. Public libraries have historically been the primary public service agencies dealing with diverse clientele. Academic librarians must rapidly catch up with them, as well as with other fields—business, education, social work—for whom the word "multicultural" is already integrated into their lexicons. Isolated academic libraries throughout the country are pioneering with public service training programs that reflect these dramatic changes in clientele. Further, general suggestions are put forth outlining the significance of shared goals, administrative support, and an understanding of the issues as necessary prerequisites to any multicultural training program.

INTRODUCTION

A multitude of issues and questions relates to training new reference librarians—what public service skills and abilities have they been taught or not taught in library school; what life skills do they bring to their reference work; once on the job, who trains them and what methods of training should be employed? Each individual brings a different combination of components to the position; on the job training must build on the new librarian's proficiencies and ex-

---

Phoebe Janes is a Reference and Collection Development Librarian and Ellen Meltzer is Head of Reference and Collection Development at Moffitt Undergraduate Library, University of California, Berkeley, CA 94720.

145

periences that are already in place. A crucial component in the training of new professionals is ensuring they are intellectually and emotionally prepared to serve the clientele of the institutions in which they have been hired.

It can be argued that the composition of college and university student bodies has altered radically in the recent past. Two decades ago or less it was a great deal easier to characterize "average" college freshmen — how they looked, sounded, and how prepared they might be to use the library. Today, any past assumptions about patrons can hinder rather than expand public service. The patrons college and university libraries now serve represent a diverse mix of cultures, ethnic origins, gender groups, ages, socioeconomic classes, and physical abilities. Public libraries have experienced and faced these changes in their clientele much sooner than have librarians in the academic setting, and we must now catch up with our public librarian colleagues.

For many librarians, the values with which we were raised and which were reinforced in library school are no longer valid in today's pluralistic setting. "Growing up in any academic environment, even in a society as multinational and diverse as the United States, we emerge with a set of perceptions that are strikingly similar and largely unrecognized by ourselves as peculiar to us. Our shared commonalities are seen best when they are not shared, or when they become uncommon."[1] The skills we need to instill in our new librarians and to reinforce in our current staffs, have consequently not only to do with traditional professional competencies that can be learned in the classroom, but also with values needed to work effectively with the increasingly diverse community of users served by us.

THE SETTING

California provides a dramatic example of the demographic change taking place in the United States. "During 1987-88, 49.9% of California's public school students were nonwhite . . . by the year 2000, the nonwhite student population is projected to be 58% of the total." The racial/ethnic makeup of immigrants from the 1950s to the 1970s has shifted from 59% European, 22% Hispanic,

6% Asian to 18% European, 41% Hispanic and 36% Asian.[2] Fall semester, 1988 was the first time there was no ethnic majority at the University of California at Berkeley—among Berkeley's 20,000 undergraduates 48.5% were whites, 26.5% Asians, 11.1% Hispanics, 7.0% Blacks, and 1.1% Native Americans.[3] Non-immigrant international students at the University of California at Berkeley have risen from 1,600 in 1973 to 2,100 in 1988.[4] The Physically Disabled Students Program at UCB estimates there to be between 500-600 currently enrolled disabled students,[5] and re-entry undergraduates in Fall 1988 numbered nearly 2,000.[6] With such demographic diversity comes economic diversity as well. In 1987, Berkeley freshmen reported average parental income of over $50,000, 18% stated that their parents earned less than $25,000, with 7% earning less that $15,000 and 6% more than $150,000.[7] These data demonstrate that students entering college today, no matter what their ethnic background, country of origin or capabilities, are entering the institution from disparate financial and environmental backgrounds.

WHY THE NEED FOR A NEW KIND OF TRAINING?

The urgent need to reassess existing training of reference librarians in the face of demographic changes is obvious. Vivian Sykes, Multicultural Librarian at University of California at Santa Cruz, explains why by identifying barriers to reference service to the multicultural library user. Such barriers, it can be argued, pertain to all groups discussed in this article:

- There are value-laden barriers to information dissemination— "Is this person asking me a valid question?"
- People at the reference desk may need special training in racial sensitivity [or cultural sensitivity or in dealing with those with physical disabilities].
- Assumptions are made before patrons open their mouths about what level of service they will need.
- [Patrons'] experience with library service may vary a great deal.
- Differences in communication styles may create barriers.[8]

Librarians must acknowledge the often difficult "truths" in Sykes' straightforward criticism. As advocates for our clientele, public service staff cannot begin to address these vital issues until we face their existence. Additionally, in the training process we must be continuously aware of how we characterize the "inadequacies" of our users. Is it only the users who lack knowledge to successfully use "our" libraries; or rather, is ethnocentricity preventing us from effectively understanding the abilities and needs of the very patrons we are attempting to serve? Patricia Tarin, in her perceptive analysis of a Rand report argues that "All of the barriers to service reported are cast in terms of inadequacies of the part of the ethnic person (the minority person 'does not know,' 'cannot make an informed choice,' 'does not perceive' . . .). These same barriers can be recast in terms that indicate what types of changes are needed [in library services]:

- Library staff do not know how to maximize potential . . .
- Library staff do not provide adequate educational and informational materials . . .
- Library staff do not feel comfortable with minorities . . . [9]

Rethinking public service attitudes mandates new perceptions, new values, and most critically, librarians who are flexible enough to realize that public service is an ever-changing process, dependent on whom we serve, not merely on who we are.

NEW PEOPLE, NEW SKILLS

What, then, are the skills librarians need to serve this changing and diverse client base? Germaine Shames provides an excellent list of attributes and skills desirable for managers in multicultural settings. These include the following:

- Self-awareness—the recognition of one's own values, assumptions, needs and limitations;
- Culture-reading—the ability to find and trace the inherent logic in each culture,
- Multiple perspectives—the ability to suspend judgment, remove one's cultural filters, and "see" through others' eyes,

- Intercultural communication skills—the ability to send and interpret verbal and nonverbal messages accurately in different cultures,
- Gear-shifting—the ability to readjust expectations, modify plans, try out new approaches, and rebound from setbacks,
- Culture-shock savvy—the ability to monitor one's own adjustment to a new culture,
- Relationship-building skills—the ability to relate to and inspire confidence in all kinds of people, and to maintain a support system, and
- Intercultural-facilitation skills—the ability to manage cultural differences and use these differences to the operations' benefit.[10]

Interestingly, the roots of these skills and philosophy were first outlined over fifty years ago by S. R. Ranganathan in his seminal work, *Five Laws of Library Science*. Ranganathan articulates the two most salient tenets of public service: First is the commitment to serve each individual regardless of who or what the individual is or appears to be; and second, the recognition of the principle that "continuous change" is a constant in the work environment, affecting librarians, patrons, and service at all times.[11]

ENSURING LIBRARIANS HAVE THE SKILLS

The mandate for public service training must be a stated and widely promulgated part of the institution's organizational goals, supported by management. These goals must be acknowledged by all members of the reference unit as a primary public service goal. Commitment on the part of the administration includes the recognition that staff will need time off from regularly scheduled activities for workshops, training sessions and continuing education activities to support this goal. Commitment on the part of staff includes not only willingness to accept and attend the training sessions, but further, willingness to initiate the necessary changes manifested in the training.

Even before such programs begin, libraries can ensure the reference staff supports the institutions' goals by including in initial job announcements for public service positions the desirability of multi-cultural experience as one of the prerequisites for the position. Course work in multicultural training in library schools would be one mechanism to partially fulfill this goal, enriching the applicant's "people" skills. DeHart points out that, "Preparation in the area of human relations, including intergroup relations, is required in all programs leading to initial teaching certification in education in Wisconsin. Program components include black, Latino, Native American, and Asian American culture and values, anti-Semitism, the culture of poverty and ageism."[12] Such coursework integrated into library school curricula would surely enrich the student's scope of knowledge. Simsova argues that "To be able to relate library service to existing needs, students should be taught the basic techniques for surveying the community . . . They should be introduced to the significant research in the field and to general principles of research methodology. In cross-cultural contacts, understanding depends on insight into how others think and feel. It is a good idea, therefore, to encourage students to undertake an in-depth case study of a minority ethnic group which is not their own. The method developed by comparative librarianship is very suitable for this purpose . . . By identifying with groups other than their own and by listening to the contributions of others in the class, students realize the relativity of their own cultural conditioning. To provide them with a conceptual framework for their pragmatic insights, they are then introduced to some theoretical concepts such as identity and prejudice."[13] One often hears the argument that it is impossible to include more courses in already crowded Library School curricula. Clearly, then, this is an even more compelling reason to ensure that new and continuing reference librarians uniformly receive on-the-job training to understand the immediate impact of demographic changes on public service.

TRAINING FOR THE NEW WORLD

New librarians come to the institution fresh from library school with a strong theoretical base, with recent, state-of-the-art information and technical skills, and enthusiasm for the profession. Education beyond the formal education must then be gained (1) on the job; (2) through deliberate self-study; (3) through institutional staff-development; and (4) through continuing education sources.[14] These are the mechanisms through which librarians gain new information; the institution, through its reward and evaluation system, must also encourage librarians to expand their knowledge and skills.

Training new reference staff requires first, the assignment of background readings on the demographic makeup of the community or student body in order to identify the constituency, and to discover what "pluralistic" means in a particular setting. By integrating such information into the initial training sessions, the new librarian learns that this aspect of the job is considered as critical to public service as reference desk procedures, collection development strategies, and the myriad other details that one must rapidly absorb at the commencement of any new position.

At the UC Berkeley Library, some 60 positions are filled each year in a variety of job classifications. Every new library employee, from photocopy repair technician to Associate University Librarian takes a two-day program entitled "New Employee Orientation Program" (NEOP). The program consists of many components, and is aimed at instructing the broadest base of all library employees. Issues covered include the complexity of working in a large, decentralized system; the organizational goals of the library; the symbiotic relationships among job classifications and between departments; and the challenge of working in a multicultural work environment. This broad brush stroke approach to library organization and mission in the academic community serves the institution well by presenting the library as an exciting, vibrant organization in which to work, and one in which both technical and public service staff share common service goals.

An ambitious in-house program at the University of Michigan aimed at educating staff to deal with pluralistic staff and clientele included the following components: a week-long workshop on racism; discussion groups; a film series; an "amity" program for new staff; a Peer Information Counseling Program for minority students, and the hiring of a Diversity Librarian.[15]

While there are many advantages to designating a "Multicultural" or "Diversity" Librarian, it is perhaps even more important to strive to create a multiculturally diverse staff. One librarian cannot be designated the "conscience" of the library; all specialists can not be from the target group.[16] While people of color and from a variety of backgrounds must be actively recruited into the profession in much greater numbers—equal at least to their representation in society—it is deceptive to think that special client groups can be well-served only by individuals from those groups. Instead our goal should be to build a diverse staff sensitive to the needs of all users and knowledgeable about different backgrounds.

A pioneering library staff training program at the University of Arizona was designed "to train staff to teach international students to use the library and at the same time, to prepare the library staff to communicate effectively with the students. Goals of the program include sensitizing the staff to the frustrations foreign students have in attempting to understand a foreign language, to the emotions of culture shock, to the awareness of one's own cultural assumptions and interpretations, and how to be effective in a culturally diverse climate." Innovative tools to accomplish these goals include the use of videotapes and a cross-cultural simulation game.[17] The English-speaking staff was shown a video which explained Inter-Library Loan procedures to them in Spanish: based on the information in the video, they were then required to fill out an ILL form properly. This program is effective by immersing staff into situations in which they are no longer comfortable as the "holders of power." Such a dramatic personal experience serves to remind us all that empathy continues to be a bridge to improved public service.

The University of California at Berkeley Library has a series of workshops for staff coordinated by the Director of Instructional Services, entitled "Training for Change." Included among the more traditional training such as "Teaching the Online Catalog" or "Managing Student Employees" are "Understanding the Hard to Understand Patron" (physically disabled students); "Patrons who speak English with Hard to Understand Accents" (international students); and a session on helping patrons with "invisible" disabilities, such as dyslexia. The primary success of these programs stems from the fact that the speakers were themselves physically disabled, international or learning disabled. Indeed the key accomplishment of these workshops was providing the opportunity for staff to relate directly and frankly with the primary group. Staff were encouraged to ask questions they would ordinarily never ask a patron (particularly a disabled person) — Does it hurt you to speak? Does it insult you if I ask you to write your question down? Staff came away with a much better understanding of the target groups; stereotypes were shattered, and in a non-threatening situation, librarians learned again how to better serve patrons.

In another context, "Donald K. Cheek urges whites to understand the black life-style by obtaining black-oriented information from a black perspective. In this way, sensitivity and understanding of black behaviors will be gained."[18] Such experiences underscore the fact that a variety of people must be involved in the training process. Learning will be most successful if planning and direct training include representatives from a variety of cultural, ethnic, gender, and age groups.[19]

Some of the training programs described here are quite ambitious in scope and could require a substantial budget to produce. However, elements of such programs might be extracted and used to bring staff to the same level of understanding and to promote the sharing of common goals. Reading and viewing of videos followed by discussion are relatively easy to implement in most settings. Arranging a program series with speakers from campus who are disabled or of international origin can be another good first step.

MAKE TRAINING ONGOING

Numerous other communities, most notably the business community, are stressing the importance of multicultural training. Such works as Pierre Casse's *Training for the Multicultural Manager: A Practical and Cross Cultural Approach to the Management of People*,[20] training and development journals in the business field, and videocassettes such as the series "Valuing Diversity" including segments on "Managing Differences"; "Diversity at Work"; and "Communicating Across Cultures"[21] should not be excluded from our own training. We must not focus too narrowly on the field of librarianship, but must scan the literature of other fields.

Once the administration and public service staff have acknowledged the need for staff training programs that explore the myriad issues related to multiculturalism, there are no absolute blueprints for success. Much depends upon the specifics of each library on how to focus and proceed. Innovations and new thinking are invited. The experts are among us. This is an important point to stress. Librarians have much to learn from those we serve; outside experts are not necessarily required. Tailoring programs for specific communities is also important. Although the word "pluralism" is used throughout this paper as an umbrella term, it is not meant to lump every group or issue together, such as racism and disability.

Another important point to recognize is that such training, in order to be effective, and to include all reference staff, is essentially never-ending; institutions must embrace the need to have continuous training programs aimed not only at new, but at continuing librarians as well. None of us assumes we have learned all there is to know about online searching, or new technologies, yet we often have no new training to deal with changing demographics — another area of "continuous change."

The excitement and challenge of public service in culturally diverse settings provide us with ongoing opportunities to learn, explore, and celebrate not only our differences, but the commonalities we share as well.

REFERENCES

1. Moorhead, Wendy, "Ignorance Was Our Excuse: BI for Foreign Students Requires a Shift in Cultural Perspective," *C & R L News* 9:586 (October 1986).

2. Gifford, Bernard, "Testing: Perils and Promises," *The Educator*, 3:7 (January 1989).

3. Simmons, W. S., "Proposal for An American Cultures Breadth Requirement: Report by the Special Committee on Education and Ethnicity," Academic Senate, University of California, Berkeley, March 29, 1989.

4. "Statistics on Non-Immigrant International Students, Fall Semester, 1988," Office of Student Research, University of California, Berkeley.

5. Interview with Ward Newmeyer, Director of Special Services, Disabled Students Program, University of California, Berkeley, May 22, 1989.

6. "Re-entry Students: A Special Volume of Undergraduate Statistics for the University of California at Berkeley, Spring, 1989," Office of Student Research, University of California, Berkeley, May 22, 1989.

7. Office of Public Information, University of California, Berkeley, January 12, 1989.

8. Sykes, Vivian, "Reference Service to the Multicultural Library User,"

Paper presented at the Fall CARLDIG workshop co-sponsored by Oakland Public Library, Oakland, California, December 2, 1988. Cited in *CARL Newsletter*, 12:2-3 (May 1989).

9. Tarin, Patricia, "RAND Misses the Point: A "Minority" Report," *LJ*, 113:32 (November 1988).

10. Shames, Germaine, "Training for the Multicultural Workplace," *Cornell Hotel and Restaurant Administration Quarterly*, 26:27 (February, 1986).

11. Ranganathan, Shiyali Ramamrita, *Five Laws of Library Science*: (Bombay, New York: Asia Publishing House, [1957]).

12. DeHart, Florence, *The Librarian's Psychological Commitments: Human Relations in Librarianship*, (Westport, Conn.: Greenwood, 1979) 7-8.

13. Simsova, Sylvia, "Library Training for Services to Minority Ethnic Groups: Concepts and General Principles," *Library Trends* 29:253 (Fall 1980).

14. Rothstein, Samuel, "The Making of a Reference Librarian," *Library Trends* 31:388 (Winter 1983).

15. *Point of Intersection: The University Library and the Pluralistic Campus Community; A Report to the Vice Provost for Minority Affairs on University Library Programs for Enhancing Diversity and Academic Excellence at the University of Michigan*. Ann Arbor: The University of Michigan Library, November 28, 1988.

16. Wertheimer, Leonard, "Library Service to Ethnocultural Minorities: Philosophical and Social Bases and Professional Implications," *Public Libraries* 26:101 (Fall 1987).

17. Louise Greenfield, Susan Johnston, and Karen Williams, "Educating the World: Training Library Staff to Communicate Effectively with International Students," *Journal of Academic Librarianship*, 12:227-228 (Spring 1986).

18. Lam, R. Errol, "The Reference Interview: Some Intercultural Considerations," *RQ*, 27:392 (Spring 1988).

19. Tucker, Michael, Baier, Vickie, and Rhinesmith, Stephen, "Before You Take Off: What Your Overseas People Need To Know," *Personnel* 62:64 (December 1985).

20. Casse, Pierre, *Training for the Multicultural Manager: A Practical and Cross-Cultural Approach to the Management of People*, (Washington, D.C.: Society for Intercultural Education, 1982).

21. "Valuing Diversity" Videocassette Series, Copeland Griggs Productions; in association with Price Cobbs, Pacific Management, San Francisco: CA: Copeland Griggs Productions, 1987.

The Ethics of Reference Service for the Public Librarian

Fay Ann Golden

SUMMARY. The ethics of library service are concepts that novice librarians must be educated to, and believe in. Supervisors must make sure that trainees understand the basic documents published by the American Library Association, *The Library Bill of Rights*, and *The Statement on Professional Ethics*. Not only the precepts of intellectual freedom, and confidentiality of library records and reference transactions are involved in observing the tenets of these documents, however. Equal treatment for all means equally courteous and thoughtful treatment of all the patrons one serves. Personal beliefs and prejudices make perfection in complying with the ideal difficult, but every librarian must try to live by the ideal in all dealings with the public. The rewards of this behavior are not only those of knowing that one has done one's best, but the contribution made to the success of the employing institution.

Librarians consider themselves professionals, members of a profession. This concept is widely accepted. The point that creates controversy and confusion is the definition of what a professional is. Levels of education are pointed to as positive proofs, but the lack of independence in being able to set up an individual practice, like that of a doctor or lawyer, is held as contradictory evidence. One point that is never disputed, however, is that a profession as a body, and its practitioners as individuals, all have certain principles that govern their conduct in performing their duties on behalf of their clients.

Ms. Golden is Director, Liverpool Public Library, 310 Tulip St., Liverpool, NY 13088.

BASIC CONCEPTS

In training new librarians in their introduction to work at the reference desk, their supervisors must make sure that they are acquainted with such documents as the Library Bill of Rights, and the Statement of Professional Ethics which the American Library Association has formulated. In most cases, newly graduated MLS's will have had an introduction in their courses to the topics of ethics and intellectual freedom. The application of these principals in the work place will involve subtleties and matters of self control that will probably not have been covered in most course offerings, however. A source for copies of these documents, and several other statements that pertain can be found in THE NEW YORK GUIDE TO INTELLECTUAL FREEDOM IN LIBRARIES, published by Intellectual Freedom Round Table, and the New York Library Association in 1987, with the support of the Social Issues Resources Series, Inc.

The Library Bill of Rights

The American Library Association affirms that all libraries are forums for information and ideas, and that the following basic policies should guide their services.

1. Books and other library resources should be provided for the interest, information, and enlightenment of all people of the community the library serves. Materials should not be excluded because of the origin, background, or views of those contributing to their creation.

2. Libraries should provide materials and information presenting all points of view on current and historical issues. Materials should not be proscribed or removed because of partisan or doctrinal disapproval.

3. Libraries should challenge censorship in the fulfillment of their responsibility to provide information and enlightenment.

4. Libraries should cooperate with all persons and groups concerned with resisting abridgment of free expression and free access to ideas.

5. A person's right to use a library should not be denied or abridged because of origin, age, background, or views.

6. Libraries which make exhibit spaces and meeting rooms available to the public they serve should make such facilities available on an equitable basis, regardless of the beliefs or affiliations of individuals or groups requesting their use.

Statement on Professional Ethics, 1981

Introduction

Since 1939, the American Library Association has recognized the importance of codifying and making known to the public and the profession the principles which guide librarians in action. This latest revision of the CODE OF ETHICS reflects changes in the nature of the profession and in its social and institutional environment. It should be augmented as necessary.

Librarians significantly influence or control the selection, organization, preservation, and dissemination of information. In a political system grounded in an informed citizenry, librarians are members of a profession explicitly committed to intellectual freedom and the freedom of access to information. We have a special obligation to ensure the free flow of information and ideas to present and future generations.

Librarians are dependent upon one another for the bibliographic resources that enable us to provide information services, and have obligations for maintaining the highest level of personal integrity and competence.

Code of Ethics

I. Librarians must provide the highest level of service through appropriate and usefully organized collections, fair and equitable circulation and service policies, and skillful, accurate, unbiased, and courteous responses to all requests for assistance.

II. Librarians must resist all efforts by groups or individuals to censor library materials.

III. Librarians must protect each user's right to privacy with respect to information sought or received, and materials consulted, borrowed, or acquired.

IV. Librarians must adhere to the principles of due process and equality of opportunity in peer relationships and personnel actions.

V. Librarians must distinguish clearly in their actions and statements between their personal philosophies and attitudes and those of an institution or professional body.

VI. Librarians must avoid situations in which personal interests might be served or financial benefits gained at the expense of library users, colleagues, or the employing institution.

Every public library board of trustees and director should be sure that these statements are incorporated in the library's mission statement and given to new employees on their first day. High ideals do no good concealed in the employee manual.

CONDUCT AT THE REFERENCE DESK

Good manners have been defined as the ability to put another person at ease. Surely nowhere is this ability needed more than at the reference desk. The first admonition for the new librarian must be to greet patrons with a smile, or at least a pleasant, open expression. (Those who master this skill find themselves being asked for directions even in the grocery store.) A colleague described a librarian as an ideal, because she rose to her feet when patrons approached and behaved as though she had waited all day for them to come ask her their questions. Adults who need help feel vulnerable, and worried that the librarian will judge them inferior because they do not automatically know how to find what they need. Children are frequently awed by the authority figure before them, and are afraid to ask questions. People who leave a library convinced that they were rebuffed by a cold manner, or a reluctance to help them, will be unlikely to return. Discontented people tend to share their resentment, and the reputation of the library, and its attraction to the public can deteriorate. Altruistically motivated staff members will be eager to provide excellent service to the patrons. Enlightened self interest dictates that presenting the best aspect of the institution to the public will ensure the success of the institution, and future prosperity for all, when patrons feel that their needs for information, and their less obvious need for an accepting manner are satisfied.

Therefore, it is necessary to provide a favorable climate for the exchange of information. The librarian must be able to draw from the client an accurate idea of the information he is seeking. A relaxed and friendly manner, reassuringly professional and confident, will set the stage for the interchange of information needed by the patron, and imparted by the librarian. The reference staff members should be trained in patience. By interrupting, or showing impatience with the person across the desk, they may curtail the reference interview, so that they misunderstand the patron's question, and give an incorrect or incomplete answer.

An inhibitor to good communication can be the prejudices that people are not even conscious they hold. Besides the more obvious biases, like racial, political or religious, which everyone condemns, there are more subtle ones. People chewing gum, girls who giggle, students who only want short books to read can always set someone's teeth on edge. Little kids who are not attractive probably are almost never greeted with a smile. All these people are deserving though, of the best that the library can offer as much as the most mannerly and adorable among us. By responding to their information search with the same enthusiasm and care as any who are "acceptable," the reference librarian demonstrates professionalism and ethical behavior.

Of course, librarians can sometimes be asked for help with questions on sensitive or embarrassing topics, or about something that strikes them as ridiculous. It goes without saying that the reference supervisor must warn new people against ever commenting to a third party about a patron's request.

QUESTIONS OF JUDGMENT

Among the issues most often discussed by librarians is the eternal homework question. How much help for school children is appropriate. Are we doing their homework for them? Or are we offering them the same help we would give an adult without hesitation? It is worth remembering that it is considered improper to pry as to the uses that a patron may make of information, if that patron is a grown up. It is surely as much a violation of a child's rights to want to know how he or she will use the information he seeks. If a librarian views his/her task as that of an educator helping the student learn how to use the library, then he is not doing an assignment for the student, he is unlocking the door that opens the world of knowledge to the student, and fulfilling his/her professional role. A child who finds the library a welcoming place, staffed by people who care about being helpful, will grow up to be a library user and supporter.

The neophyte reference worker must be taught to use judgment in measuring the amount of time spent on each question. When the desk is busy, with the phone ringing, and clients lining up, it is necessary to ration the attention that can be spent on each. The temptation is there to hurry through dealing with the difficult or unpleasant person, rather than objectively to help each patron as fully as possible, given the restraints of time, and the number of other people waiting for help. The librarian should not allow herself to get caught up in an interesting though complex question, while letting others wait. It is courteous to acknowledge those who are waiting, and sometimes help them to get started on their searches, then to return to the longer, more complicated one. This demands an ability to pursue several subjects at once. The skill to divide one's attention successfully is necessary to develop so that patrons do not get exasperated by waiting, only to leave before they receive any help.

When new people are getting used to the pressures of public service, they may be thrown by the occasional obnoxious patron. It could be a demanding, condescending, or hostile manner that is difficult to deal with. It could be a lack of personal hygiene that is offensive. Although there are limits beyond which a librarian should not be pushed, in most cases, courtesy and patience can defuse a situation, and result in a satisfactory conclusion to the reference search. A new staff member must also be trained when to determine that a situation has become serious enough to require help, and even to ask for rescue by the security staff.

QUESTIONS OF DISCRETION

Related to the issue of even handed treatment of all patrons is that of the use of interlibrary loan. Some institutions limit the availability of ILL to certain ages, or to certain types of material. Sadly, there are some librarians who are reluctant to offer ILL to children despite what the institutional policy may be. This, of course, is unconscionable. A free and equal access to all sources of information for all is a basic tenet of the Library Bill of Rights and the Statement on Professional Ethics. By the same token, to ask whether material is needed for a scholarly purpose or for leisure reading by an adult is unethical. Naturally, children should not be prohibited from using adult materials. New professionals must be reminded of these important points as methods of teaching children and the rest of the public to trust their librarians.

In building this trust, it is essential to instill in new people the doctrine of the confidentiality of library records, patron files, the uses of computer aided searches, and circulation of materials. Attempted violations of this principle have ranged from FBI requests that personnel report people with foreign-sounding names using research sources to business people wanting the registration files for mailing lists. Although it may be necessary to tell a relief reference colleague that "so and so has been looking for everything on training golden retrievers" if the search is still going on and the first person is heading off to lunch, it is not all right during lunch to tell anyone that "so and so came in to find THE ILLUSTRATED JOY OF SEX" (giggle, giggle). Confidentiality is not only ethical; in most states, now it is a matter of law.

Impartiality and objectivity are certainly ethical principles that govern librarianship as other professions. It can be distasteful to a neophyte to find herself/himself looking for topics that are contrary to his/her tastes, or beliefs. Looking for books on dressing game for someone who hates hunting and trapping may be repugnant. Helping someone find arguments in favor of the Pro Choice movement may seem an impossible chore to someone who is a firm adherent of Right to Life. Yet the demands of the job are that the professional librarian performs these tasks as thoroughly as though they are for subjects that are agreeable.

Another issue of impartiality to be discussed in training new employees is that of the treatment of special people. If the Mayor calls up with a question in the middle of a busy day, does everyone else get held up while His Honor gets service? Of course, if the Mayor's office has supervision over the library's budget, the issue may not be easy to resolve. If the budget gets cut, all the customers suffer. Still, morality dictates that all the tax payers deserve equal treatment, and equal access to the library's materials and services.

JURISDICTIONAL ISSUES

There are some jurisdictional issues that a new librarian may not have authority to oversee, nor may need to deal with directly; however, employees should understand matters that the public may question them about, so that they can explain the library's position. For instance, the question of charging fees for nonresidents is sometimes a hotly-debated issue. A city council with budget problems may not see the desirability of funding library use for residents of neighboring communities that contribute nothing to the support of the institution. At the same time, the growing movement in information science toward the sharing of resources is one that students will have discussed in library school. Both sides of this debate have arguments that are supportable. Whichever is the one that governs the particular library, the new employee must understand and be ready to clarify, so that the institution sustains its credibility with the public. The reference librarian is the person that the public sees as representing the library, each must be trained in what the library stands for, and be ready to support the institution. Any misgivings they have should be shared internally, as much as possible.

COLLECTION DEVELOPMENT
AS AN ETHICAL EXERCISE

Even if a new reference person has no responsibilities right away for selection, a successful career will eventually lead that person to fulfilling that task. The supervisor should be ready to discuss the complexities of the job in preparation for the future. Among the ethical controversies involved is that of answering popular demand even with questionable materials. Examples that come to mind are the microwave cookbook that may contain unsafe directions, or diet books that physician columnists in the mass media warn may be dangerous. A recent case involved a computer whiz who crashed a network supposedly by using information from a hackers' handbook. The police wondered in the press that the library circulated a book that advised how to break the law. The library's sensible answer was that the book did not so much advise on breaking the law as teach how to protect computers from hackers. The question that always must be asked is where does professional judgment end and censorship begin. Does the librarian refrain from buying material that some opinion holds might be harmful? Or does professional objectivity dictate that the librarian must trust to the personal judgment of the members of the public to read and evaluate ideas and advice intelligently in order to make an intelligent and informed decision? Whatever is the decision of the person in charge of acquisitions, the new librarian must be ready to give the public a thoughtful answer to queries about selection.

RESTRICTIONS ON ACCESS

Ethical treatment of the public also demands that practices that make portions of the collection difficult to obtain must be limited. The hoary device of the Closed Shelves has been eliminated in most modern libraries. Labeling books and some forms of nonprint materials is considered another form of censorship by most intellectual freedom organizations. Keeping children from the adult room in the library is also an antiquated form of discrimination. Charging fees for services can be conceived of as a method of limiting access, and a form of censorship. Indeed, budget constraints have been used as excuses for self censorship by several institutions.

CONCLUSION

In the course of training new reference librarians, it becomes apparent that ethical treatment of patrons will facilitate an easy and fruitful reference interview, and a productive search for the information that the patron needs. Courteous and friendly behavior will set apprehensive people at ease, and make it easier for the librarian to make sure of the real object of the reference question, and will save time and frustration for all. The long term effect of being able to efficiently and pleasantly satisfy the needs of the patrons will be to build a good public image for the library, ensuring its support, financially and politically.

REFERENCES

Katz, Bill, and Ruth Fraley. *Ethics and Reference Services*. New York: The Haworth Press, 1982.
Intellectual Freedom Round Table, New York Library Association. *The New York Guide to Intellectual Freedom in Libraries*. New York, 1987.
Library Video Network. *The Difficult Reference Question*. Baltimore, 1985.
Library Video Network. *Does This Answer Your Question?* Baltimore, 1985.
Library Video Network. *If It Weren't for the Patron: Evaluating Your Public Service Attitude*. Baltimore, 1988.
Library Video Network. *The Library Show: Merchandise It!* Baltimore, 1985.

Reference Training
in California Libraries —
Back to Basics

Mary Layman
Sharon Vandercook

SUMMARY. CORE — California Opportunities for Reference Excellence — is an LSCA project designed to improve basic reference skills and collections in public libraries in California. The primary audience for the project is paraprofessionals in small and rural system branches. The project has purchased basic reference materials for participating libraries in English, Spanish, and a variety of Asian languages, to reflect the ethnic diversity of the State. Basic reference skills have been taught throughout the State, and a cadre of trainers have been created to teach a multiple-day, intensive reference skills workshop. Additionally, workshops dealing with special populations have been provided to participating libraries. A number of detailed training products have been developed by CORE and distributed to public libraries in the State to continue teaching efforts.

INTRODUCTION

Outside of its large cities, the reality of library service throughout much of California is one of small, isolated branches, often with poor collections and dedicated but untrained staff. California is physically awesome, and branches exist both in spare desert areas and mountain communities inaccessible in winter. Even before the devastating effects of Proposition 13 and its aftermath, these li-

Mary Layman is Project Director for CORE, 1707 Essex St. #46, San Diego, CA 92103. Sharon Vandercook is Project Manager for CORE, SJVIS, 2420 Mariposa, Fresno, CA 93721.

167

braries were underfunded, and cuts since then have left many without funds to do basic training and collection development.

In an effort to improve the level of reference service in the State, the California State Library in 1987 funded CORE: California Opportunities for Reference Excellence. This LSCA (Library Services and Construction Act) project is primarily a training grant, however, it was felt that there was little point in training staff when they often had almost nothing to work with to answer questions. To overcome the collection problem, CORE has purchased, over the past two years, over one-half million dollars in basic reference materials.

Of the approximately 1000 public library outlets in California, about half have taken part in the project. The majority of the participating libraries are small and rural, and most are branches of California's county library systems. Typically the branches are staffed by paraprofessionals, often working alone. Over half of the participating branches are open less than 40 hours per week.

DECENTRALIZED PROJECT ORGANIZATION

The grant was awarded to the San Joaquin Valley Cooperative Library System, which has a history of creative initiatives for rural libraries. The Cooperative hired a director for the project using an interesting approach. The Cooperative headquarters is in Fresno, California, but it was decided that the project director could live anywhere in the State. Project Director Mary Layman lives in San Diego.

The Project Director, working as an independent contractor out of her home, is in close contact (telephone and electronic mail) with Project Manager Sharon Vandercook, whose primary job is with the Cooperative in Fresno.

There have been advantages and disadvantages to this management method. The Project Director has had the freedom to subcontract with printers, suppliers, clerical assistance, and other needed support systems without involving the bureaucracy of a government agency to any great degree. This has permitted rapid production of materials, reports, and mailings. At the same time, the fiscal agent for the project, Fresno County, has been able to keep close watch on expenditures.

On the other hand when a project staff meeting has been required, it has involved a five hour drive or a two hour plane ride.

As it turns out, meetings have seldom been needed. Telephone and electronic mail, and, to be sure, the compatibility of the project staff, have made communication smooth and effective. Alvin Toffler's cottage office described in the *The Third Wave* has become a reality in the CORE project. Bureaucracy has been kept to a minimum, and creativity and efficiency have been, on the whole, enhanced. Project staff has been able to appropriately divide tasks — the director handling administration, communications, materials ordering, publishing, and most of the teaching work; the manager writing curriculum materials, supervising materials distribution, and teaching.

CORE's organization demonstrates that flexible, distributed management can be used to carry out a complex, expensive and diverse project.

MATERIALS — WHAT'S NEEDED

California State Librarian Gary Strong, immediately upon funding the grant, selected two committees to assist the project. The Advisory Committee, consisting of three librarians, helped set some broad project directives at the beginning. The Curriculum Committee with seven members, selected the reference books to be purchased and provided advice on curriculum material preparation.

In October, 1987 the Curriculum Committee met to prepare a list of basic reference books that members felt should be in all branches, regardless of physical size, number of clients, or hours of operation. (See Appendix.) Participating jurisdictions selected needed materials from the list for their branches and CORE placed the orders.

In its second year the project focussed attention on the ethnic diversity of California, and purchased basic reference materials in Spanish and a variety of Asian languages. (See Appendix.)

Training supported use and familiarity with the purchased tools.

TRAINING AND CURRICULUM DEVELOPMENT

Project staff and the Curriculum Committee developed a detailed list of skills and attitudes which every staff member should know. It included, for example, understanding the library's mission statement, respecting the privacy of patrons, knowing how to read a chart, and how to use key reference tools. Early in the project a decision was made to try to teach each concept in a variety of formats, over time, so that a person would be exposed to the same concept in many different ways.

The formats used by the project, after some consideration, are a four-hour basic reference workshop, a series of miniworkshops,[1] a multiple-day intensive reference skills workshop, four-hour special population workshops,[2] a reference tool correspondence course, a reference manual, and a first day packet to welcome new employees.

Teaching manuals and accompanying student materials have been published for each of the workshops. These materials, packaged in a box, have been distributed to participating libraries and to interested libraries outside the State.[3]

SPREADING THE WORD

For many branch staff CORE training sessions were the first formal training they had ever received, and for others it had been some years since their jurisdictions had been able to devote any resources to training.

In order to ensure that all staff had at least a basic introduction to reference service, the CORE staff developed a four-hour Basic Reference Workshop, which staff presented to over 1000 people throughout the state. If CORE funds purchased even one book for a branch, someone from the branch was expected to attend a Basic Workshop session. Distances can be formidable in rural California, which is one reason so few training sessions are held in many of the State's libraries. It is not uncommon for a branch to be located almost two hours from its central library. In addition, since many branches have only one person working in them, workshop attendance requires closing the branch or hiring a substitute (often difficult in small towns).

To overcome some of these problems, CORE staff made a commitment to take the Basic Workshop to the staff that needed training, and to pay for substitutes. Mary Layman, Project Director, left her home in San Diego in mid-July, 1988 and did not return again until mid-August, traveling throughout Northern California. Workshops sometimes had 40 attendees, sometimes four. However, those four might not have been trained at all if a special session had not been scheduled for them.

This "personalized touch" was appreciated by participants, and has added to the success of the project. Library staff attended sessions in their own system or a nearby system, and used the basic reference books purchased by CORE in the training.

CORE quickly realized that it would be impossible to reach everyone in the State who needed training, much less to continue training beyond two years (the length of the grant). Therefore, the "trickle down" approach was implemented.

During the first year of the project 100 library staff from participating libraries, professionals and paraprofessionals, were taught to teach the Basic Reference Workshop and provided with curriculum materials. They are encouraged to present it whenever they feel it is necessary.

During the second year, approximately 70 librarians and paraprofessionals have been taught to teach a multiple-day reference behaviors workshop.[4] Each trainer will teach representatives from five branches—a team of two teaching ten branches—during the next two years.

The jurisdiction headquarters have also been supplied with the Basic Reference Workshop teaching materials, and will receive the teaching manuals for the special populations workshops.

This cadre of trainers will help to keep the spirit of CORE alive—teaching manuals are detailed and all supplies are provided so that the workshops can be repeated as often as necessary.

BASIC WORKSHOP COMPONENTS

The Basic Workshop introduced key ideas to staff, many of whom had never been formally exposed to these concepts. The mission of the library as a place to get information, the idea that the library serves all patrons equally, basic reference ethics like unbiased service and respect for client privacy were combined with practical exercises using some of the basic reference tools purchased by the project. Attendees brought their branch copies of these books to work with.

A large part of the workshop discusses model reference behaviors and information needed by the librarian to correctly answer a question (see Appendix). The behaviors, developed by Ralph Gers and associates, are expanded on and reinforced in the multiple-day reference workshop.

The reference manual, correspondence course, mini-workshops, first day packet, special population workshops, and the multiple-day reference workshop build upon the concepts presented in the Basic Workshop.

CORE PRODUCTS

As has been indicated, the learning philosophy followed by CORE has been one of multiple, varied reinforcement of basic reference skills. Products designed by CORE work together and separately to achieve this end.

All curriculum materials have been created with the idea that they will be used by library staff in a variety of settings. Clear instructions are provided for their use, and they have been distributed to all participants. The ability of an LSCA project to be replicated is one of the criteria for success of such projects in California, and CORE has aimed at replication from its inception.

The Reference Correspondence Course was modeled on an existing course from the San Joaquin Valley Cooperative and gives basic lessons on reference book use. Staff can work with materials in their branch or system, at their own pace.

The Reference Manual is comprehensive yet generic, covering reference behaviors, approaches, where to look, reminders on networking, and other topics.

All materials are in loose-leaf format; CORE or the individual jurisdiction may add other material to any product.

Teaching manuals are accompanied with a supply of student materials, and CORE is committed to at least one update of reference tool exercises.

Since CORE has so many aspects in both training and collection development, the project prepares a quarterly newsletter which is sent directly to each participating branch. The newsletter reports on CORE activities and provides a continuing education section on reference tools (see Appendix).

EVALUATION

Prior to CORE no one had attempted such an indepth training program for the State's library paraprofessionals, so the project has been seen as a potential source of information on reference abilities. Dr. Terence Crowley, San Jose State University, has contracted with CORE to evaluate various aspects of the project. His findings will be published at the end of the grant.

Participants in all workshops have been asked to complete evaluation forms. These evaluations have generally been very positive. Basic Workshop attendees wanted more practice time with reference tools and more practice with model reference behaviors, which was an encouraging sign that training was desired.

WHAT HAS BEEN LEARNED TO DATE

The project has revealed a number of things about how to approach and manage such a massive undertaking:

1. Even though the audience may have many different levels of experience and ability, it is important to provide a basic level of training, to bring everyone to the same place, before going on to more advanced concepts.
2. It is important to provide funding for hiring substitutes so that staff may attend workshops. It is an added benefit if the jurisdiction will then send the substitutes to be trained!
3. It is important, whenever possible, to provide training where staff is rather than expecting them to travel long distances to training sessions.
4. It is important to provide those you wish to be trainers (individuals and/or jurisdictions) with ready-made training packages. These packages should be detailed and complete.
5. It is important to reinforce and repeat each learning concept in

different ways over a period of time for training to be effective.
6. It is important to keep communication flowing on all levels. Administrators, supervisors, and staff need to be aware of what kinds of training are available, when and where workshops will be held, what the content of the training is and what will be expected of the learners. In a state the size of California, this becomes a formidable task.

CORE staff is excited and pleased at the success of the project. It's goal is large: to improve the overall basic reference service in the state. While CORE may not be the total answer to that goal, it is a definite step in the right direction.

NOTES

1. Mini-workshops are 20-30 minute exercises working with one concept, such as reading a chart. They are designed to be used at staff meetings or other staff gatherings. They can introduce or reinforce (depending on when they are used) a skill or idea quickly.

2. Special population workshops are working with Spanish-speaking patrons, working with Asian language-speaking patrons, and working with physically handicapped patrons. Dr. Brenda Dervin, Ohio State University, is teaching the ethnic workshops and Dr. Kieth Wright, University of North Carolina, is teaching the physically handicapped workshop. Each workshop has been offered five times around the State between the months of March and September, 1989.

3. For information about CORE curriculum materials contact Sharon Vandercook, SJVIS, 2420 Mariposa, Fresno CA 93721, 209-488-3229.

4. The reference workshop created by Transform, Baltimore, Maryland was selected by CORE staff and curriculum committee as the format for intensive reference skills training. Ralph Gers, Nancy Bolin and their associates are the authors. Mr. Gers and Ms. Bolin have provided five multiple-day training sessions around California to "train trainers." Those interested in further information about the intensive reference training should contact Transform, 5726 Springing Step, Columbia, MD 21044.

APPENDIX 1

BASIC REFERENCE MATERIALS LIST

World Almanac
Random House Unabridged Dictionary, 2nd Edition
Bartlett's Quotations
Chilton's Auto Repair
Consumer Reports Annual Buying Guide
AMA Family Medical Guide
American Heritage Larousse Spanish/English Dictionary
Rand McNally Road Atlas
Goodes World Atlas
Emily Post Etiquette
How to Write Better Resumes, Adele Lewis
Dictionary of First Names, Kolatch
Worldmark Encyclopedia of the States
Turabian Guide for Writing Papers
Occupational Outlook Handbook
Webster's Secretarial Handbook
Webster's Geographical Dictionary
Webster's Biographical Dictionary
Physician's Desk Reference
Nutrition/Food Composition Guide, Bowers & Church
Lasser Income Tax Preparation Guide
Sunset California Missions
World Book Encyclopedia
Zip Code Directory
U.S. Government Manual
California County Fact Book
California Journal Roster
Almanaque Mundial
Chilton Manual de Reparacion de Automoviles
Guia Completa de la Salud Familiar
Diccionario del Espanol Chicano

In addition, at the end of the first grant year, one set of
McGraw-Hill Science and Techology Encyclopedia and one set of
Enciclopedia Barsa were offered to participating libraries.

APPENDIX 2

SPANISH AND ASIAN MATERIALS LIST

Spanish

Como reparar 500 problemas de la casa
Diccionario de mejicanismos
Diccionario etimologico comparado de los apellidos espanoles,
    hispanoamericanos y filipinos
Farmacodependencia: la enfermedad
Fiestas de Mexico (one in English, one in Spanish)
Frases celebres de hombres celebres
El gobierno y los presidentes de los Estados Unidos de America
Historia de los Estados Unidos
Manual de primeros auxilios
Resumes que consiguen empleos
Urbanidad y buenas maneras
Sus derechos

Japanese

Amerika joho Q & A (American Information Q & A)
Amerika kurashi Q & A (American Life Q & A)
Amerika seiji keizai hando bukku (Hndbk. of Am. Politics & Econ.)
Jidosha yogo handobukku (Hndbk. of Automobile Terminology)
Shitte okitai Amerika no horitsu (Wanting to Know Am. Law)
Q & A Amerika no zeikin hyakka (Q & A Am. Taxation)

Chinese

Chien ming mei kuo li yu tzu tien (Concise Dic. Am. Slang)
Ju ho shen ching mei-kuo chien cheng (How to Apply for Visa...)
Wang kung tzu k'ai chiang (Mr. Wang Talk Show)
Mei kuo cheng fu chien chieh (Intro. U.S. Government)
Mei kuo shih (History of U.S.)

Vietnamese

Phep ngua va tri benh (Medical guide)
Thu tu giao thiep hang ngay (English-Vietnamese Letters...)
Nganh co khi o to: sach huan nghiep (Automotive Trades...)
Tu dien Anh Viet Anh thong dung (English/Vietnamese Dict.)
Van pham Anh ngu (toan bo) (English Grammar...)
Nhung dieu can biet tai Hoa Ky (Manual on U.S. Life...)
Tu hoc khai thue (Income tax)
Tuc ngu ca dao & dan ca (Vietnamese folk literature...)

Thai

Prapenee Mongkol Sumkan Kong Thai (Thai ceremonies & traditions)
Tamra Raksa Sukhaphab Nai Muang, Nauk (Health book...)

Korean

Etsensu Yong-Han sajon (English-Korean Dictionary)
Muyok Yongo 300 munye (300 Patterns Business English)
Miguk pomnyul haendu puk: imin saenghwal ul wihan (U.S. law)
Irol ttaen yoroke: chadongcha unggup suri (Car repair)
Sisa TOEFL

Spanish materials ordered from: Hispanic Books Distributors, 1665 W. Grant Road, Tucson AZ 85745

Asian materials ordered through: ASIA, 2225 W. Commonwealth Ave, Suite 315, Alhambra CA 91803

APPENDIX 3

MODEL REFERENCE BEHAVIORS*

Approachability
  Smiles
  Makes Eye Contact
  Gives Friendly Greeting
  Is at Eye Level
Comfort
  Speaks in Relaxed Tone
  Goes with Patron
Interest
  Maintains Eye Contact
  Makes Attentive Comments
  Gives Full Attention
Listening
  Does Not Interrupt
  Paraphases
  Clarifies
Inquiring
  Probes
  Verifies
Searching
  Finds Answer in First Source
  Searches Other Sources
  Keeps Patron Informed
  Offers Referral
Informing
  Speaks Clearly
  Checks If Answer Understood
  Cites the Source
Follow-up
  Asks "Does this completely answer your question?"
  Asks Other Follow-up Question

INFORMATION NEEDED BY LIBRARIAN TO ANSWER QUESTION

1. Purpose (why information is needed)
2. Deadline (when is information needed)
3. Type and Amount (in what format(s) and how much)
4. Who (experience patron brings to question)
5. Where (what prompted the question)
6. The Basic Question (make sure patron and librarian agree on what the question really is)

*These behaviors are copyrighted by Transform, Columbia, MD

APPENDIX 4

EXAMPLE OF CONTINUING EDUCATION SECTION OF CORE NEWSLETTER

Practice Session--CORE Tools

Almanaque Mundial,·1989

(Answers in next newsletter)

1. In the section marked "Fisica/Matematica/Quimica (see "Contenido" at the beginning of the book) find "English Measurements"and the "Greek Alphabet". Are they listed in the index?

2. Is there a chronological history of India?

3. What page does the "Calendar of Events" begin on? In that section, what is the gemstone listed for the month of March and what page is it on?

Answers to Questions from Bartlett's Quotations, 15th edition, in the last newsletter:

1. Dorothy Parker (look in index under "dust").
2. "Ten Days that Shook the World" (look in author table of contents in front of book)
3. "It is completely unimportant. That is why it is so interesting." Agatha Christie (unimportant versus important, interesting rather than "of interest").
4. Earl of Chesterfield in "Letters to His Son, July 20, 1749").

The Role of Multitype Networks in Providing Continuing Education for Reference Workers

Sara Laughlin
Karen Nissen

SUMMARY. Continuing education for reference workers has been neglected in the professional literature. This article describes the experience of a multitype library network, identifies models for developing programs and presents an argument for the involvement of networks in continuing education for reference workers.

INTRODUCTION

The days are gone when a reference librarian could take a course in library school, find a job and gain all the skill and experience needed on the desk. Or are they? Darlene Weingand suggests that the "shelf life" of the MLS is currently 5 years and ". . . the rate of societal change continually challenges that estimate."[1] She concludes that librarians now entering the profession can expect to spend more hours in continuing education activities than in the MLS degree program.

In large and small libraries, in school and public and research libraries, reference workers face a new wilderness of sources, formats, patron demands and technological innovations.[2] How they address the issues of information access and automation in the next few years may well determine whether their patrons receive first class service. For many in the field, though, the impact of expanding technology is elusive, the commitment of resources required to

Sara Laughlin is Coordinator and Karen Nissen is Program Manager, "The Library Network," 112 North Walnut, Suite 500, Bloomington, IN 47408.

179

change from old models to new seems staggering. The need for training for nondegreed library workers is well documented, as are programs offered by state library agencies in some states.³ This article describes the experience of one Indiana regional multitype network and offers a rationale for the involvement of networks in continuing education for reference workers.

WHAT THE LIBRARY NETWORK IS

Multitype networks come in all shapes and sizes and they have been organized for a variety of purposes. William and Sandra Rouse point to four important factors in the emergence and growth of networks over the past twenty years: a tightening economy and rising materials costs, new technology, a shift in the focus from storing books to serving patrons, and the profession's endorsement of network activity.⁴ In response to these factors, regional multitype networks were organized in Indiana under state statute to provide interlibrary loan, reference referral and continuing education.

Stone Hills Area Library Services Authority, recently nicknamed the Library Network, is one of the Indiana multitype networks. It serves 53 member libraries in a 4,300 square mile area of southern Indiana. Twenty-four members are school corporations (122 individual school buildings), 17 are public libraries, 7 are academic libraries and 5 are special libraries. Included among the members are the major research libraries at two state universities, some of the smallest public libraries in the state, elementary schools with no library staff and a maximum security federal prison.

Predominantly rural, the Library Network area includes 10 counties, three of which have scattered town libraries but no countywide library service. The 1980 census showed that the population in the area is older and median income and educational levels are lower than the Indiana averages.

The Library Network is fortunate to have two library schools within its boundaries.⁵ The school's faculty and libraries are invaluable sources of information. They offer many courses in the reference area, ranging from basic reference skills and science, social science and humanities bibliography to online searching. Their focus is on graduate education for those who want to become professional librarians; their continuing education emphasis likewise is directed to their alumni's professional concerns.

For nearly fifteen years, the Library Network has been engaged in assessing needs, conducting workshops, routing professional journals and consulting with individual librarians.

The Library Network and other regional networks in Indiana publish regular newsletters and calendars that contain literally hundreds of continuing education opportunities each year. Since 1985, the calendar has been available online on ALANET, through a bulletin board maintained by the Library Network. The online calendar is used as the source for regional newsletters and in planning on the local, regional and state level. Many libraries use the calendar as a primary source for identifying CE opportunities for themselves and their staff.

CERTIFICATION IN INDIANA

Indiana has mandatory certification for public librarians, as do 22 other states. In 1941 the Indiana General Assembly adopted the Library Certification Law, creating a Library Certification Board to prescribe and define grades of public library service and to provide examinations for and issue certificates to librarians.[6] Almost 50 years later, the Certification Board still holds examinations that allow public librarians to be certified without taking MLS coursework. Supporters of the system contend that library trustees are not trained in library functions and are dependent upon certification to aid them in hiring qualified librarians. Others argue that the system is outmoded, that the examination method allows librarians to become certified without adequate training, and that certification doesn't protect the public from unqualified practitioners since there is no continuing education requirement.[7] However outmoded, certification affects primarily directors of public libraries in the Library Network area, since most of the libraries are small enough not to have professional requirements beneath the director level.

Certification requirements for school teachers (including media specialists) have recently been updated.[8] School media specialists must have a teaching license issued by the Department of Education with at least a minor in School Media. Those entering the teaching profession after 1986 cannot get life licenses as earlier graduates could, but must update continuously to maintain their licenses. This new ruling has yet to affect most of the working media specialists in the Library Network area, since they already have life licenses. It also doesn't affect library aides or volunteers, who make up the majority of school library workers in the area. These individuals are not certified in any way; nor do most have any training.

Academic librarians, not subject to state certification requirements, are nevertheless tenure-track. In order to meet the requirements for tenure or promotion, academic librarians are required to conduct research, engage in professional activities, or teach. These expectations force academic librarians to be more active in continuing education as well as in other areas. Library workers beneath the professional level face no certification requirements and in general fare no better than their public library and school media counterparts in receiving training.

CONTINUING EDUCATION IN INDIANA

In 1980, the Indiana State Library published *The Continuing Library Information Media Education Plan for Indiana* (CLIME).[9] Written by a committee broadly representative of the Indiana library community, the plan defined continuing education as "Planned learning experiences . . . designed primarily to increase the competence of practitioners . . . to provide quality library/media/information services to all residents of the nation; and enrichment of library/media/information careers." The *CLIME Plan* recognized that lifelong learning is necessary for individuals to be able to meet the challenges of highly accelerated change. It defined continuing education activities to include both formal and informal situations.

The *CLIME Plan* called for a statewide needs assessment of library workers in every type library to be conducted, proposed roles and responsibilities for those agencies that were major providers of continuing education, suggested resources that would be necessary and established goals for communication, recognition and evaluation of continuing education.

In 1982, the State Library completed work on the needs assessment recommended in the *CLIME Plan*. The needs assessment identified broad topic areas and correlated them to information about professional status, years of experience and geographic region, but problems related to the random sampling mechanics and the length of the survey made detailed correlation difficult, if not impossible. As a result, the Library Network could identify popular topics that had been selected by all respondents in the area, but not, for example, by public library directors with 10 years of experience.

From the *CLIME Plan* also came the Indiana Committee for the Approval of Providers (ICAP), which has the authority to approve quality program providers. ICAP granted approval to the Library Network as a provider of quality continuing education in 1986. Unfortunately, ICAP is limited to approving sub-state providers like the regional networks, not statewide providers like the associations and library schools. Those groups must turn to CLENE or other national organizations, which adds another layer of complexity to the process.

Continuing education opportunities abound for Indiana library workers. The Indiana Library Association, the Indiana Library Trustee Association and the Association for Indiana Media Educators have annual conferences and district meetings each year, in which they address topics of concern to their members. The Indiana State Library and Department of Education offer workshops and in-service training on an irregular basis. The regional networks offer workshops, roundtables and tours.

In 1989, the Library Network and other regional networks in Indiana administered an LSCA grant that installed CD-ROM workstations and databases in 58 Indiana public libraries. The libraries were awarded equipment based on the strength of their applications and their commitment to maintain the database subscriptions for two years after the grant. They were also required to attend a two-day training workshop, and agreed to conduct searches for other libraries. In all, 131 databases have been installed and reference workers around the state are rapidly learning to search and print citations. For many, it is their first exposure to microcomputers. For almost all, it is the only automation they have. It is too early to assess the project's impact on information delivery or the new issues CD-ROM will raise for reference workers in southern Indiana.

THE PROBLEM

Many library workers find these library school courses, statewide workshops and conferences to be out of reach. They must cover the reference desk while they are away, not an insignificant problem for small libraries and schools. The registration fee and travel expenses are often a problem for libraries with no continuing education budget.

Most important of all, they must want to learn something new, and frankly many do not have either the internal or external motivation to do so. They are protective of their "professional" status, resistant to change, and see a need for training as an admission of insufficiency. Even though the Library Network offers continuing education units (CEUs), most receive no recognition for them. Boards and superintendents reinforce the static view of library service. They don't understand the need for updating and improvement of skills, even at the most basic level.

This lack of motivation has been apparent in the "Take Home Education" project, a correspondence study series co-sponsored by the Indiana regional networks and the Indiana University School of Library and Information Science. For the past three years, 3,700 free copies of five "Take Home Education" articles written by leading library educators from Indiana University have been distributed statewide in network newsletters that reach every type and size library. Topics have included delegation, communication, organizational and personal goal-setting, evaluation of public services and evaluation of personnel. For each article, fewer than 50 individuals paid the $10 or $15 to register for the CEU credit, available upon completion of an essay examination. Fewer than half of those that registered completed the examination. Distance was not a factor, since the articles came to the library; cost was minimal; CEU credit was offered. What seems to have been lacking was the interchange of ideas that is gained in a workshop discussion and any real motivation to attend.

Experience with the Take Home Education project echoes the dilemma that the National Commission for Libraries and Information Services published in their report on continuing education in 1974.[10] Continuing education modes found most effective by library practitioners were attendance at professional meetings, participation on professional committees or task forces, and attendance at workshops. Home study materials and correspondence courses were least often used. The report concluded: "The importance of attending professional meetings and participating in professional committees or on task forces is given high ranking, but there is a serious question concerning how much opportunity paraprofessionals have for involvement in this type of activity. Concern is deepened by the fact that types of individualized learning such as home study and correspondence courses, which could be made available to paraprofessionals on an equal basis with all other levels of library personnel, rank at the bottom of methods used."[11]

In summary, Indiana efforts to certify librarians and media specialists, define continuing education needs, accredit continuing education providers and present continuing education offerings have been scattered, inconsistent and inadequate to the challenges facing library workers. They have for the most part neglected those beneath the professional or administrative level. In this, they don't differ from the national failure to achieve the coordinated articulated infrastructure recommended eighteen years ago.[12]

THE LIBRARY NETWORK'S CONTINUING EDUCATION PROGRAM

The Library Network adopted a long-range plan in 1987.[13] Based on needs expressed by the hundreds of individuals who gave input and ideas for the Plan, a Support Staff Task Force was created to investigate the specific interests and requests for continuing education opportunities.

In 1988, the Support Staff Task Force surveyed the staffing of member libraries in an effort to determine what the ratio of professional to support staff was and how many volunteers and students were working in area libraries.[14] The survey showed that 38% of the paid staff were certified professionals and 62% were support staff. When student assistants and volunteers were included, they accounted for 63% of the work force. Two-thirds of the public libraries operate with a single certified librarian who does everything in the library. Half of the schools have certified full-time media specialists; the rest are staffed by either part-time professionals, library aides or parent volunteers. Half the academic libraries are one-person operations and all the special libraries are operated by part-time staff with no library training.

Based on the survey and discussions with key administrators in the area, the Support Staff Task Force presented two "Library Workers" workshops in 1988. Each included breakout sessions for those working in public services and technical services. The public services section focused on basic reference sources, interlibrary loan and the reference interview. The workshops were short (half day) and inexpensive. They were offered at two locations on different dates, so no one had to travel further than 50 miles. The presenters for the public services section were staff from the Library Network's Reference Centers and the two state university libraries. They shared information on basic reference sources and on their libraries' unique collections and reference strengths. As much as possible, the reference books being discussed were available at the workshops for participants to handle. Handouts outlined the sources discussed and included the names and phone numbers of the presenters. Videotapes used in the workshops are available on loan from the Library Network.

In addition to providing practical information about job responsibilities, the workshops had the goal of increasing awareness of the value of being part of a network of library workers. Participants were very enthusiastic about the workshops, making comments like "Just what I needed to learn!" and "Hope you have more of these." They also wrote, "I received ideas that can be implemented at our library and now know we can request help from others," and "I am so pleased that this group is now available and I look forward to learning about future workshops," and "I learned of new places to find information or call and ask for information."

The *Turning Point* newsletter produced by the Support Staff Committee for library workers also attempts to provide a regular reference feature in the form of a review column. The criteria for reference books reviewed is not that they are new or specialized, but that they have multiple uses and are affordable.

In 1989 the Support Staff Task Force surveyed the Library Network members about specific reference training needs. Although results are not yet complete, the survey shows the strongest need for information on reference and research strategies, basic and new reference materials, reference for school libraries, community information and vertical files, and local history. The second level of need is for help in referring reference questions, online databases and CD-ROM products, and children's and young adults' reference services. Respondents would like to visit reference departments in other libraries, but do not feel that their own library has anything of interest. They also indicate interest in attending a reference roundtable on a quarterly basis, but feel their library couldn't host one because of space shortage. Three quarters of the respondents did not want to be interviewed on a reference topic for the newsletter.

THE CHALLENGE

Library workers will continue to be the largest group of information service providers in the Library Network area for the foreseeable future. No other provider group is addressing their continuing education needs. As information delivery becomes more sophisticated, it will be ever more important that reference workers be well-grounded in the basics, since as Edward Jennerich concludes, reference interviewing skills will transfer from one information format to another.[15]

The best argument for the continuing education of reference workers is made by Marty Bloomberg, who points out: "The library's patron puts trust in the library to perform its duties competently and the librarian makes a claim to be able to do this best because of special training. The patron must depend on the library to offer good service, since he or she is often in no position to judge the quality of that service."[16]

The Library Network faces a major challenge in reaching and teaching library workers in reference, but there are many models. William Young has described the McGill University reference training manual and other efforts aimed at entry level librarians.[17] The Maryland studies and peer coaching methods offer promise of improving reference service in small libraries that have small budgets and few staff.[18] With a small but current reference collection and a staff trained in probing and followup, reference accuracy can be dramatically improved. Kenneth Tewel and Carol Kroll report on a successful program of staff development and peer support among school media specialists in the Nassau School System.[19] Roberta Walters and Susan Barnes describe a reference service training program at the UCLA Biomedical Library that is based on goals, objectives and competencies.[20] The common denominator in all these programs is that they are structured and lengthy, making them costly in terms of time and personnel, and they focus on reference interview skills with opportunities for practice and feedback over a period of weeks.

The models have pinpointed the need for careful assessment of the problem and consideration of the methods of teaching and learning. A successful program directed at training reference workers must take into account the importance of peer coaching and the reference interview as well as basic sources, must focus on needs of people rather than books, must be nearby and inexpensive. It must introduce reference workers to the larger library world and motivate them to use continuing education to improve skills in the future.

The Library Network has a state mandate to provide continuing education and a good track record in planning and conducting continuing education programs. It has task forces of library workers and professionals to give advice and work on planning and evaluation of continuing education. It has a regional union list of professional materials, a newsletter especially for library workers, a collection of videotapes for continuing education, a correspondence study series, a professional journal routing service, and offers workshops several times a year. State funding is available to the Library Network to subsidize continuing education planning, so registration fees are low. When programs are offered in more than one location, library workers can travel shorter distances.

Small libraries expect the Library Network to play a central role in meeting their continuing education needs, partly because they cannot do it alone and partly because they know other agencies cannot help. Conducting their own continuing education for reference workers will be out of reach, due to the complexity of planning and the long-term commitments required. The models above suggest that it is now essential for planners to understand learning and teaching styles, assessment techniques and learning transfer methods, in addition to basic and new reference sources, interview techniques and technological innovations. A recent study in a Midwestern state by Verna Pungitore confirms that public library directors consider regional networks to play an important role in the flow of information among public library directors and various change agents including library schools, associations and state agencies.[21] In the Library Network, the library schools will help, but the task is outside their primary mission. The state associations are busy answering the needs of their members, few of whom are library workers from small libraries. State agencies are too distant, both in miles and in outlook.

Because of the mounting cost and complexity of providing continuing education for reference workers and the need for the continuing education to be delivered inexpensively and within a reasonable distance, regional library networks must take the lead in providing continuing education for reference workers in small libraries.

REFERENCES

1. Darlene Weingand, "Continuing education programs and activities," in *Education for Professional Librarians*, (White Plains, NY: Knowledge Industry Publications, 1986), 223, 225.

2. The Library Network has defined as "library workers" those individuals that have little or no library training. Library workers may hold titles ranging from "director" to "assistant circulation clerk."

3. Nicky Stanke, "Training the nondegreed library worker: How it is and how it should be," *Public Libraries* 27:2 (Summer 1988), 79-81.

4. William B. and Sandra H. Rouse, *Management of library networks; policy analysis, implementation and control*, (New York: Wiley Interscience, 1980).

5. The Indiana University School of Library and Information Science is the only ALA-accredited program in the state. Indiana State University also offers graduate courses through its Department of Library Science.

6. Indiana Code 20-14-12. The Official Rules and Regulations were revised and adopted by the Indiana Library Certification Board in 1974.

7. Unpublished sunset review report issued by the Indiana Legislative Services Agency, 1989.

8. 511 Indiana Administrative Code 10-3-1, Section 1, Subsections A, B, C, D, issued April 25, 1988.

9. Continuing Library Information Media Advisory Committee, Indiana State Library, *Continuing library information media education plan for Indiana:*

Official report, compiled by Sabra Stockey, (Indianapolis: Indiana State Library, 1980).

10. *Continuing library and information science education: Final report to the National Commission on Libraries and Information Science*, (Washington, DC: American Society for Information Science, 1974).

11. Ibid, p. 66.

12. Guidelines Subcommittee of the Staff Development Committee, Personnel Administration Section, Library Administration Division, American Library Association, "Guidelines to the development of human resources in libraries: rationale, policies, programs and recommendations," *Library Trends* 20 (July 1971), 111-115.

13. *Excellence at the basic level; a long-range plan, 1988-1993*, (Bloomington, IN: Stone Hills Area Library Services Authority, 1987).

14. "Staffing Patterns in Member Libraries Surveyed," *Turning Point* 1:1 (June 1988), 2.

15. Edward Jennerich, "The art of the reference interview," *Indiana Libraries* 1:1 (Spring 1981), 7-18.

16. Marty Bloomberg, *Introduction to public services for library technicians*, 4th ed., (Littleton, CO: Libraries Unlimited, 1985), 24.

17. William Young, "Communicating with the new reference librarian: the teaching process," *Reference Librarian* 16 (Winter 1986), 223-32.

18. Sandy Stephan and others, "Reference Breakthrough in Maryland," *Public Libraries* 27 (Winter 1988), 202-203.

19. Kenneth J. Tewel and Carol Kroll, "Empowerment for the school media specialist: Moving from reactive to proactive," *School Library Media Quarterly* 16:4 (Summer 1988), 244-248.

20. Roberta J. Walters and Susan J. Barnes, "Goals, objectives and competencies for reference services: A training program at the UCLA biomedical library," *Bulletin of the Medical Library Association* 73 (April 1985), 160-167.

21. Verna Pungitore, "The flow of information among public library directors and library change agents: an exploratory study," *Journal of Education for Library and Information Science* 29:4 (Spring 1989), 276.

Getting to the Core: Training Librarians in Basic Reference Tools

Ellen Berkov
Betty Morganstern

SUMMARY. The Anne Arundel County Public Library developed a three phase reference project. During Phase I (12 months) a committee conducted a study of the reference holdings among the 13 branches and developed a core list of 250 reference titles for each branch. In Phase II (six months) the library explored ways to have staff learn to use these reference titles. Each branch would develop a lesson plan, questions/activities, to teach both the preparer and taker the organization and content of a reference title. A training team presented a workshop on examination of reference titles and preparation of lesson plans. Participants practiced both. In Phase III (14 months) each branch develops its own lesson plan on a subject area of the core list. After all plans are developed, one plan is sent to each staff member monthly to complete. At the end of Phase III, an evaluation mechanism will be initiated to test the transfer of learning.

Branch A owns *Thomas' Register* but not branch B. Geographically isolated Branch C subscribes to *Value Line*, while Branch D, with twice the circulation, doesn't. Branch E's manager wants to drop its subscription to the building code that Branch F is requesting. Newly built Branch G has the current edition of the *McGraw-Hill Encyclopedia of Science and Technology*, but the set at Branch H dates to its opening 15 years ago.

Sound familiar? Problems like these confronted the suburban

Ellen Berkov is Reference Librarian and Betty Morganstern is Information/ Programming and Outreach Librarian, Anne Arundel County Public Library, 5 Harry S. Truman Parkway, Annapolis, MD 21401.

Anne Arundel County (Maryland) Public Library when it began to evaluate the reference collections in its 13 branches in the spring of 1987. Located in a rapidly growing area between Baltimore and Washington, D.C., the library system is in a state of growth as well with 13 branches and plans underway for at least three additional branches.

The collections in the nine community branches varied the most. While the large collections at the county's two area branches and the intermediate collections at the two next-biggest branches received fairly even support from the materials budget, by the time yearly reference collection decisions were made for the smaller branches, money was starting to run out.

Community branch reference collections all began life with healthy diets of capital funding, but they grew unevenly thereafter. Who got the last dollop of reference dollars was decided title by title, taking into account circulation, proximity to larger branches, branch lobbying, and community profiles. This cumbersome approach left the materials management department, which orders the system's books, open to charges of unfair treatment by the branches that didn't get those last copies of the *Gale Directory of Publications*.

The Anne Arundel County Public Library administration decided that community branches that were expected to provide a uniform level of reference service needed the same core of basic reference tools. Its commitment to a core reference collection would demand a sizable and continuing influx of time and money to bring and keep branches up to standard. At a time when a subscription to the *Encyclopedia of Associations* costs as much as a set of semi-precious jewelry, the library system wanted to make sure its money was well spent. It not only created a core reference list, but also required all branch staff to be trained to use the materials on the list. All branch information staff at Anne Arundel County Public Library meant some 124 people including 45 professionals, 41 paraprofessionals (who have had 72 hours of library training in addition to a bachelor's degree), and 36 hourly staff (who have at least a bachelor's degree, but some have no additional library training).

PHASE I:
PREPARING THE CORE REFERENCE LIST

The committee of public service and materials management staff members who prepared the core reference list wanted to meet several objectives. The committee wanted to create a hard-working document in which each title filled a branch reference need. It wanted the titles on the list to be easy to obtain and to update, and it wanted a document that could be modified as sources changed. Most of all, it wanted the core list to be a blueprint for even-handed branch reference collection development that could be used for many years to come.

None of the Maryland library systems contacted by the Anne Arundel County Core List Committee could provide reference lists that were currently in use. A 1986 list from Illinois' Suburban Library System became the model for Anne Arundel County Public Library. This list, unlike others the committee had reviewed, arranged material by subject heading rather than by call number. The staff also liked the division of the Illinois list into two parts: the basic core list and a reference supplement containing suggested titles with widely varying price tags. This design made the list both easier to update and more suited to the differing budgets of the Illinois member libraries.

The Anne Arundel County Public Library's 250 item core list incorporates this Chinese menu, pick-one-from-column A approach. For instance, the business section of the list requires branches to own "a directory of information and assistance for small businesses." This supplement then lists two suggested titles: *Insider's Guide To Small Business Resources* at $24.95 and *Small Business Sourcebook* at $125.00. If one of these titles becomes dated or goes out of print, the materials management department can add a new suggested title to the supplement. Computerization has also made it easier to update the lists and to send periodic revisions out to the branches.

At a series of monthly meetings, committee members tackled a total of 24 subject areas, two or three at a time. Librarians came prepared not only to recommend specific titles, but also to decide on the numbers of each type of material needed (three sets of multi-volume encyclopedias), the level of the material (one juvenile encyclopedia and two adult sets), and the currency of the material (no encyclopedia more than four years old). Certain internal battles were waged between public service committee staff: "Every branch needs the *Directory of Medical Specialists*," and materials management committee members: "Do you realize how much that costs?" but the determining question was "How often will this reference title be used?"

The core reference list does not aspire to be to our library system what a cultural literacy list is to a great books program. Not all subject areas are represented on the list, and those included are not represented equally. The three top subject areas, Law and Government with 33 items, General Sources with 31, and Business with 20, contain the sources that answer the highest number of patron inquiries. (These sources probably also eat up the highest proportion of the reference budget; almost half of them need to be updated at least yearly.)

Conversely, the core list gives minimal representation to several subject areas, despite the large number of reference tools available on them. The Antiques and Collectibles section requires libraries to own only two items: a guide to antiques and collectibles and a price guide. Anne Arundel County's antique buffs don't ignore the library system, but the committee felt that their specialized interests and questions could be handled best by the circulating collection and by referral to the county's two area libraries or Maryland's State Library Resource Center, the Enoch Pratt Free Library in Baltimore.

The majority of titles on the core reference list were drawn from heavily used reference materials in the collections of the four large branches. This meant that staff members could recommend the reference titles they used most, and that staff members in those branches would already know how to use them. Just as important, the system could save time and money by ordering more of the same titles it already owned. Though not even the two large area libraries owned all the items on the core list, the purchasing staff spent most of its effort on finding and filling in the holes in the collections of the nine community branches.

The library administration approved the core list in July of 1988. Six months later, Anne Arundel County Public Library branches owned most of a uniform collection of basic reference tools. In those six months, the staff charged with ordering material had reason to applaud the flexible format of the list and the computer software on which it was stored, as they made substitutions for out-of-print items.

PHASE II:
TRAINING STAFF TO USE THE REFERENCE TOOLS ON THE CORE LIST

You are a librarian at a small branch on the western edge of the county. Your information staff consists of two paraprofessionals and three hourly staff. In the last month, you have received 100 new reference books: mortgage tables, business directories, scientific encyclopedias, building and electrical codes. You (A) breathe in that printer's ink and throw up your hands with joy, (B) breathe in that printer's ink and throw up your hands in despair, or (C) shelve the new books and stick with your old standbys when answering your patrons' reference questions?

With the influx of large numbers of new reference tools into the branches came the challenge of training the staff to use them. Although staffs in the four large branches were familiar with most of the items in the core collection, Anne Arundel County Public Library staff members who operated the community branches had last used many of these sources in library school, in paraprofessional training, or on their last job. The library administration backed the establishment of a core list as part of the library system's long range plan commitment to accurate and timely responses to information requests; but even the community branches most actively providing reference service might be intimidated by the sheer quantity of what they needed to master.

Before deciding on any training plan, the library system tried to familiarize the information staff with the core collection concept. At their monthly meetings, branch managers learned how the collection was progressing. Each information staff member received a copy of the completed list. As material began arriving, the branch managers decided as a group how they wanted their staff to learn the sources.

Lesson Plans

The branch managers elected to have each branch responsible for creating a lesson plan for one or more subject areas of the core list. A lesson plan was defined as a series of questions and activities which enable both the preparers and the takers of the plan to learn the organization and content of reference titles. The completed plans would go out, once a month, to the branches' full-time and hourly staffs. Branch managers would take responsibility for evaluating their information staffs' monthly results.

But just what should a lesson plan look like? What kind of guidelines would information staff need to work with to create a plan? Including everybody in lesson plan creation meant that the staff had to learn how to look at reference books: their formats, scopes, and individual features. But just how do you squeeze the essence from a reference book? An administrative decision was made that before tackling the actual lesson plans, the staff needed a refresher course in reference book evaluation.

Enter a training committee. With branch and administrative representatives from the team who prepared the core list as well as a staff development resource person, this four person committee brought reference and training expertise to the task.

Monthly half-day meetings of the training committee began in July. Training dates were set for the following January (with 124 people to train and groups much larger than 40 too unwieldy, training would be presented three times). Sessions would be mandatory for all information staff to attend and, three hours each, the norm for Anne Arundel County.

Philosophical questions were abundant during the training meetings. How can you present a training workshop on reference that will hold the participants' interest? How do you teach what is inherently a very personal skill? The group struggled. In previous in-house training evaluations, information staff had asked for more sessions with reference tools. How could this hands-on concept be incorporated into training sessions with 40 people?

Workshop Design

From all of these questions, two training objectives emerged:

1. To identify techniques on how to examine a reference book—one hour.
2. To practice those techniques using sources from our reference collection—one-and-a-half hours.

To add credibility to the training, the group decided early on to include an outside presenter to develop this concept of how to examine a reference book. Bob Burke, who came highly recommended from the Enoch Pratt Free Library in Baltimore, was the first choice. Mr. Burke's approach was to include using a handout he adapted from Louis Shores' "Checkpoints for the Evaluation of Reference Books" (Appendix A) to examine his personal collection of arcane reference tools and found that in most cases they demonstrated the lack of some essential ingredient for ease of use or quality of information. For instance, Mr. Burke taught the groups about reference book bias by questioning an encyclopedia article on the F.B.I. with the signature J.E.H. Bob's ability to make reference book evaluation enjoyable instead of a dull, though necessary, chore set the tone for not only the rest of the workshop, but for the eventual creation of the branches' lesson plans.

To give a preview of future lesson plan activities, the training group developed first a pre-workshop assignment for all information staff to complete *before* the training session. Basic sources were used in the assignment—*Readers' Guide to Periodical Literature* and *Magazine Index*.

Hands on Success

The trainers then turned to the training session itself. Again, basic reference sources from the "General Sources" section of the core list, familiar to most staff, would be used. Workshop attendees would be divided into eight groups, five members each. Each group as a team would have no more than three reference titles assigned to them to work on during the session.

Some examples:

Group 1 *Famous First Facts*
Guinness Book of World Records

Group 2 *World Almanac*
Information Please Almanac

During the session, Group 1 and Group 2 then would be instructed: (1) to examine the tools at their table using the techniques explained by the reference expert earlier in the workshop, (2) develop three questions on "arrangement," "format," "scope," etc. of the sources, (3) develop three reference questions which could be answered using the tools and (4) record questions on one color-coded form and answers (citing source) on another color-coded form. Fifty minutes was allotted for this section.

After the 50 minutes lapsed, Group 1 and Group 2 would switch their color-coded forms and their reference tools. Group 1 would answer Group 2's questions and vice versa — this would be done in 25 minutes.

To accomplish the above, trainers found the following crucial to the success of the "hands-on" reference tools segment:

1. Secure enough copies of reference titles so each staff member at a table will be able to examine one title.
2. Provide explicit verbal and written instructions to the groups.
3. Time sections carefully and revise as necessary.

The workshops proved extremely popular with the staff. Participants mentioned two high points when evaluating the sessions. First they loved the presenter, and second, the groups appreciated the chance the workshop gave them to use their newly taught skills to ask and answer reference book questions. Inventing, not answering, the questions proved to be the more difficult task for workshop participants. After learning from the first set of evaluations that the staff felt rushed creating seven or more questions in only 50 minutes, the presenters upped the time for question preparation to 70 minutes. Evaluations from the subsequent groups still mentioned lack of time for question preparation as the session's biggest drawback. Answering the questions, on the other hand, took less than 25 minutes for most groups. Clearly, drawing up the lesson plans would be a harder task for the Anne Arundel County staff than taking them.

PHASE III: PREPARING LESSON PLANS ("IT TOOK MORE TIME THAN WE EXPECTED")

After the training workshop, the task of creating lesson plan guidelines and of assigning core list segments to branches went to one librarian. This coordinator sorted out which of the 250 core list titles the branch lesson plans should cover, and which of the 24 subject areas would be allotted to the system's 13 branches. Not all subject areas of the core would be tackled in lesson plan format, just those deemed of highest priority. Branches had six weeks to create lesson plans using the talents of their information staff and the services of hourly staff if possible.

Lesson Plan Tips

A tips sheet on how to prepare a lesson plan went out to each branch with the list of their assigned books. Staff were given specific guidelines that stated lesson plans should include:

1. At least one reference question per title that reflects the "essence" of a particular title, i.e., nothing that is obscure in the title.
2. Two other kinds of activities: at least one compare and contrast and one other activity such as a crossword, mix and match, etc.

In addition, to build upon their earlier training, staff were told to create questions like the ones they'd made up for the workshops. Branches determined the format questions should take. Creativity was encouraged. Each branch was also sent a copy of the Louis Shores' checklist and a sheet of helpful hints. "Appoint your own coordinator," branches were told. "Treat the assignment as librarians who want to teach other librarians." Other tips encouraged branches to try working in teams, and pick the best questions from a pool of questions and not to wait until the last minute. (The tips sheet also stated the assignment should take two hours for the other branches' staff to complete.) "Have fun with it," it concluded.

Six weeks later 13 lesson plans, complete with answer keys and source lists, made their ways to the plan coordinator. Branch comments indicated that the staff found developing lesson plans for core list sources tremendously educational. Even those sources familiar to staff members held surprises. "Did you know that was in there?" became a standard question, rivaling, "I don't know how we can be expected to do this in six weeks, but I must admit I'm learning a lot."

Staff members faced two main problems as they worked on the lesson plan — lack of time and missing materials. Routinely, branch staffs found that "getting to the essence" of reference tools took longer than they'd expected. What information did one book contain that another book lacked? What special features made a book particularly useful? How could this all be presented so that by the time branches took the 12th lesson plan they would still retain some enthusiasm? Struggling with these questions during February and March, traditionally marathon months for information staffs everywhere, was no easy job.

Missing or out-of-date material proved to be a second problem. Some branches had not received copies of all the reference sources covered in their assignments. New editions of material hadn't arrived, or looseleaf portions of books had disappeared. The discovery of these problems, though aggravating, proved to be a useful check on the status of the core list collections. When possible, updates were ordered and rushed to the branches. A few sources were stricken from the core list.

Taking the First Lesson Plan

The plan coordinator now faced the task of getting the first plan out to the branches. Twelve branches had sent in plans that could be photocopied for each staff member. The 13th branch had sent in an actual board game they developed on legal sources called "You Be The Judge" which could not be photocopied. "Statistics" became the first plan for 12 branches to answer in April 1989. The branch that prepared the "statistics" plan would work on the game "You Be The Judge" complete with its color coded cards, token and dice. This process will continue through April 1990 with 12 branches working on one plan and the other on the game.

"Statistics" covered the *Statistical Abstract of the United States*, the *County and City Data Book*, "Statsline," the statistical recording issued monthly by the Library of Congress, and three state and local statistical sources. The plan contained one page of reference questions covering each source, one page of compare-and-contrast questions, a crossword puzzle page, and an optional "circle the numbers" puzzle.

No one breezed through this assignment. Although the plan takers have been tempted to take short cuts by simply using the indices and ignoring the prefaces, introductions, and those boring "how to use this book" instructions; by the assignment's end most of them had to dig into the intros, read those pesky little footnotes, and rummage through the appendices. For the most part, staff response was positive.

As the process continues branch procedures for checking results will vary, and each branch manager will decide what steps to take with a staff member whose answers are incorrect or incomplete. Evaluations compiled by the branch manager from staff comments will go back to the project coordinator.

So far, few staff members see the assignments as a dreary chore. To keep flagging spirits high through April of 1990, the training committee is using some public relations techniques. Flowers were sent out to branches to thank them for completing their lesson plans. The library's monthly newsletter will recognize staff achievements. The real reward, however, will be the increasing confidence with which staff members can go to reference sources to answer patrons' questions.

Plans to evaluate the entire core lesson plan project in July 1990 have been discussed. Under consideration is a survey of the entire information staff to determine how well staff members use these titles to answer specific reference questions.

The Future of the Core Reference Collection

The Anne Arundel County Public Library has built a collection development and training plan that can serve it well for many years to come, but only if the system continues to work on it. Nothing changes faster than information. Last year's lesson plans go out of date with this year's new titles. Core collection priorities change and publishers are fickle.

All new information staff members and substitutes will have to complete the 13 lessons as part of their orientation and training. To be effective learning tools for these new staff members, lesson plans will require revision as new editions of sources arrive. Already, some branches have had to send in updates to their plans: new state and county budgets have come in since the plan deadline, and the county executive has issued a new set of major goals and objectives. The responsibility for keeping the plans current is an important one and will go to a reference materials committee consisting of branch and administrative representatives.

Some core collection titles have already been eliminated from the core list. They may have been duplicated by other titles, or they may have gone out of print. Community branch staffs may discover that they do not use all the sources in the collection. This committee will need to address these issues.

Creating a core reference collection has made sense for the Anne Arundel County Public Library System. A patron walking into any of our full service branches can now expect to find the same resources and staffs trained to use them. Ordering reference material has become not only more equitable, but more streamlined. Any new community branch the county builds will now receive the same reference tools as its peer branches. Any tests and surveys constructed to evaluate reference service countywide can depend on reference collection uniformity.

Building the core collection has been like laying a road. At first, in the planners' imaginations, it lay before them smooth and fast. Digging out its path and grading its foundation took a lot of toil, but now the library system can offer a community branch reference collection that, with yearly attention to holes, can benefit users for many years to come. With this basic road built, the system can now turn its attention to its superhighways: the reference collections of its major and area branch libraries.

REFERENCE

Shores, Louis. "Shores' Checkpoints for the Evaluation of Reference Books," *Basic Reference Sources*. Chicago, American Library Association, 1954: 134-135.

APPENDIX A

EVALUATING REFERENCE BOOKS

I.   AUTHORITY
     A. Reputation of author

     B. Reputation of publisher

     C. Is work completely new or revised?

II. SCOPE
     A. Does book fulfill stated purpose?

     B. What is the range of subject matter covered and what are the
         limitations? How does this work compare with others in the
         same field?

     C. How up to date are the articles, bibliographies, and/or
         statistics?

     D. Are bibliographies supplied? Are the sources cited current and
         authoritative?

III. TREATMENT
     A. How thorough, reliable and complete are the facts?

     B. Is there any bias displayed regarding controversial issues?

     C. Is the level of writing for average readers or for scholars,
         for adults or for children?

IV. ARRANGEMENT
   A. Are contents arranged by subject, geographic location, or by chronological sequence? If classified according to subject, is the arrangement letter by letter or word by word?

   B. Is access to contents facilitated by index and use of cross references?

V. FORMAT
   A. Do binding, paper, type and layout meet standards?

   B. If illustrations are used, are they of good quality? Do they aid the reader in understanding the text?

VI. SPECIAL FEATURES
   A. What special or unusual features distinguish this source from similar ones?

N.B. List based on Shores' checkpoints for the evaluation of reference books.

Self-Directed, Contract Learning
for the Reference Librarian

Ruth J. Patrick

SUMMARY. Earlier articles on continuing education for reference librarians describe the major methods used and their shortcomings. The premise of this article is that reference librarians will be able to make the greatest gain in their continuing education if they develop a long-range plan instead of relying on isolated, sporadic, unrelated or unvalidated activities. Self-directed contract learning can be the cornerstone of a long-range plan for continuing education.

This article reviews the earlier literature, describes the eight steps of the contract learning process and presents several sample contracts. It describes the experiential learning model and learning styles. It also expands on the steps of identifying learning needs and resources by describing specific competencies for reference librarians and by listing a wide range of available learning resources.

The rapid changes in our society affect the library and, especially, the reference librarian. In the 1970s, computer networks revolutionized technical services. Transformation of the labor-intensive operations of acquisition and cataloging created the national bibliographic databases that can be used to locate any recent book or periodical in any library in the United States. In the 1980s, this revolution advanced into public services, especially the reference desk.[1] The online catalog, online searching of data bases, and CD-ROM indexes are changing reference services. The library profession, primarily through the library schools and associations, tries to meet the need for the continuing professional development of reference librarians to keep up with these changes by offering classes

Ruth J. Patrick is Dean of Library Services, Maureen and Mike Mansfield Library, University of Montana, Missoula, MT 59812.

and workshops. But many reference librarians are unable to attend these offerings by reason of their distance or cost.

My premise is that the reference librarian who develops a long-range plan instead of relying on isolated, sporadic and unrelated activities will make the greatest gain in continuing education. The cornerstone of this plan is contract learning. This article reviews the earlier literature of continuing education for reference librarians, describes the eight steps of the contract learning process and presents several sample contracts. It describes the experiential learning model and learning styles. It also expands on the steps of identifying learning needs and resources by describing specific competencies for reference librarians and by listing a wide range of available learning resources.

DEFINITION OF CONTINUING EDUCATION

For the library profession, continuing education:[2]

- Implies lifelong learning to keep an individual up-to-date with new knowledge; it prevents obsolescence.
- Includes updating a person's education (e.g., makes an individual's education comparable to that of a person receiving a like degree or certificate now).
- Allows for diversification to a new area within a field (e.g., supervisory and management training).
- Assumes that the individual carries the basic responsibility for his or her own development.
- Involves educational activities beyond those considered necessary for entrance into the field.

These elements of life long learning, updating, diversification, individual responsibility, education beyond the entrance degree, can be effectively addressed by self-directed, contract learning.

BACKGROUND

A search of the library literature revealed very few articles addressing continuing education for reference librarians. One article directly on this topic was written in 1980 by Margaret F. Steig.[3] She, too, notes the paucity of articles on the topic amid the flood of materials on continuing education in librarianship. She further observes that the literature is written from an administrator's or educator's point of view, not from the perspective of the practicing librarian. From that perspective, what remains the same is at least as significant as what technology has altered. Steig identifies the constant elements of reference service: patrons with information needs, the almost infinite universe of knowledge, and the method by which the reference librarian links the two. The techniques of analysis, memory and imagination remain the same.

Steig shows that, until 1980, continuing education efforts for reference librarians focused on reference materials, reference techniques and interpersonal relations. Subject knowledge, an indispensable component of the reference librarian's expertise, has been ignored. This neglect is, at the very least, impractical; as Steig argues, the greater the reference librarian's knowledge of the subject, the more likely the librarian is to be perceived as giving good service. Steig speaks eloquently of the importance of liberal education to a reference librarian. Liberal education provides a person with subject knowledge and standards of judgment and cultivates the imagination. Steig's recommendation on how to continue one's liberal education and increase subject knowledge will always be valid: read, read, read. She suggests that the reference librarian design a satisfying, individualized educational reading program. She also recommends taking university courses in nonlibrary subjects.

In 1982, Charles A. Bunge reported on the results of an informal survey of reference librarians in large and medium-sized public and academic libraries who were asked how they kept up-to-date on reference materials and techniques. The most frequently reported strategies were professional reading, staff meetings, staff sharing, and conferences, workshops and other meetings outside the respondents' libraries.[4]

A year later, in 1983, Rothstein, in a major review of library education for the reference librarian, notes that most of the writings about reference education deal with it as it has been conducted in the accredited library schools, although most reference education is gained outside the library school.[5] Rothstein identifies four main ways by which further education may be pursued. The first is "on-the-job-training" and is the learning that comes with the experience of doing reference work. New librarians learn from contact and discussion with other, more experienced reference librarians. They learn about the collection, the users and searching shortcuts.

The second way is self-study, as Steig suggested, by reading and taking courses. Rothstein points out that, since these efforts are private, it is difficult to judge the effectiveness or even the existence of them. Third is staff development — programs planned, financed and supervised by the employing institutions. Rothstein did not find many references to the existence of such programs in the literature.

Fourth, there is continuing education — programs conducted by agencies other than the employing institution. Continuing education providers include professional library associations, library schools, commercial vendors, and bibliographic utilities. Rothstein concludes that although the number of offerings for reference librarians is large, the programs have been unsatisfactory. The deficiencies are those of continuing education generally: lack of coordination, sequence and a recognition system. "In short, the librarian has too little incentive or opportunity to pursue a thorough, systematic and convenient program of relevant professional studies over the long run of his or her career."[6]

The conclusion to be drawn from the work of Steig, Bunge and Rothstein is that continuing education for the reference librarian requires techniques and procedures not yet commonly practiced. The method should be both effective and reasonably easy for working reference librarians to use. Self-directed, contract learning meets these requirements.

CONTRACT LEARNING

Contract learning is a process based on research about adult learning. It acknowledges that adults are highly self-directed when they go about learning something and that when they learn on their own initiative they "learn more deeply and permanently than what they learn by being taught."[7] A learning contract is developed in eight steps. These steps are detailed by Malcolm Knowles in *Using Learning Contracts*.[8]

Step 1 is to diagnose your learning needs. A learning need is the "gap between where you are now and where you want to be in regard to a particular set of competencies."[9] Step 2 is to specify your learning objectives. Translate each learning need into a learning objective. The objectives need to be clear, feasible, personally meaningful, measurable as to accomplishment, and at appropriate levels of specifity or generality.[10] The objectives should describe what you will learn, not what you will do to learn it. State your objectives in the terms that are most meaningful to you—the acquisition of new knowledge, the ability to search a new CD-ROM index, a direction of growth such as increased sensitivity to the cultural differences of foreign students.

Step 3 is to specify your learning resources and strategies. Once you have listed your learning objectives you need to identify how you will accomplish each objective. Identify the resources (material and human) and the strategies (techniques and tools) you will use. Step 4 is to specify evidence of accomplishment. After you have identified the learning resources and strategies you will use to accomplish your learning objective you need to describe what evidence you will collect to indicate the degree to which you have achieved each objective.

Step 5 is to specify how the evidence will be validated. You need to vary criteria according to objective. For knowledge objectives, appropriate criteria might include comprehensiveness, depth, precision, clarity, scholarliness, and authentication and usefulness. Appropriate criteria for skills objectives may be poise, speed, flexibility, gracefulness, precision, and imaginativeness. Once you have specified the criteria, you need to indicate the means you propose for judging the evidence. "For example, if you produce a paper or report, whom will you have read it, and what are those persons' qualifications? Will they express their judgments by rating scales, descriptive reports, evaluative reports, or how?"[11]

Step 6 is to review your contract with consultants. Reviewing it with two or three colleagues, supervisors, or other expert resource people will strengthen the quality of the contract. Here are some questions you might ask your consultants:[12]

• Are the learning objectives clear, understandable, and realistic; do they describe what you propose to learn?
• Can your consultants think of other objectives you might consider?
• Do the learning strategies and resources seem reasonable, appropriate, and efficient?
• Does the evidence seem relevant to the various objectives? Would it convince your consultants?
• Can they suggest other evidence you might consider?
• Are the criteria and means for validating the evidence clear, relevant, and convincing?
• Can your consultants think of other ways to validate the evidence that you might consider?

Step 7 is to carry out the contract. As you proceed you may discover that your ideas about what you want to learn and how you want to learn it change. If this happens, revise your contract as you proceed. Step 8 is to evaluate your learning. One way to ascertain that you have learned what you wanted to is to ask the consultants in Step 6 to examine your evidence and validation data and judge your accomplishments.

SAMPLE LEARNING CONTRACTS

An example of what a learning contract looks like will help illustrate how this process of self-directed learning works. Figure 1 shows a sample contract for a reference librarian who has identified the need to learn how to plan for CD-ROM services. Resources or strategies that could be used in addition to those listed are: Attend a conference to see the CD-ROMS available and to see demonstrations and to attend programs on the topic of CD-ROMS; and, discuss with your supervisor such variables as cost, scope of coverage, that will be relevant to assessing this technology for this library. A striking feature of this plan is the combination of a variety of learn-

Reference Librarian Learning Plan[14]

Overall Goal: To review new technology for possible implementation.

Objectives:	Resources:	Evidence:	Criteria:	Target Date:
To assess the CD-ROM technology and indexes for possible implementation.	1. Review recent articles on use of CD-ROMs in libraries and on methods of assessing new technology in libraries.	Prepare a paper describing possible CD-ROMs that are available and recommend an action for the library.	1. Collect feedback from supervisor about usefulness of paper.	January 1990
	2. Obtain several test CD-ROMS from vendors to get hands-on experience with them and to test user reaction, ease-of-use, and satisfaction.		2. The recommended action will be implemented.	
	3. Interview by telephone librarians at other libraries who have already implemented CD-ROMS to find out how they went about deciding which CD-ROMS to acquire.			
	4. Talk with other librarians at the library to obtain their ideas and knowledge about CD-ROMS that they have obtained from their reading or from attendance at conferences or visits to other libraries.			

FIGURE 1. Reference Librarian Learning Plan[14]

213

ing resources and strategies, from reading to consulting other people to hands-on experience. Also notable is how closely related the learning plan is to an immediate task the librarian is faced with at work—recommending a plan for CD services.

Figure 2 illustrates a learning need more closely related to an individual than to a library in general. It focuses on a behavioral change and on learning that would develop the ability to understand and work effectively with others.

NEEDS ASSESSMENT

A list of competencies developed for the reference librarian by Suzanne H. Mahmoodi and others can be used in assessing learning needs.[13] The competencies are detailed and related to the tasks, responsibilities and duties of the reference librarian. Although this list was developed to help persons working in small and medium sized public libraries (serving populations of up to 50,000), these competencies will be an excellent start for reference librarians working in larger public libraries or in school, academic, or special libraries. The competencies are grouped into five areas: research skills—the ability to gather information on whatever subject interests the library user; communication skills—the abilities to interview the user to determine the user's need and to communicate to others about the library and how to use it; managing skills—the ability to plan and organize services and to formulate and implement policies; knowledge of the community—ability to identify current information needs of the users and to predict future needs; knowledge of information resources—familiarity with the entire library collection and the wide range of other resources available. This competency list was revised in 1986 and needs to be updated again in the competencies listed for teamwork, management and technology.[16]

Each of these five areas comprises from five to ten specific competencies. For example, the library worker skilled in communication is able to:[17]

Student:
Cluster: Human Resource Management
Competency: Accurate self-assessment
Goal: To seek help to improve on soliciting and accepting criticism

	Actions	Target Dates for Completion
Educating myself about the competency	Read <u>Managing Self-Esteem in Organizations</u>	3/25
Practice and application of the competency	1. Meet with my former superior, with whom there has been an undercurrent of attempts to get past the barriers I have erected. Request his assessment and his help, including honest criticism.	
	2. Meet with my present superior, who has been through a similar exercise and who seems willing and anxious to practice all the various competencies. Ask for his evaluation of my diagnosis and his help in overcoming my resistance.	3/30
	3. Practice openness through use of Positive Regard Indicators with subordinates. Gauge reactions and, when timing is right, request help.	Ongoing
Feedback plans	Document each instance of criticism and follow up with person who gave it (3 months?) to see if he or she perceives any improvement.	Ongoing

I can anticipate the following obstacles:
    Personal: My tendency to respond to critical remarks with witty sarcasms will not disappear overnight.
    Situation: Past history of being unwilling to accept constructive criticism has made subordinates, superiors, and peers unwilling to come forward with comments.
Sources of help: Personal friends whom I can ask for assistance.

FIGURE 2. AMA Competency-Development Plan[15]

- Write clearly;
- Use interviewing techniques to determine an individual's information needs;
- Use nonverbal communication effectively;
- Teach individuals or groups how to use information sources;
- Evaluate the individual user's response to information provided;
- Mediate between users and information sources, translating information into terms used by both;
- Work with individuals, local media and other groups using appropriate techniques to promote reference service;
- Respond to all users appropriately and fairly;
- Convey knowledge of materials and services to the public;
- Use questionnaires and discussion techniques.

After identifying the competencies you wish to acquire, your next task is to assess the gap between where you are now and where the model says you should be in regard to each competency. The Mahmoodi guide presents a detailed process for this task.[18] The reference librarian evaluates his or her ability for each of the forty competencies and determines how important each competency is to performing the reference function for his or her position. The librarian determines the areas for improvement by subtracting the rating of importance from the rating of ability. The larger the negative number, the greater the need for improvement. These areas for improvement are the learning needs.

The learning needs can be grouped into results expected and kinds of learning.[19] The results expected can be knowledge, skills or attitudes. The kind of learning can be conceptual, technical or human. Figure 3 presents examples of learning needs for the reference librarian in each of these six categories. Other assessment inventories are relevant to reference librarians. The Myers-Briggs Type Indicator evaluates workers according to the ways they like to perceive situations and make judgments about them. The Personal Profile System helps people understand how they work with others.

Whatever system of competency assessment the librarian may use, the result of the assessment may well be perception of the need

RESULTS EXPECTED

KINDS OF LEARNING	KNOWLEDGE (Awareness of facts, ideas and concepts relevant to a task, a function or an organization)	SKILLS (Ability to apply knowledge proficiently in a manner appropriate to the situation)	ATTITUDES (A position, and often behavior, that indicates opinion, disposition, or manner with regard a person, a thing, or situation)
CONCEPTUAL (Ability to formulate, understand, and apply concepts and ideas)	trends in reference service	how to plan for CD-ROM services	desire for quality work
TECHNICAL (Ability to apply a particular art or skill)	the new CD-ROM indexes	how to search new CD-ROM indexes	receptivity to using new methods
HUMAN (Ability to understand and work effectively with others)	interpersonal communication principles	how to supervise student assistants	feelings of prejudice

FIGURE 3. My Learning Needs and Expected Learning Results[21]

to learn additional competencies. In order to do so efficiently, the librarian should understand the theory and styles of learning.

LEARNING THEORY AND STYLES

Being aware of learning theory and styles will help the librarian to become an effective self-directed and independent learner. Kolb's experiential learning model emphasizes the important role that experience plays in the learning process.[20] (See Figure 4.) The four-stage cycle begins with concrete experience, which is the basis for observation and reflection. The learner uses these observations to build a generalization from which new implications for action can be deduced. These implications serve as guides to create new experiences.

To learn effectively, learners need four different kinds of abilities. They must be able to:

- Involve themselves fully, openly, and without bias in new experiences;
- Observe and reflect on these experiences from many perspectives;
- Create concepts that integrate their observations into logically sound theories;
- Use these theories to make decisions and solve problems[22]

Kolb developed the Learning Style Inventory to measure differences in learning style. The advantage to the learner of using the Inventory is increased awareness of both the learning process and the person's own style of learning. People who are familiar with the

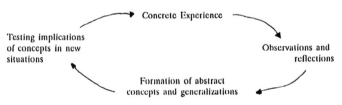

FIGURE 4. The Experiential Learning Model

learning process and with their own learning styles should be able to become better independent and self-directed learners and to maximize the effectiveness of the contract learning process.

LEARNING RESOURCES

A knowledge of the learning model and of his or her learning style should assist the learner in selecting learning resources and strategies related to learning needs. As an example of how you might identify learning resources, let's suppose that one of your learning objectives is to improve your ability to organize your work efficiently so that you can accomplish twenty percent more work in a day. Possible learning resources and strategies for you to consider are:

- In the library, find books, articles, videos, or audio cassettes on how to organize your work and manage time, and read, watch, or listen to them.
- Interview three reference librarians on how they organize their work, then observe them for one day each, noting techniques they use.
- Select the best techniques from each librarian you've observed, plan a day's work, and have a colleague observe you for a day, giving you feedback.
- Review offerings of various continuing education providers, such as library associations, universities or colleges in your area, for a workshop on time management and attend it.

The key point in this example is that there is a wide range of possible learning strategies that go beyond merely reading or attending a workshop. The Mahmoodi guide presents a long list of learning resources that are available to match your learning needs. The various formats and techniques are grouped by type of learning need for which they are especially effective.[23]

- *For obtaining information, ideas, or concepts*: audio media (audio tape, radio, telephone conferencing), books/journal articles, classes/courses, correspondence study/courses, discussion groups, films/television/videotapes, filmstrips/slides, forums/panels, lectures, programmed instruction/computer-aided instruction, seminars, symposiums/colloquiums.

- *For learning by demonstration and observation*: conferences/conventions, demonstrations/exhibits, field trips/tours.
- *For practicing skills, techniques, and thinking processes*: case studies, clinics, committees/task forces, critical incidents, role playing simulation/games.
- *For increasing in-depth understanding*: coaching, job instruction, job rotation, laboratory training, sabbaticals.
- *For meeting a variety of learning objectives*: institutes, workshops.

Another way of discovering what learning resources are available is to review the offerings of a wide range of continuing education providers. Library education programs, community colleges, and vocational-technical institutes in your area provide classes, short courses and workshops. State library associations and other professional associations, state library agencies, library systems, bibliographic utilities, regional networks, online database vendors, library consultants, and commercial providers such as Careertrack provide workshops, conferences, program meetings, and other one-time learning opportunities. Toastmasters' training is available everywhere and has rigorous and comprehensive learning programs for communication and leadership skills. The Association of College and Research Libraries (ACRL) offers continuing education preconferences that relate to learning needs reference librarians might have. The 1989 American Library Association (ALA) Annual Conference offered the following preconferences: Stress Management for Librarians, Librarians as Supervisors, Managing Student Workers in Academic Libraries, Approaches to Managing the Problem Patron. These courses are among twenty-six available for local presentations and also offered by state library association conferences, library schools, libraries, universities or other professional groups. Several of these are directly related to needs of reference librarians: Public Services Under Pressure, An Introduction to Maps in Libraries: Maps as Information Tools, and How to Teach Science Reference Materials: A Workshop for Librarians Who Serve the Undergraduate. The Reference and Adult Services Division (RASD) of

ALA also offers conference programs of interest to reference librarians.

Some on-the-job activities also address learning needs: coaching, job rotation, emulating the behavior of another reference librarian or person who is effective in the areas of your learning needs, accepting or seeking advice from others on how to do better, taking special assignments, serving on task forces and committees, making presentations on the topic, and job exchange.[24]

Other compilations of learning activities are given in the provider approval system of the National Council on Quality Continuing Education for Information, Library and Media Personnel.[25] One list is of formal group educational activities in planned programs. Examples are academic courses taken for credit or audit, institutes, seminars, short courses, workshops or lecture series. A second set, formal individual activities, includes home study programs, academic independent study, internships, fellowships, education for an advanced degree or post-master's certificate, or audiovisual activities.

Informal group activities, a third cluster, include journal clubs, study groups, library/information/media association meetings, and lecture series. The National Council recommends that these activities be accompanied by written summaries. Self-teaching activities constitute a fourth group. Examples are the use of non-supervised audiovisual devices, educational television without local supervision, and the use of programmed educational materials such as teaching machines. A fifth sort of activity is consultation, and a sixth is self-assessment by taking appropriate tests and audits. Seventh is publication. Examples are articles in recognized journals to report research findings or to share information, technical reports, books or book reviews, and presentations or exhibits to professional audiences; an eighth activity is teaching.

Ninth is participation in association activities (national, state, regional, or local office; committee work; conference attendance if submitted with a written summary). The tenth and last group of learning activities is described simply as other learning experiences. This option recognizes that, as broad as these lists are, individuals may identify other learning activities that meet their needs and that other educational activities may develop to assist individuals in their pursuit of learning. As you can see from this compilation of learning resources, a wide range of opportunities is available.

EVIDENCE OF ACCOMPLISHMENTS AND LEARNING

A fundamental necessity in any learning process is to ascertain if indeed learning did take place. For continuing education, an additional key determination is whether or not the learning is improving the practice. These examples of evidence that learning objectives have been achieved will help the learner to determine if learning did take place.[26]

Types of Objective	*Examples of Evidence*
Knowledge	Reports of knowledge acquired, as in essays, examinations, oral presentations; annotated bibliographies.
Understanding	Examples of utilization of knowledge in solving problems, as in action projects, research projects with conclusions and recommendations, plans for curriculum change, and so on.
Skills	Performance exercises, videotaped performances, and so on, with ratings by observers.
Attitudes	Attitudinal rating scales; performance in real situations, role playing, simulation games, critical incident cases, and so on, with feedback from participants and/or observers.
Values	Value rating scales; performance in value clarification groups, critical-incident cases, simulation exercises, and so on, with feedback from participants and/or observers.

The Continuing Library Education Network and Exchange Round Table (CLENE RT) of the American Library Association is concerned about improving the quality of continuing education and the transfer from workshop to worksite. For example, two recent programs aimed at continuing education providers focused on the fundamentals of skills transfer, the typical barriers to effective learning, and specific training techniques that can be used during workshops to assist learners in making the connection between workshop and workplace.[27]

An example of a transfer technique is a form used to encourage participants to choose the most important idea they identified at a session and to work with a partner on accomplishing some action based on the idea.[28]

1. Write down the most important idea you identified during the session.
2. How will you use this idea?
3. When will you put it into action?

Although this technique is geared to workshops, it might help generate ideas about other ways to ensure transfer of learning.

To develop a plan for your own continuing education you may need to begin with your career goals. What do you plan to be doing five years from now? Let's say you've been a reference librarian for three years. In five years would you like to be head of a reference department? If you don't know, then you might want to back up and do some career planning. You might even want to take a step further back and do some life planning.

This model of self-directed learning for the reference librarian is rigorous and demanding. Nevertheless, any reference librarian who allows it will be ready for the revolution that is taking place in public services.

REFERENCES

1. Brian Neilsen, "The Role of the Public Services Librarian: The New Revolution", *Rethinking the Library in the Information Age Volume II* (Washington, DC: U.S. Government Printing Office, 1988), p. 179.

2. Elizabeth W. Stone, Ruth J. Patrick, and Barbara Conroy, *Continuing Library and Information Science Education: Final Report to the National Com-*

mission on Libraries and Information Science, (Washington, DC: U.S. Government Printing Office, 1974), pp. 2-3.

3. Margaret Steig, "Continuing Education and the Reference Librarian in the Academic and Research Library", *Library Journal*, December 15, 1980, pp. 2547-2551.

4. Charles A. Bunge, "Strategies for Updating Knowledge of Reference Resources and Techniques", *RQ*, Volume 21, Number 3, Spring 1982, pp. 228-232.

5. Samuel Rothstein, "The Making of a Reference Librarian", *Library Trends*, Volume 31, Number 3, Winter 1983, pp. 375-399.

6. *Ibid*, p. 391.

7. Malcolm S. Knowles, *Using Learning Contracts*, San Francisco: Jossey-Bass, Inc., Publishers, 1986, p. 27.

8. *Ibid*, p. 27.

9. *Ibid*, p. 28.

10. Malcolm S. Knowles, *Self-Directed Learning: A Guide for Learners and Teachers*, Chicago: Follett Publishing Company, 1975, p. 36.

11. Malcolm S. Knowles, *Using Learning Contracts*, San Francisco: Jossey-Bass, Inc., Publishers, 1986, p. 31.

12. *Ibid*, p. 31-32.

13. *Self Assessment Guide for Reference*, St. Paul: Office of Library Development and Services, 1986, pp. 15-18. This guide is available for sale from CLENE Publications at the American Library Association Office in Chicago.

14. (Adapted from Knowles, *Using Learning Contracts*, San Francisco: Jossey-Bass, Inc., Publishers, 1986, p. 184.)

15. (Adapted from Knowles, *Using Learning Contracts*, San Francisco: Jossey-Bass, Inc., Publishers, 1986, p. 194.)

16. Telephone Conversation with Suzanne H. Mahmoodi, June 21, 1989.

17. *Ibid*, p. 4.

18. *Ibid*, p. 15.

19. Barbara Conroy, *Library Staff Development and Continuing Education*, Littleton: Libraries Unlimited, Inc., 1978, p. 10.

20. David A. Kolb, "Learning Styles and Disciplinary Differences", *The Modern American College*, San Francisco: Jossey-Bass, Inc., 1981, p. 235.

21. (Adapted from Conroy, p. 10 and *Self Assessment Guide for Reference*, p. 21.)

22. David A. Kolb, "Learning Styles and Disciplinary Differences", *The Modern American College*, San Francisco: Jossey-Bass, Inc., 1981, p. 235-236.

23. *Self Assessment Guide for Reference*, pp. 22-24, based on Conroy, *Op. Cit.*, p. 75-79.

24. *Self Assessment Guide for Reference*, p. 37.

25. *Ibid*, p. 21-22.

26. Malcolm S. Knowles, *Using Learning Contracts*, San Francisco: Jossey-Bass, Inc., Publishers, 1986, p. 30.

27. *CLENEXCHANGE*, March 1988, p. 1.

28. *CLENEXCHANGE*, December 1987, p. 5.

III. MANAGEMENT

The Developing Reference Librarian: An Administrative Perspective

Helen H. Spalding

SUMMARY. The learning of librarians continues beyond the awarding of the MLS. Continuing professional development is necessary for librarians to anticipate and position themselves for the changing information field and changing client needs. Practitioners on all organizational levels must recognize and support the importance of this activity. Administrators are accountable for providing clear institutional values and job expectations, and for creating an environment and incentives that nurture professional development. Librarians have the individual responsibility to recognize personal strengths and developmental needs, to realistically assess career changes and educational opportunities, and to contribute to the professional development of their colleagues throughout the profession.

Much of what applies to the professional development of reference librarians applies as well to librarians in other areas of specialty. Development depends upon the partnership of the librarians, the employer, and colleagues in the profession at large. Each has a stake in keeping librarians intellectually and emotionally engaged in

Helen H. Spalding is Associate Director of Libraries, University of Missouri-Kansas City, 5100 Rockhill Road, Kansas City, MO 64110.

their work. And each has the responsibility to support individual change and growth. Development issues are different for the new librarian, the experienced professional, and library managers, but librarians in each of these roles expect institutional encouragement to develop professionally, and have a responsibility to provide similar support for their colleagues.

To be curious about what goes on in the worlds that surround us—our small personal world and the larger one out there, beyond our workaday reach—is to enlarge and enrich our lives. But to be curious within our professional lives is something else. It is the quality that moves us ahead, makes us more useful, even changes the world a little bit. Without it we are condemned to be ordinary. With it we have a shot at being part of the future. To be caught up, captured, magnetized by an idea larger than oneself, to be riveted by one's work in the world, is the very goal of work itself.[1]

JOB DESCRIPTION

No one way exists to structure the reference position that all will find satisfying for the length of a career. But by continually reviewing and analyzing position responsibilities in light of changing resources, client needs, staff preferences, and external environment, there is less likelihood that a librarian feels stuck in the rut of a job with no stimulation, surprises, or reward. An obvious opportunity for such review is when a position is vacated. Once the vacated position and those related to it are examined and reorganized, the advertisement must then clearly represent the institution's values and the position's requirements. Martell describes how integrating quality of work life concepts with the job creates an enriching position for dynamic librarians.[2]

KNOW THYSELF

Librarians as job candidates have the responsibility of realistically evaluating prospective job opportunities. One must have enough self knowledge to recognize strengths, weaknesses, and true motivations for entering the field of librarianship or looking at particular openings. If going to library school was a means to getting a job, any job, and getting a job is the final career goal, new librarians should not be surprised if employers look instead at those who view being hired as the beginning of a new phase in the learning adventure of life. If job hunting is a result of resentment that in the current position time must be taken from the reference desk for bureaucratic paperwork, for decision making to allocate constrained resources, and for resolving personnel problems, one should think seriously about the implications of looking for positions with increased management responsibility.

This is not to say that administrators expect a candidate to completely foresee what one's day to day work will entail, or how one will change during tenure in the position, or exactly where this position will lead one's career. The quality of the staff is the most crucial factor in the organization's ability to secure resources, adapt to change, and deliver quality service. Turnover is costly, and risk taking occurs with every new hire, for each new person brings changes to the organization as a whole. Employers want to find not only librarians to perform the duties as they are currently described, but to find those who also can evolve with inevitable change. Provision of a challenging assignment and professional development opportunities are for naught if the librarian does not feel the position builds upon strengths, provides growth in weaker areas, and is leading to the work/lifestyle envisioned for oneself. The match of these expectations with a particular position in a particular institution should be delineated from the printed advertisement, and clarified in the interview.

CLEAR EXPECTATIONS

On both sides, the interview should not be seen as a finalizing process as much as a development process. There should be no expectation that once hired, the librarian is settled until retirement. Each of us has heard from a librarian who feels betrayed after a decade in the position for which s/he was hired, when s/he is asked to learn new skills, or even change positions completely. And all of us have known department heads who feel personally used and resentful when a librarian joyfully announces having been recruited for a more responsible position in another library, because of the expertise gained on the job partially as a result of investment by the supervisory department head. In an organization committed to professional development, a positive climate is in place where department heads view their support of developing librarians as a contribution not only to their library, but also to the profession at large. Both the subordinate and supervisor expect to learn from each other and stand ready to adjust to inescapable change.

The interview is an opportunity to define what attracted the applicant to the position and what future career development is planned. The administration can ensure that the institution's mission, setting, style, and values are communicated. An honest discussion of both the difficult issues and the advantages that characterize the library and the daily work, ensure that acceptance of an offer is based on a realistic assessment. Later dissatisfaction will be less a result of disillusionment than that of actual change in the institution, position, or person. The use of a search committee, and the involvement of other library staff in the interview process serve as ongoing staff development. As managers explain the institutional setting and priorities, regular reinforcement is provided for staff as well. As candidates' questions get answered, all gain a better understanding of the ambiguous or conflicting perceptions that need further discussion and resolution within the organization. Employees feel greater loyalty to an organization if the work is challenging, the expectations clear, and role ambiguity is reduced.[3]

This emphasis on the importance of mutually clear expectations at the point of hiring is intentional. The quality of its personnel determines the ability of a library to reach the excellence to which it aspires. A major factor for job candidates considering offers can be the intellectual stimulation, personal enjoyment, opportunity to learn, and rapport they perceive they will gain through interaction with the current staff.

TRAINING

All levels of library staff should view their relationship at work as a team developing the library's services and its individual staff parts to be the best that they can be. This developmental perspective implies change. In an organization made up of diverse individuals with different personal motivations and professional goals, it is to be expected that all will not develop at the same pace or in the same direction. A challenge for managers is to provide the creative, nurturing environment that enables the library's services to keep pace with changing external pressures, and yet supports individual development.

It is helpful if there is the understanding that the profession as a whole benefits as a librarian develops increasing self awareness and skills, even though such development may result in the person selecting a different position, or leaving the profession entirely. A librarian who has self knowledge and a thorough understanding of the library in which she works, and who chooses to take a different position where s/he finds a more comfortable fit, is leaving for the right reasons. Staff development is a motivation for librarians to stay in an organization, but also can enable them to better assess personal abilities and goals in relation to the library's expectations, leading to a productive career change.

Administrators who perceive the hiring and retention process as one of staff and organizational development will plan a thorough and sequential training program for any new hire, regardless of past experience of the individual.[4] Feeling comfortable with new job duties at the side of a more senior colleague, adjusting to the unique style, politics, and relationships of the new setting, and reinforcing the service orientation and institutional values can be accomplished through such a training program.[5]

DEVELOPMENT CLIMATE

Continuing assessment of external and internal pressures enable an institution to prepare for changing service expectations and delivery capabilities. Integrating professional development opportunities with ongoing organizational redesign provides institutional flexibility and a climate for constant skill enhancement and retooling. Personnel policies should clearly reflect a concern for the development of human resources. An established staff development program should be addressing needs at all staff levels. Examples of relevant professional development programs include dual job assignments,[6] job sharing,[7] joint appointments, temporary appointments, job exchanges, sabbaticals, assessment centers,[8] designated research time, job rotation, teaching, management internships.[9] Our faculty colleagues face the issues of providing encouragement for young faculty to reach tenure, and tenured faculty to remain fresh.[10] Some of their development programs are applicable to the library setting, and include research, travel, service, counseling, and re-training incentives.[11]

Importing speakers and trainers to give lectures and workshops in basic reference and communications skills, as well as providing information on new reference tools and techniques are useful for even the most experienced reference librarian. Workshops aimed at teaching grantsmanship, applied statistics, personal computer facility, and research skills can be especially productive. (Release time to do research is no incentive for the librarian who was not trained in graduate school to produce research.[12])

Certainly involvement of staff on all levels of the organization in committee work, goal and budget planning, and priority setting engages them more fully. They have a greater sense of mutual commitment and recognition. The librarians better understand the constraints within which the administration must operate and feel a necessary part of the management process. Settings where employees have more feedback, appreciation, autonomy, responsibility, and supervisors skilled in human relations are less likely to leave.[13] Providing stress and time management programs may help equip librarians with skills to better manage the personal attitudes and choices that affect their job satisfaction.[14] Because time and cost are the major impediments to staff development participation,[15] administrators need to design opportunities with sensitivity to these factors.

The climate that cultivates professional growth is a part of a dynamic institutional setting. Brian Champion describes the difference encouragement of innovation in librarians can have on the development of their enthusiasm and expertise, as well as the improvement of the library's ability to accommodate change.[16]

MANAGEMENT COMMITMENT

Supervisors have a responsibility not only to train and evaluate job performance, but also to take a personal interest in the professional growth of those who report to them. Management, in partnership with staff, must continually examine organizational structure and communication for their impacts on professional development and satisfaction. The administration must do its job of securing resources, managing efficiently, serving as an advocate for the unit, and maximizing opportunities for favorable unit visibility. Of course, performance and attitude problems must be addressed. Colleagues recognize when a discrepancy exists between an organization's aspirations for excellence, and its avoidance of tough personnel decisions. Not only is there unfairness in asking others to work around a problem employee, suggesting that different standards exist for different individuals, but there also is deceit implied by the pretense. Such duplicity leads to erosion of hard won trust and open communication within an organization. To expect people to perform responsibly and stretch their capabilities also may mean confronting them with hard truths concerning areas in which they may need to improve to achieve their professional ambitions. Good performance evaluation programs reiterate institutional values and expectations, recognize achievement, provide mutual accountability, and identify developmental needs.[17]

Because less and less external praise is received the further one progresses administratively, it often is hard to remember how meaningful directly expressed appreciation is to employees. Praise is a motivator that inspires one to do more and binds one in a commitment to the institution. If employees are respected and valued as individuals, their self-concepts are strengthened and confidence in delivery of service results. The role modeling and mentoring managers can provide are crucial obligations.[18] Some libraries have formal mentor-protege programs that enable not only direct supervisors, but also other experienced librarians to enter into mutually rewarding developmental relationships with librarians exploring career development.[19] Exemplifying a personal commitment to professional development, learning from those with whom one works, involvement in professional activities, and continuing study make inspiring impressions. In allocating resources to staff development activities, managers demonstrate greater stewardship if they do not pursue their own professional activities at the expense of opportunities for others in the organization.

Although turnover is expensive, administrators cannot afford to be paternalistic or territorial about "their" staff. It may be okay for librarians to develop, outgrow a particular setting, and move on. An opportunity for reorganization or resource allocation may thus be created. Support of individual career development can bring beneficial visibility for the institution as its "graduates" populate the nation. Positive partings contribute to the forging of broader networks of colleagues at other institutions with new ideas, potential job candidates, consulting expertise, fresh contacts, and honest feedback. The same potential exists even for librarians who decide through much self examination and dialogue with their mentors to leave the profession. Administrators should be motivated to provide professional development not only to retain good staff, but also to enable staff to go where they will do best. Just as directors value staff who grow with a job and develop the skills required by new services and technology, they must guard against the personal tendency to want a smoothly running organization to be locked in time without the threat of change. As people grow, they change, and their change influences the organization.

AS TIME GOES BY

Of course, development issues are not just for beginning professionals. It is hard to mentor and inspire if one is dissatisfied with one's own career choice or current responsibilities. Smith and others have described the influence a burned out administrator can have on an entire organization.[20] We need to be aware of why we chose this profession, what turned us on in the first place. We must look for the newness in our jobs that can keep them fresh. A catalyst may be a particularly interesting patron; the maturing of a subordinate; new topics or questions being raised by patrons and staff; changing political, curricular, fiscal dynamics of the campus; or new concepts or contacts gained at meetings. What is to be learned each day, with each encounter? How can this learning lead to personal growth and rejuvenation of excitement about a future in the profession? Senior staff must recognize the value of learning from their less experienced colleagues. Openness to that which each person brings to the organization can lead to mutual growth and satisfaction.[21]

Judith Hegg found that, "The longer librarians had been employed by a library the more likely they were to have participated in no continuing education activities in the past year and the longer they had served in their library careers in total, the less likely they were to have engaged in continuing education."[22] And that, "Women, the youngest, the newest to the profession, and those employed in institutions granting faculty status were more likely to participate in course work, workshops, and attendance at conventions."[23] Administrators must give attention to incentives and meaningful experiences that will appeal to and lead to further development of experienced professionals.

PERSONAL COMMITMENT

As much as library administrators may dispense in the way of sensitivity, nurturing, and stimulation, they cannot be responsible for the individual happiness or satisfaction of an individual. Self awareness on the part of the professional is needed to recognize that personal choices are being made in accepting a particular position, in bringing an attitude to the performance of the job duties, in investing oneself in professional growth, and in setting career goals. Librarians should suggest potential development opportunities and alternatives so that as a team they can work with their supervisors to design programs that can mutually benefit the individual and the institution. It is difficult for an institution to respond when a person is vague about aspirations, what constitutes personal job satisfaction, and specific development preferences. "SOME people CAN change CERTAIN aspects of themselves and their behavior if they WANT to badly enough and if they are WILLING to WORK hard enough at it."[24]

At a certain point, one is in a position to gain satisfaction in giving back to the profession through mentoring others, publishing, and teaching. Indeed, these contributions should be viewed as a professional responsibility. Senior librarians have the opportunity to guide and inspire not only those with whom they work daily, but also those entering the profession and those employed at other libraries. More of an effort should be made to share explicitly with each other how we individually stay fresh and interested in what we do. Certainly, senior staff members can share with newer professionals the fulfillment they derive from these activities, including the professional networks and personal friends one builds along the way. One cannot assume that by example alone skills, experience, attitudes, professionalism, and enthusiasm will be passed along.[25]

A WORTHY RISK

Staff development is a shared responsibility that recognizes that change is inevitable in oneself, others, the library, the parent institution, the profession, and society. All affect one's work, motivation, and career plans. Being sensitive to staff development needs and expectations, and proactively recognizing opportunities for development involve risk. Librarians, including the administrators, may reject growth opportunities, or take advantage of them and develop in an unexpected direction, possibly affecting the organization with startling results. Without investing in staff development, individuals and libraries risk an even worse fate, that of becoming stale, burned out, or irrelevant. A proactive stance empowers, reducing the negative impacts of risk. When one takes responsibility in the development process, one is more aware of possibilities, develops alternatives, and thus has greater control of one's fate. Such empowerment on the part of individual librarians, whatever their place in the organization, brings confidence and vivacity in oneself, and in the pursuit of excellence in one's career and institution.

REFERENCES

1. Weintraub, Stanley, "Curiosity and Motivation in Scholarship," JGE: THE JOURNAL OF GENERAL EDUCATION 38, no. 3 (1986): 160.

2. Martell, Charles and Mercedes Untawale, "Work Enrichment for Academic Libraries," THE JOURNAL OF ACADEMIC LIBRARIANSHIP 8, no. 6 (1983): 339-343.

3. Neal, James G., "The Turnover Process and the Academic Library." ADVANCES IN LIBRARY ADMINISTRATION AND ORGANIZATION 3 (1984): 50-51.

4. Creth, Sheila D., EFFECTIVE ON-THE-JOB TRAINING: DEVELOPING LIBRARY HUMAN RESOURCES (Chicago: American Library Association, 1986).

5. Jones, Dorothy E., "I'd Like You To Meet Our New Librarian: The Initi-

ation and Integration of the Newly Appointed Librarian," THE JOURNAL OF ACADEMIC LIBRARIANSHIP 14, no. 4 (1988): 221-224; Karen Y. Stabler, "Introductory Training of Academic Reference Librarians: A Survey," RQ 26 (1987): 363-369.

6. Linsley, Laurie S., "The Dual Job Assignment: How It Enhances Job Satisfaction," in ACADEMIC LIBRARIES: MYTHS AND REALITIES (Chicago: Association of College and Research Libraries, 1984): 146-150.

7. Bobay, Julie, "Job-Sharing: A Survey of the Literature and a Plan for Academic Libraries," JOURNAL OF LIBRARY ADMINISTRATION 9, no. 2 (1988): 59-69.

8. DuBois, Henry J., "Assessment Centers for the Development of Academic Librarians: A Foot in the Door," THE JOURNAL OF ACADEMIC LIBRARIANSHIP 14, no. 3 (1988): 154-160.

9. Townley, Charles T., "Nurturing Library Effectiveness: Leadership for Personnel Development," LIBRARY ADMINISTRATION & MANAGEMENT 3, no. 1 (1989): 16-20.

10. Baldwin, Roger G. and Robert T. Blackburn, eds., COLLEGE FACULTY: VERSATILE HUMAN RESOURCES IN A PERIOD OF CONSTRAINT, New Directions for Institutional Research, no. 40 (San Francisco: Jossey-Bass, 1983); Chandra M. N. Mehrotra, ed., TEACHING AND AGING, New Directions for Teaching and Learning, no. 19 (San Francisco: Jossey-Bass, 1984).

11. Roever, James E., "The Over-The-Hill Gang: A Problem For All Seasons," ACA BULLETIN 53 (1985): 60-62; John Lee Jellicorse and James G. Tilley, "Promoting Vitality After Tenure," ACA BULLETIN 53 (1985): 65-69; Jack A. Fuller and Fred J. Evans, "Recharging Intellectual Batteries: the Challenge of Faculty Development," EDUCATIONAL RECORD 66, no. 2 (1985): 31-34.

12. Emmick, Nancy J., "Release Time for Professional Development: How Much for Research?" in ACADEMIC LIBRARIES: MYTHS AND REALITIES (Chicago: Association of College and Research Libraries, 1984): 130.

13. Neal, "The Turnover Process and the Academic Library," 57; Diane B. Rutledge, "Job Permanency: The Academic Librarian's Dilemma is the Administrator's Challenge for the 1980s," THE JOURNAL OF ACADEMIC LIBRARIANSHIP 7, no. 1 (1981): 29, 41.

14. Smith, Nathan M. and David T. Palmer, "Reference: Rewards or Regrets, Believing Makes It So," THE REFERENCE LIBRARIAN 16 (1986): 271-281.

15. Neal, James G., "Continuing Education: Attitudes and Experiences of the Academic Librarian," COLLEGE & RESEARCH LIBRARIES 41, no. 2 (1980): 132.

16. Champion, Brian, "Intrapreneuring and the Spirit of Innovation in Libraries," JOURNAL OF LIBRARY ADMINISTRATION 9, no. 2 (1988): 35-43.

17. King, Patricia, PERFORMANCE PLANNING AND APPRAISAL: A

HOW-TO-BOOK FOR MANAGERS (New York: McGraw-Hill, 1984); Clive Fletcher and Richard Williams, PERFORMANCE APPRAISAL AND CAREER DEVELOPMENT (London: Hutchinson, 1985); Robert D. Brown, ed., PERFORMANCE APPRAISAL AS A TOOL FOR STAFF DEVELOPMENT, New Directions for Student Services, no. 43 (San Francisco: Jossey-Bass, 1988); PERFORMANCE APPRAISAL IN RESEARCH LIBRARIES (Washington, D.C.: Office of Management Studies, 1988).

18. Wall, Celia, "Self-Concept: An Element of Success in the Female Library Manager," JOURNAL OF LIBRARY ADMINISTRATION 6, no. 4 (1985/86): 53-65.

19. Roberts, Deanna L., "Mentoring in the Academic Library," COLLEGE & RESEARCH LIBRARIES NEWS 47, no. 2 (1986): 117-119.

20. Smith, Nathan M. and Howard C. Bybee and Martin H. Raish, "Burnout and the Library Administrator: Carrier or Cure," JOURNAL OF LIBRARY ADMINISTRATION 9, no. 2 (1988): 13-21.

21. Durrant, Stephen W., "The Myth of Mentoring," ADFL BULLETIN 19, no. 3 (1988): 44.

22. Hegg, Judith L., "Continuing Education: A Profile of the Academic Librarian Participant," JOURNAL OF LIBRARY ADMINISTRATION 6, no. 4 (1985/86): 49.

23. Ibid., 56.

24. Anderson, A. J., "Do People Change Their Management Styles and Practices as a Result of Taking Courses and Attending Workshops? JOURNAL OF LIBRARY ADMINISTRATION 6, no. 4 (1985/86): 3.

25. McNeer, Elizabeth J., "The Mentoring Influence in the Careers of Women ARL Directors," JOURNAL OF LIBRARY ADMINISTRATION 9, no. 2 (1988): 23-33.

Continuing Professional Education:
A Management Development Approach

Rosie L. Albritton

SUMMARY. Continuing Professional Education may take many different forms. An Integrative Model of Management Education that stresses a synthesis of knowledge, skills and attitudes will be presented in this article as a theoretical foundation for formulating the goals, objectives and activities associated with a continuing library education program. For the individual, the concept of self-assessment will be emphasized as a key component of an organizational model or for self-initiated continued learning. The instructional framework for implementing the model features a Leadership Development Hierarchy that moves the learner in the direction of becoming a fully functioning and effective leader-manager librarian. Application of the model is demonstrated by an overview of the Intern-Scholar Leadership Development program at the University of Missouri-Columbia Libraries.

Ms. Albritton is Assistant-to-the-Director of Libraries for Research, Grants & Planning, and Director of the Intern-Scholar Program, University of Missouri at Columbia, Columbia, MO 65201. During the academic year 1989-90, the author will be a Doctoral Fellow, Graduate School of Library and Information Science, and Research Assistant, Library Research Center, University of Illinois at Urbana-Champaign, Urbana, IL.

The Intern-Scholar program at the University of Missouri-Columbia Libraries was funded by the Council on Library Resources (CLR) Recent Graduates Internship Grant #3103.

The author wishes to thank Lori Campbell, Special Projects Assistant and recent graduate of the University of Missouri School of Library and Informational Science, and Kyung Park, Graduate Research Assistant and Doctoral candidate in Educational and Counseling Psychology for their assistance during the intern program, and the preparation of this article.

INTRODUCTION

In order to function effectively as a professional, one must have continuing learning experiences to reinforce his or her formal education. Due to the rapid growth in new knowledge and technology, it is estimated that within 10 to 12 years of receiving their formal professional education, most librarians will become approximately half as competent as they were upon graduation to meet the demands of their profession. "Degree obsolescence is today's way of life. The 'half-life' of knowledge in any given profession may now be as little as two to three years. The degree, in short, is today only the beginning of the education of a professional" (Frandson, 1980, p. 61).

Numerous reasons or causes for obsolescence, which is defined by Dubin (1972, p. 468) as "the normal decremental process that responds to updating efforts," and by Knox (1979, p. 133) as "less than optimal proficiency for current profession performance," have been cited. Some of these include: the rapid rate of societal change and the current technological and knowledge explosion (Frandson, 1980); lack of retention of knowledge and skills gained during preparatory education and experience (Dubin, 1972; Frandson, 1980); lack of desire and effort to increase proficiency (Knox, 1979); changes in societal expectations (Knox, 1979); and shifts in the concept of best practice and once accepted knowledge (Frandson, 1980).

One way to combat obsolescence is to continually learn new knowledge and skills. The focus and format of the learning endeavor will differ with each individual's needs, interests, and learning abilities. However, there is no doubt that, to remain a competent professional, an individual must continually be involved in some type of learning. According to Dubin (1972):

A highly trained person must constantly renew . . . knowledge. The goal is not merely to keep knowledge already acquired during the period of formal education. Much more than this — for past knowledge may become outdated — the aim is constantly to recharge the batteries that motivate and trigger self-renewal by keeping abreast of new knowledge that is constantly being added to by research and publication. (p. 468)

Continuing professional education, as used in this article, refers to keeping up to date and professionally competent in a continuous education mode. Continuing library education was defined by Stone (1986) as: ". . . all learning activities and efforts, formal and informal, by which individuals seek to upgrade their knowledge, attitudes, competencies, and understanding in their special field of work (or role) in order to: (1) deliver quality performance in the work setting, and (2) enrich their library careers" (p. 489-90).

A more detailed definition of continuing education was also cited by Stone (1986). This definition was developed by the library/information leaders who founded the National Council on Quality Continuing Education for Library/Information/Media Personnel (1980),

Continuing education is a learning process which builds on and updates previously acquired knowledge, skills, and attitudes of the individual. Continuing education comes after the preparatory education necessary for involvement in or with information, library media services. It is usually self-initiated learning in which individuals assume responsibility for their own development and for fulfilling their need to learn. It is broader than staff development which is usually mitigated by an organization for the growth of its own human resources. (p. 1)

The term continuing professional development was broadly defined by Horner (1987) as including: (a) all relevant learning experiences after any initial formal training period; (b) professional, staff, career development, and related personal development; (c) planned and unplanned learning exercises; (d) formally taught and informal (e.g., self-directed) projects; and (e) learning through reflection on experience and mutual self-help.

Continuing professional development activities (Horner, 1987) may include:

— courses (e.g., in-house, university, full or part-time, day release, evening, etc.)
— conferences, seminars, workshops and visits
— current awareness: books, journals, magazines, tapes, video
— distance learning experience (e.g., correspondence, extension courses)
— special project work or assignment
— undertaking research, writing or training activities
— independent learning initiatives
— planned job rotation, extending breadth of experience
— job exchanges and visiting appointments
— sabbaticals and paid educational leave
— self-development workshops and counseling (including, for example, working on interpersonal skills, creativity, leadership style, stress management and relaxation)
— membership in related professional associations

According to Nadler (1980), the term *human resource development* (HRD) has gained acceptance as the broad heading for learning activities provided by organizations. Under this umbrella, organizations offer learning experiences related to (1) the current job of the individual; (2) a different, but identified job; and (3) the possible directions of the organization and society. These three types differ in how they are designed, in the expectations of the learner and the sponsor, in the responsibilities of the providing organization, and in the way they are evaluated.

Nadler (1980) offered the following distinctions: Present-job learning = Training; Different-job learning = Education; and Future Directions learning = Development.

For the purposes of this paper the terms continuing education, continuing professional education and continuing library education will be used interchangeably, and will refer to the learning processes and activities by which librarians seek to expand and improve knowledge, skills and attitudes related to their professional careers. Development, as contrasted with education, will be viewed as a broader term that encompasses the whole complex process by which librarians as individuals learn, grow, and improve their abilities to perform professional tasks. The term development is future oriented and focuses on long-range planning. These distinctions in terminology will be explored in more detail when the theoretical program models are discussed later in this paper.

The purpose of this paper is to present a model of the continuing professional development process that could provide a conceptual framework for individuals and organizations to follow in planning continuing education activities. For the individual, the continuing professional development (CPD) process is likely to involve four recurring phases: self-assessment, planning, implementation, and review/evaluation. Self-assessment will also be highlighted as a key strategy in the organization model.

An Integrative Model of Management Education that stresses a synthesis of knowledge, skills and attitudes will be presented as the theoretical foundation for planning the goals, objectives and activities associated with a continuing library education program. Following the discussions of the individual and organization models, an illustration of how the two models were applied to the development and implementation of a continuing professional education program for beginning university librarians will be presented.

THE ORGANIZATIONAL MODEL: AN INTEGRATIVE MANAGEMENT EDUCATION APPROACH

Planning a comprehensive continuing education program requires the purposive use of resources. *Effectiveness* as a professional implies ability to achieve desirable results. This outcome is based on an appropriate repertoire of *knowledge*, *attitudes*, and *skills*. *Knowledge* consists of retained observation, facts, and interrelationships and the ability to manipulate the various elements. It is based on our intellect. *Attitudes* are our predispositions to act and react in predictable ways. They are often emotionally rooted. *Skills* are the ability to do things, to use the knowledge, to mobilize personality resources in order to carry out certain activities, to accomplish specific tasks (Hawrylyshyn, 1983).

Knowledge, attitudes, and skills are interrelated and influence each other. The best combination of knowledge, attitudes, and skills varies according to the nature of the organization, and the level of responsibility or function. Yet the process by which one acquires knowledge, attitudes, or skills varies greatly. Knowledge is acquired through a cognitive, intellectual process. Attitudes are acquired through experiential conditioning, i.e., through a more effective, emotional process. Skills are acquired through practice (Hawrylyshyn, 1983).

With the above learning processes, learning methods should be chosen to be compatible with learning processes for different learning categories. This *integrative* approach is summarized in Figure 1, which shows the skeletal configuration of the integrative model, focusing on interrelationships between *objectives, learning categories, learning processes,* and *teaching methods.*

A management development approach is, thereby, proposed as a sound theoretical foundation for planning a continuing professional education program in academic libraries. A comprehensive program that builds on the five parts of the integration model should be expected to foster a high level of growth and development for the individual and effective functioning for the organization. Management development is indeed a form of continuing education. However, management development is but one of several related and overlapping activities aimed at improving the effectiveness of organizations such as libraries.

The idea of development, as discussed earlier, provides a new focus. Development is not the same as learning (incremental acquisition) or change (a response to an external stimulus) or innovation (something new) or growth (more of the same), though it may include such things. It is concerned with the whole person and the whole life cycle. The other activities are: training, management education, and organization development. While all of the above have complementary roles and use some of the same techniques, they have different objectives and methodologies. Definitions by Hawrylyshyn (1983) attempt to point this out:

Management education aims at developing a broad range of abilities, based on appropriate knowledge, attitudes and skills, to enable managers and librarians to cope with a large variety of tasks in a large variety of organizational, library, or situational contexts. It is not, therefore, task or organizational specific. It is broader in scope,

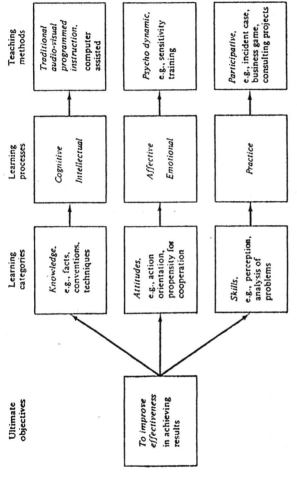

Management education – an integrative model.

Source: *Management Development and Training Handbook.* 2nd Ed. B. Taylor and G. Lippitt (Eds.) London: McGraw-Hill, 1983, p. 251.

FIGURE 1

has a longer scale than has training, and is more person-oriented than job or task-oriented.

Management training is to develop highly specific and immediately useful skills. It is intended to prepare people to carry out well-known tasks in well-defined job contexts. While training can be given in external programs, to develop skills common in most libraries, training programs are normally organized internally when library-specific practices must be taught. The whole activity is task-oriented, as people are being prepared to accomplish specific tasks.

Management development encompasses the whole, complex process by which professionals as individuals learn, grow, and improve their abilities to perform professional tasks. Librarianship, as well as management, is a practice-oriented profession. The concentration of librarians' and managers' activities lie in practical results. Learning must, therefore, be practice linked. Management development involves, first and foremost, learning on the job through experience. Learning on the job can be, and often is, enhanced and accelerated by a variety of activities, such as development-oriented performance appraisals, career planning, job rotation, participation in task forces, project teams, and special assignments. Occasional participation in formal training or educational programs should be an integral part of the overall professional development.

To get a successful continuing professional education program off the ground, it is important that both individual prospective participants and their organizations see some benefit in it for them; wherever possible individual and organization needs and purposes should be related. The responsibility for an individual's professional growth should be shared between him or her and the organization. Stone (1986) outlines several objectives and policies for consideration in planning continuing library education programs; the five listed below relate to learning principles and management concepts:

— appropriate applications of learning theory and adult education principles should be used to enhance the quality of CE
— reorganized management concepts should be used to strengthen CE quality

- CE should be perceived as not an end in itself, but as a means to an end — i.e., quality service to the public
- the methods of CE should be planned and conducted using three modes of education: inquiry, instruction, and performance
- the primary responsibility for learning should rest on the individual.

THE INDIVIDUAL:
THE SELF-ASSESSMENT APPROACH

The acceptance of one's self, which is at the heart of confident leadership, comes primarily through developmental programs which are grounded in a sound behavioral framework. Self-confidence comes both from experience and personal development. Personal development can be greatly assisted by developmental programs which nurture the participant's self-awareness and understanding of his or her relationship style to others.

Self assessment, including career and life goals should be the first step in an individual's continuing professional development (CPD) process. The four phases for the individual CPD process as outlined by Horner (1987), are (a) Self-Assessment, (b) Planning, (c) Implementation, and (d) Review/Evaluation. The model for promoting individual growth and development is outlined as follows:

1. Self-Assessment

- recognizing your need for CPD is half the battle; consider where you are in competence and any gaps; willingness to learn, change, adapt.
- what are your career goals? professional goals? how important, relatively, are security, status, job satisfaction challenge, personal achievement?
- consider short-term and long-term futures

2. Planning

— discuss with colleagues, friends, boss, etc. how best to meet needs; develop a strategy for identifying and assessing options and using various appropriate sources available; consider a written plan:

   — regular perusal of journals for current awareness
   — conferences/seminars as relevant
   — courses of different types
   — time commitment — should be realistic

3. Implementation

— personal discipline to avoid side-tracking; motivation
— reflection on experience

4. Review/Evaluation

— carried out during and after learning phases, and at least annually: what has been learned? what goals achieved? how is career developing? any attitude changes which are relevant? putting new insights into practice/influencing policy? follow-up? future needs?
— this takes one back to Self-Assessment and a new learning/ development phase.

Self-Assessment enables one to develop a greater self-awareness of interests, abilities and desires for the future — of where they are and where they are going — and actively pursue their interests. Self-assessment leads to self-understanding and eventually to self-development. It is from a sense of self that leadership behaviors emerge.

Kouzes and Posner (1987) explained the connection between self-development and leadership development (a potential outcome of continuing education), as follows:

The mastery of the art of leadership comes with the mastery of self. Ultimately, leadership development is a process of self-development. The quest for leadership is first an inner quest to discover who you are. Through self-development comes the confidence needed to lead. Self-confidence is really awareness of and faith in your own powers. These powers become clear and strong only as you work to identify and develop them. (p. 298)

A self-assessment and self-development approach is concerned not with the transmission of knowledge, but with seeking to help individuals understand their own personal learning and development processes in a way which increases their capacity and ability to take control and responsibility for learning and developing from personal experience (Taylor and Lippitt, 1983).

Self-Assessment/Self-Awareness principles are key components of the conceptual framework to be described in this paper. They fall under the umbrella term, "personal/interpersonal growth and development." See Figure 2 for an illustration of the tri-leveled *Leader-Manager Librarian* conceptual framework. This theoretical model was created and designed by the author, to provide a sense of focus and direction to planning the educational and behavioral objectives for a professional development program at the University of Missouri-Columbia; known as the Intern-Scholar Leadership Development Program and funded by the Council on Library Resources

FIGURE 2. The Leader-Manager Librarian: A Conceptual Framework for a Continuing Professional Development Program*

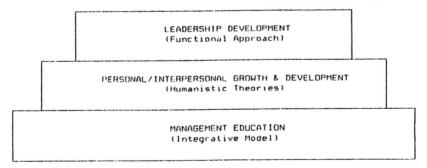

*This model was developed to provide educational and behavioral foundations for the University of Missouri-Columbia's CLR Intern-Scholar Leadership Development Program.

(CLR). The remainder of this article will describe the program and its implementation based on the Leader-Manager Librarian conceptual model.

APPLICATION OF MODEL:
PROFESSIONAL DEVELOPMENT AT THE
UNIVERSITY OF MISSOURI-COLUMBIA LIBRARIES

The University of Missouri-Columbia's Intern-Scholar Program was designed to prepare junior librarians for leadership by helping them develop self-knowledge, and interpersonal and management skills. The program was developed by the author and Dr. Thomas Shaughnessy, Director of Libraries. Funded by the Council on Library Resources from June 1986 to early 1989, the program was based on a definition of leadership that integrates personal qualities with technical knowledge and skills. Interns participated in four types of activities: (1) inhouse seminars on communication, self-development, group dynamics, and teamwork; (2) coursework in business administration, management, behavioral science, social science, and higher education; (3) mentorships with senior librarians; and (4) administrative internships with high-level campus administrators. The program gave librarians a wider perspective on academic librarianship and the context in which university libraries operate.

Initial seminars were devoted to individual assessment through techniques such as the Myers-Briggs Type Indicator. These instruments aided the participants in formulating personal goals for the internship. Later meetings included exercises that tested creative thinking, leadership abilities and cooperative decision-making. Discussions after the exercises encouraged self-analysis and application of the exercises to real-life situations. Through shared activities in the seminars, the interns formed a support group for each other as beginning librarians. In a relaxed environment, without distractions, the group compared experiences and provided mutual encouragement that made transition into the profession of librarianship easier.

A unique aspect of the Intern-Scholar program was the out-of-library into-campus experience of University coursework for credit, to augment seminar discussions and provide an opportunity for in-depth study of various topics relating to management. The courses ranged from Economics to Sociology to Psychology to Higher Education to Business Administration and Management.

The Mentorships had benefits for the mentor as well as the protege. Renewing enthusiasm, transmitting goals and values, establishing a warm collegial relationship, sharing experiences, networking, and exposure to new approaches through association with a recent-graduate were among the benefits the mentors derived from the relationships.

Another unique feature was the campus-wide administrative internships. This component was developed to give junior librarians an understanding of the University's environment outside the boundaries of the library. The internships with high-level campus administrators developed on an individual basis according to the interests of the intern and the programs within each assigned department.

A resource notebook entitled DEVELOPING LEADERSHIP IN ACADEMIC RESEARCH LIBRARIANSHIP accompanied the program. Compiled by the project directors, the book was designed for the interns to use as a self-teaching resource to supplement other program activities and to use as a tool for future reference. The resource notebook has been revised and published as a sourcebook for libraries (Albritton and Shaughnessy, 1989).

The program was based on The Integrative Model of Management Education (Hawrylyshyn, 1983); (2) Personal/Interpersonal Growth and Development (Beck, 1986) and (3) Leadership Development (Bennis, 1985; Kouzes and Posner, 1987 and Hitt, 1988). The basic core of the model is the *integrative approach* that emphasizes the interrelationships among three learning and development categories: knowledge, attitudes and skills. This approach proposes that the process by which one acquires knowledge, attitudes or skills varies greatly, and that learning methods should be chosen to be compatible with learning processes for different learning categories. The integrative model focuses on the development of an educational program that effectively combines objectives, learning categories, learning processes, and teaching methods.

The objectives of the grant program were reviewed by CLR vice president D. Marcum in the Foreword of the recent book (Albritton and Shaughnessy, 1989) based on the program:

> The CLR Internship for Recent Graduates program was developed to encourage libraries to create opportunities for their newest professional staff members. CLR offered the grant program because of its conviction that libraries have an obligation to continue the professional education of recent graduates of MLS programs who are hired for positions in research libraries. (Albritton and Shaughnessy, 1989, Foreword)

In accepting the CLR's support of this program, the UMC Libraries made a strong commitment to professional continuing education and staff development. While the Intern program was funded to develop an innovative, unique, and scholarly in-service program to enhance and extend the formal training of new librarians, it also provided the framework for expanding the scope and depth of current ongoing, library-wide staff development and continuing education programs.

The conceptual framework for the Intern-Scholar program was designed to move the learner in the direction of becoming an effective leader-manager (as described by Hitt, 1988), within his or her organization. Therefore, the key educational objective of the intern-scholar program was to introduce the concept of the *Leader-Manager librarian* to new librarians as a developmental model that can be applied to a formal training program or used as a guide for self-directed continued learning.

The Leader-Manager concept is based on the premise that every librarian has a certain amount of leadership potential and that this potential can be further developed. The theme of this model is that librarians can *learn* how to become effective leader-managers. By learning and applying known principles of leadership, management and human development, all librarians can improve their position on the leader-effectiveness scale.

In developing the instructional framework for the program, a leadership development hierarchy (see Figure 3) was proposed that would establish an instructional methodology for operationalizing the three components of the theoretical model (management educa-

FIGURE 3. A Leadership Development Hierarchy*

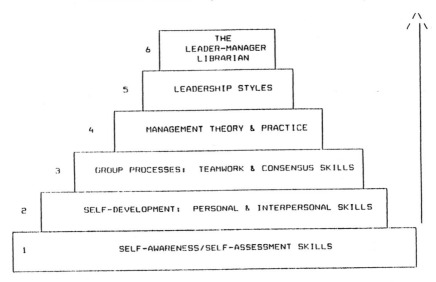

*This model was developed to support the instructional and behavioral objectives of the University of Missouri-Columbia's CLR Intern-Scholar Program.

tion, personal/interpersonal growth and development and leadership development). The leadership hierarchy is essentially an expanded version of the tri-level conceptual model. The hierarchy consists of five steps that lead to a sixth level representing a fully-functioning leader-manager librarian.

The steps in the leadership development hierarchy are: (1) Self-awareness/self-assessment; (2) Self-development (personal and interpersonal); (3) Group Processes; (4) Management theory and practice; and (5) Leadership styles. These steps were used to formulate the instructional framework, including format and methods. The framework included: program activities, resource methods, teaching methods, topics/subjects for presentation; literature resources and desired program competencies. These parts of the instructional framework are illustrated in Figure 4. As previously noted the self-assessment/self-awareness principles are thoroughly covered in all segments of the program.

Four categories of data will be used to evaluate the program:

```
                    Subject Areas

    1.  Self-Awareness/Assessment
    2.  Self Development:  Improving
        Interpersonal Skills
    3.  Professional Growth and Development
        (including career planning)
    4.  Leadership in Organizations
    5.  Teamwork and Consensus Building
    6.  Libraries, Technology and Change:
        The Leadership Challenge
```

```
        Activities                      Literature
      and Materials                     Resources

 1.  Workshops/Seminars          1.  Human Resource Development
 2.  Resource Readings           2.  Organizational Psychology
 3.  Coursework                  3.  Organizational Development
 4.  Mentorships                 4.  Human Resource Management
 5.  Internships                 5.  Training and Development
 6.  Guest Speakers              6.  Management
 7.  Survival Group              7.  Library and Information Science
     Exercises                   8.  Business Administration
 8.  Special Projects and        9.  Public Administration
     Presentations              10.  Social Psychology
 9.  Panel Discussions
10.  Conferences
```

```
      Teaching Methods                  Desired Competencies


 1.  Experiential Activities     1.  Self-Assessment Skills
     Games                       2.  Self-Development Skills
     Simulations                 3.  Group and Organizational Skills
     Role-playing                4.  Management Skills
 2.  Case Studies                5.  Leadership Skills
 3.  Discussions
 4.  Lecturettes
 5.  Group Projects
```

FIGURE 4. The Leader-Manager Librarian: Instructional Framework for a Continuing Professional Development Program

(1) new skills, (2) changes in feelings/attitudes, (3) self-assessment of development and advancement, and (4) initiative. The categories of new skills, development/advancement and initiative will be used to establish guidelines for long-term evaluation and follow-up plans over the next 3-5 years. However, feelings/attitudes were recently

assessed with a survey questionnaire, and preliminary analysis of the responses indicates that all parts of the program had significant value for the intern participants.

CONCLUSIONS

All libraries must look for ways to develop the skills of current staff members while continuing the day-to-day work of the library. In terms of continuing education and leadership development, new programs must be developed that include learning experiences and opportunities that go beyond developing the skills for accomplishment of tasks. These training and professional development programs should be designed to improve the abilities of staff in broader areas, such as *human relations, management and supervision, planning, decision-making, and coping with organizational change* within the context of contemporary higher education. These programs must have both educational and behavioral foundations.

Continuing professional development and continuing education may take many different forms. It may be informal and completely within the work experience of the individual, or it may be formal with detailed plans. The nature of the situation determines the formality, the detail, the responsibility and the methods of planning.

A management development approach based on an integrative model that stresses a synthesis of knowledge, skills and attitudes should foster a high level of growth and development for the individual librarian and promote effective functioning for the organization. The Leader-Manager Librarian model offers an instructional framework for developing leadership potential. By learning and applying known principles of management, leadership and personal development, call librarians can become fully-functioning leader-managers.

The CLR Recent Graduate Intern program (Inter-Scholar Leadership Development model), at the University of Missouri-Columbia, has served as a vehicle for implementing unique and innovative methods for advancing the library profession, promoting continuing professional education, leadership development, and allowing new librarians the opportunity to participate actively in the library and the university. One-day programs do not constitute "development," unless they are part of an ongoing process. Therefore, the use of a combination of instructional methods is fundamental to the goals of a comprehensive educational program.

REFERENCES

Albritton, Rosie L. "The Intern-Scholar Program at the University of Missouri-Columbia Libraries." *Show-Me Libraries* (June 1987): 9-18.

Albritton, Rosie L. "Leadership Development." *College and Research Libraries News* (Nov. 1987): 618-23.

Albritton, Rosie L. and Thomas W. Shaughnessy. 1989. *Developing Leadership Skills: A Sourcebook for Librarians*. Englewood, CO: Libraries Unlimited, August 1989.

Beck, Arthur C. and Ellis D. Hillmar. 1986, *Positive Management Practices*. San Francisco: Jossey-Bass.

Bennis, Warren and Burt Namus. 1985. *Leaders: The Strategies for Taking Charge*. New York: Harper & Row.

Dubin, Samuel S. 1972. "Obsolescence or Life-Long Education: A Choice for the Professional." *American Psychologist* (27): 486-98.

Frandon, Phillip E. 1980. "Continuing Education for the Professions." In *Serving Personal and Community Needs Through Adult Education*. E. J. Boone, R.W. Shearon, and E.E. White, editors. San Francisco: Jossey-Bass, p. 61-82.

Hawrylyshyn, Bohdan. 1983. "Management Education—A Conceptual Framework." In *Management Development and Training Handbook*, 2nd edition. Bernard Taylor and Gordon Lippitt, editors. London: McGraw-Hill, p. 245-56.

Hitt, William D. 1988. *The Leader-Manager*. Columbus: Battelle.

Horner, David J. 1987. "Continuing Professional Development Revisited." *Adult Education* (Sept. 1987): 133-37.

Knox, A.B. 1979. "The Nature and Causes of Professional Obsolescence." In *The Evaluation of Continuing Education for Professionals: A Systems View*. P.P. LeBreton, *et al.*, editors. Seattle, WA: Division of Academic and Professional Programs, Continuing Education, University of Washington, p. 133-54.

Kouzes, James M. and Barry Z. Posner. 1987. *The Leadership Challenge*. San Francisco: Jossey-Bass.

Nadler, Leonard. 1980. "Human Resource Development for Managers." In *Serving Personal and Community Needs Through Adult Eduation*. E.J. Boone, R.W. Shearon and E.E. White, editors. San Francisco: Jossey-Bass, p. 82-96.

National Council on Quality Continuing Education for Information, Library and Media Personnel. 1980. *A Program for Quality in Continuing Education for Information, Library, and Media Personnel, Policy Statement and Criteria for*

Quality, vol. 1. Washington, D.C.: Continuing Library Education Network and Exchange, p. 1.

Stone, Elizabeth W. 1986. "The Growth of Continuing Education." *Library Trends* (Winter 1986): 489-513.

Taylor, Bernard and Gorden Lippith. *Management Development and Training Handbook*, 2nd edition. London: McGraw-Hill, 1983.

Mentor Meets Telemachus: The Role of the Department Head in Orienting and Inducting the Beginning Reference Librarian

Tara Lynn Fulton

SUMMARY. This paper explores the various ways in which the reference department head serves as a mentor to the beginning reference librarian. It does so through the analogy of the relationship of Athena-Mentor and the protege, Telemachus, in Homer's *Odyssey*. In both cases, the mentor supports and guides the initiate, provides a role model to observe, coaches and tutors for competent performance, serves as an advocate and sponsor for the newcomer, and gives advise and counsel along the way. The department head is responsible for more than orientation to the institution and training in specific areas of responsibility. S/he ensures that the beginning librarian learns to apply the theory presented in library school to everyday practice, and thereby to define him/herself as a professional. An extensive list of additional resources is provided.

TELEMACHUS' EDUCATION AND INDUCTION

In Homer's *Odyssey*, Odysseus is called into the Trojan War when his son, Telemachus, is just an infant.[1] He entrusts the care of his son to his faithful friend, Mentor, who educates and guides the boy through his childhood and adolescence. As rumors spread that

Tara Lynn Fulton is Head of the Reference Department, E.M. Cudahy Library, Loyola University of Chicago, 6525 N. Sheridan Road, Chicago, IL 60626.

Odysseus has been killed in the war, suitors begin to court his mother, Penelope, and to wreak havoc in the court of Ithaca. In his youth, Telemachus feels powerless to deter the suitors, and lacks the confidence and strength to confront them. He is still a boy and not yet ready to succeed his father as head of court.

When Telemachus reaches his late teens, the goddess Athena takes the form of three people (Taphian, Mentes, and later Mentor) and convinces the boy to go in search of his father. This is Telemachus' initiation journey, during which he is transformed from a boy into a man. In fact, he undergoes his own odyssey, which parallels that of his father. Thus it is actually Athena and not Mentor himself who has the most profound effect on Telemachus' development. She gives him advice which transforms him from a passive observer into a future leader who is actively controlling his destiny. She jolts him out of a pessimistic, inactive state into one of determination. His attitude toward both the suitors and his mother changes as soon as he resolves to undertake the voyage, and his newly found confidence agitates the suitors to plot against him while he is away. Although he is still an awkward youth, his dreams and his courage are heroic and it is clear that he is destined to assume his inherited role.

Athena accompanies Telemachus on this journey and ensures that he encounters the people and situations he needs to face to become a man. She cannot simply tell him his father is alive: he must go through the ordeal to emerge as an independent person. Telemachus travels to Pylos, where he seeks information on his father from Nestor, and to Sparta, where he talks with Menelaus. Nestor and Menelaus provide him with historical and cultural information about the Trojan War which will help him prepare for the future. During this time he also learns to conduct himself among strangers, to use his powers of reasoning and his intelligence to make decisions, and to accept responsibility.

Whenever he hesitates or flounders, Athena is there to encourage him, to reassure him, and to guide his thinking, as is evidenced in the following passage, in which she appears to Telemachus as Mentor and convinces him to visit Nestor.

But clear-headed Telemakhos replied:
"Mentor, how can I do it, how approach him?
I have no practice in elaborate speeches, and
for a young man to interrogate an old man
seems disrespectful—"
But the grey-eyed goddess said:
"Reason and heart will give you words, Telemakhos;
and a spirit will counsel others. I should say
the gods were indifferent to your life."[2]

By the end of this journey he is taking initiative and demonstrating the skills needed to stand beside his father,

When Telemachus returns, he finds that Odysseus has also returned, and father and son are reunited at last. They plan together to fight off the suitors. Athena assumes her traditional form as a bird, and guides the spears and arrows in their favor. The suitors are massacred; Odysseus and Telemachus arise victorious. Telemachus now finally emerges as a man.

THE REFERENCE DEPARTMENT HEAD AS MENTOR

The term "mentor" derives from its first use, in Homer's *Odyssey*.[3] Thus originally "mentor" alluded to a loyal and trusted guide, and the mentor-protege relationship was a long-term, intimate one in which the ultimate aim was to make the protege a more competent, mature, self-sufficient individual. In his book on adult development, Daniel Levinson writes:

> The true mentor . . . fosters the young adult's development by believing in him, sharing the youthful Dream and giving it his blessing, helping to define the newly emerging self in its newly discovered world, and creating a space in which the young man can work on a reasonably satisfactory life structure that contains the Dream.[4]

Use of the term has evolved over time to refer much more generally to a counselor, instructor, support person, master, groomer, leader, guru, exemplar, teacher, coach, role model, guide, tutor, confidant, nurturer, advisor, advocate, sponsor, or protector. Thus the mentor serves in some ways as parent, peer, friend, and supervisor, and attends to both the pragmatic and the psychological needs of the protege.[5] Ideally the department head serves all of these roles for the beginning reference librarian, as Athena-Mentor did for Telemachus.

INITIATION OF THE BEGINNING
REFERENCE LIBRARIAN

The story of Telemachus' initiation into manhood is a classic example of the process of maturation into new responsibilities and new situations. The many phases and levels at which a beginning reference librarian must be integrated into his/her first professional position can likewise be seen in this context. Let's look now at five facets of this process and the ways in which the department head serves as a mentor throughout them.

A. Education and Preparation:
Mentor as Advisor and Teacher

The role that Odysseus' old friend Mentor played is similar to the educational role of the library school. As Telemachus was growing up, he acquired the general knowledge base of his culture, as well as its philosophical base — its norms, its ethics, its mission. He was made aware of the duties and responsibilities he could expect to assume as a leader in the house of Ithaca, and observed the conduct expected of someone of his stature. He was exposed to, and in some cases minimally trained on, some of the tools of his trade.[6] All of this was background preparation for his eventual entry into the adult (or, in our case, the professional) world.

The time came when Telemachus was ready to step into that world. It was Athena who prompted and oversaw his rite of passage. One might argue that the ordeal of interviewing for one's first library position is challenging enough in itself to assure one a place in the ranks! Recruiters, including department heads, do play a role in influencing the self-confidence with which initiates traverse the path, and this process does involve considerable testing of courage and stamina. However, that is only the beginning of the odyssey.[7]

B. Applying Library School Theory in Practice: Mentor as Exemplar, Master, and Role Model

Once on the job, the new reference librarian must learn to use the knowledge gained in library school and apply it to everyday library practice. As this process takes place, it is the department head who helps to ensure that librarians do not lose the wholistic, conceptual approach that was instilled in them in library school.[8] Librarians who bury themselves in the details of daily operations soon lose sight of their mission: they become parochial and shortsighted, no longer the reflective practitioners the MLS degree intended for them to be. To avoid this, the department head must make opportunities for conversation, projects, and learning available to the new recruit to help him[9] see the relevance of his education to his current position.

Three areas in particular warrant attention: relation of library to community, diversity of professional roles, and ethics. Library school stresses the interrelationship between a library and the organization or community of which it is a part, including missions, attitudes, use patterns, financial support, public relations and the like. The new librarian should be made aware of both factual or documented relationships between his new library and the clientele/support base, as well as perceived relationships from all points of view. Only then can he truly understand the context in which he is functioning. The question of alternate and conflicting professional roles is another area in which the fledgling librarian has received some introduction.[10] The teacher vs. intermediary debate, for example, has ramifications in all of the "core tasks" of librarianship.[11] The new librarian is likely to find himself torn between what he feels he ought to be ideally and how he is treated or what is expected of him in reality. There is also tension between present roles and anticipated future roles and service needs, and the relationship of this struggle to library school curriculum is not readily apparent.[12] Through the process of self-analysis and situational analysis, the young professional comes to define himself and the roles he feels most comfortable and most committed to playing. Here the mentor must be careful to guide but not to control the young protege's search, so that the new librarian becomes not a reflection of what he sees modeled around him, but a truly unique individual in the way that he balances and manipulates his roles as librarian.

It is especially important that a sense of professional ethics be ever-present in the new recruit's mind. Terms such as intellectual freedom, free-vs.-fee service, confidentiality, and the equality of service take on new meaning in the light of the decisions professionals make every day.[13] Modes of conduct must be made consistent with organizational values and norms if the newcomer is to have clear direction and focused energy towards good performance.[14]

The department head naturally serves as a role model and master craftperson whom the apprentice can observe and with whom he can discuss his thoughts. The department head should also be sure that theory is woven into the department's service policies and into the management and operational practices the recruit observes. Furthermore, the new librarian must learn to perceive and integrate the relationship between the conceptual and the applicable for himself; Socratic questioning is one of the most effective teaching methods known for development of these critical thinking skills.[15]

C. Orientation and Job Skill Training: Mentor as Coach, Guide, Instructor, and Tutor

First order of business in a training program[16] is orientation to the physical surroundings and to the local ways of doing things. Taking tours of the library building and of the campus or community, meeting key players, reading policy and procedure manuals, seeing how supplies and materials are ordered, noting the layout and arrangement of the reference room, reviewing personnel matters and organizational structure, and visiting special collections are methods used to cover this territory.

Next comes training in specific job skills. As stated, it is assumed that all inductees have some basic skills in most of these areas, although some of the skills may be rusty as well as superficial. Much like an apprentice, the librarian must practice, refine and develop his talents in all areas of reference librarianship. Studying specific reference tools, observing senior librarians as they conduct reference interviews, practicing search strategy on challenge questions, reviewing videotapes of instruction classes, and verifying difficult citations in various online systems are examples of ways in which these skills are honed.

In many cases it is also necessary that general skills be transferred or applied to specific contexts. Mostly notably, this applies to the area of automation. While beginning librarians may be aware of various OPAC and CD-ROM systems, for example, it is not until they have to work with and teach specific packages that they acquire an intimate knowledge of those tools. Reference librarians are also frequently asked to serve as bibliographers in subject areas that are only vaguely familiar to them, and the department head must open doors for them to meet with faculty, to take classes, or to conduct research in order to learn the literature of these fields. If decision-making and planning are to be part of the person's accountabilities, he will need assistance in outlining factors to consider, brainstorming problem-solving options, and using logic. Participatory management is one of the most empowering methods to establish independence in this regard.[17]

No less challenging is the task of helping professionals learn to balance these various job responsibilities, to manage their time well, and to cope with stress.[18] While certainly not one of the aspects of training that can be expected to be accomplished in the first several months on the job, it is imperative that one get started right away learning to set priorities and manage paperwork well: it is easier to maintain good habits than to break bad ones. And, after all, that's what the training process is all about!

D. Social and Political Integration: Mentor as Advocate, Confidant, Counselor, Groomer, and Sponsor

In the courts of Sparta and Pylos, Telemachus got the information he needed, but he was unfamiliar with their customs and thus did so in some awkward and apparently rude ways. There are ways to get things done effectively, and there are ways to get things done correctly. The department head must see to it that the new librarian is counselled in the organizational climate and culture in which she/he is operating.[19] How is communication handled—privately or in the group settings, in writing or verbally, directly or through unit heads? What level of creativity, initiative, risk taking, and independence is expected, tolerated, or appreciated? Who holds power in the organization based on rank, seniority, savvy, smarts, and connections to the grapevine? Too often it is assumed that young professionals will pick up on clues on their own, and that the degree to which they demonstrate savvy in the political arena is a matter of personality. Not so, I would argue. If the department head is willing to speak candidly about "what's really going on," the new librarian is less likely to commit costly faux pas and will be integrated more quickly and more easily into the organization. Attendance at department, library-wide, and committee meetings is an excellent way for newcomers to observe organizational dynamics in action.

The daily life of the reference librarian is spent with users, colleagues, supervisors, administrators, support staff—people! Interpersonal and communication skills are an essential component of public services job descriptions, and it is the department head's responsibility to ensure that the interactions a new librarian has with all of these people are positive and fruitful.

Of course, we *hope* that individuals who choose reference librarianship as a career path and who graduate from library school are essentially suited to and well-equipped for work with others.[20] But there is a big difference between getting along with others and being appreciated and liked by others, and an even bigger difference between being accepted in the organization and being recognized by the administration. More importantly, there is a big difference between competent service and high quality, one-on-one attention to users' needs. A professional needs interpersonal and communication skills to do his/her job and also to maintain and enhance his/her status as a professional. Beginning librarians need to spend considerable amounts of time observing interactions, talking through how to present ideas in different contexts, and practicing and receiving feedback on their ability to listen, explain, articulate, question, and establish rapport. Because of the variety of styles and techniques used to interact and communicate, it is best if the department head ensures that professionals have the opportunity to work with and observe a representation from a wide spectrum of these approaches.

E. Surviving Initiation: Mentor as Guru, Leader, Nurturer, Protector, and Support Person

Through the odyssey of induction, skills and knowledge are what the inductee must master to be accepted as a full-fledged adult/ professional. However, acquisition of skill and knowledge has important prerequisites, of which ability is only one component; training must attend to those prerequisites. I refer here to motivation, to attitude, to philosophy, and to commitment.[21]

One of the major roles Athena played for Telemachus was that of security net. Telemachus' voyage was a precarious and frightening one, full of storms and omens. In the end, of course, he arose a stronger and more courageous individual who knew his own will and his limitations. But along the way he lost his sense of direction, lost his faith, and lost his confidence in himself. One's first professional position is a similarly trying time, and the beginning reference librarian needs the encouragement and support of his colleagues and supervisor. It is during this time that one establishes long-term patterns of handling problems, of dealing with stress, and of coping with adversity. It is imperative that the department head be empathetic rather than judgmental during this period, that she be ready to help the neophyte pick up some broken pieces and move on. Just as Athena-Mentor allowed Telemachus to learn from his mistakes, so should new reference librarians be assured that they are expected not to be perfect, but to try.[22]

In this capacity the department head shows her true colors as a leader and a visionary.[23] The performance standards and the goals set by the department head serve as a beacon to the inductee on his odyssey, just as Athena guided and steered the young Telemachus towards his destination. In this way, the mentor sets a path not just for the current voyage, but for the protege's self-actualization and career development in general.[24] With this extra level of support and leadership, the young reference librarian is ready to look beyond the present transition phase to the opportunities ahead, both within the library and in the profession.

HOMER IS ATHENA-MENTOR:
AUTHORING THE INITIATION PROCESS

We have looked at the ways in which a mentor interacts with a new initiate to provide him with the guidance, insights, and experiences he needs to become a more self-sufficient, more self-reliant, and more competent individual. All of this takes place on the surface, in the written text of the Odyssey. Let's look now behind the scenes at what Homer has Athena-Mentor thinking, feeling, and doing to set up the plot of the adventure, for much of the department head's role in conducting training happens long before the beginning reference librarian arrives on the scene.[25]

The department head is responsible for the knowledge, skills, attitudes and values of reference librarians. She must assure that the librarians are not only competent today, but that they are prepared for future developments as well. Since she is dependent on them to develop and implement reference services, she works on developing them both individually and as a team. And since all human service organizations must operate as businesses in some regards, efficiency and effectiveness are essential.[26] In other words, the first question she asks herself is, "Why train?"[27]

"Why" is a philosophical question. Deciding one *ought* to do something does not guarantee that one will decide *to* do something. So the manager must decide "whether" to train. Athena was a very busy goddess; yet of all the people in Greece at that time, she chose to devote her attention to Telemachus, and apparently she had the blessing of the other high-ranking gods and goddesses to do so. Support for and commitment to the training program is essential on all levels. As sources in the literature bemoan, most of our library training programs are half-hearted attempts that do not meet their goals fully.[28] The department head must devote considerable time and energy communicating the need for training to others and garnering the necessary resources to conduct training.

Only within the realistic framework of support can the mentor begin to plan "what" to teach. Athena, too, apparently did her own version of needs assessment, goals establishment, objectives formulation, performance standards setting, and content outlining. A department head's thought processes should be much more apparent and formal, preferably written down in the form of a checklist and/ or a plan.[29] We have already looked briefly at possible content elements for an initiation process in the previous section.

Based on instructional principles, this content must then be translated into a workable training plan—the "who," "where," "when," "how," and "how much" of it all.[30] Athena did not directly impart all of the information to Telemachus: rather, she lined up a series of people, places, objects, and events that were intended to convey content. Similarly a department head will involve other reference librarians, representatives from throughout the library, automated and audiovisual sources of information, self-instruction and practice projects and a variety of other opportunities in the training plan. She also controls the timing, pacing, and scheduling of training, determining how much is reasonable to expect the new person to absorb and determining which content is prerequisite to other content. It is she who determines how much of the training will take place on the scene, in private study, outside the library, etc. Telemachus' odyssey was a smaller, controlled version of his father's, commensurate with his stage of development, and designed to be most effective for that individual at that time under those circumstances. Athena planned some elements of the odyssey, allowed other elements to evolve naturalistically based on Telemachus' own initiative and needs, and monitored the whole voyage to ensure its ultimate success. She was, in other words, both author of and player in the initiation process.

WHAT TELEMACHUS TAUGHT ATHENA-MENTOR: EVALUATION OF TRAINING

The department head must take a further step after planning and implementing a training program: she must evaluate it.[31] Throughout the odyssey, there are times at which one decides to change course. Planning carefully includes making room in the plan for alterations, serendipity, and experimentation. After all, if one hopes to instill a sense of curiosity and appreciation for taking risks in the initiate, then one has to be ready to demonstrate the same! A generic training calendar and checklist does not take into account the needs of the individual, with his special talents and areas of weakness, and therefore it is imperative that one continually modify the plan to maximize those strengths and to confront areas of concern. While a written training plan ensures careful thinking and assists in communicating the plan to the new librarian and to others, it should not be stagnant.[32] In this way, each initiate contributes to the improvement of the mentor and the mentor's plan.

We must not overlook the fact that the department head, and in fact the whole department, also learns from the new initiate and from the experience of mentoring. Every time a supervisor works with a new employee, a door is opened for the supervisor to expand her own spectrum of management style to accommodate the new person and to reflect on oneself as supervisor. We also speak frequently in the library world of the value of hiring "new blood" for the fresh ideas and perspectives they bring; through their eyes existing staff are able to look in the mirror and perceive themselves in this new light. New librarians help to improve service by pointing out where policies and procedures are unclear, how operations might be streamlined, and what areas of staff development are needed by everyone, not just for the new kid on the block. In short, the induction process is an opportunity for the department head and the department to evaluate and improve itself. The new reference librarian reciprocates department orientation and training by educating and training the department.

CONCLUSION

The process of planning, conducting, and evaluating a training program for a beginning reference librarian is at once a very challenging, taxing, and exhausting experience and a unique opportunity to contribute simultaneously to an individual's and to the profession's improvement. The parallel of the department head to Athena-Mentor seems an appropriate one, for one feels throughout the process that god-like qualities are needed to carry on with the odyssey. The fate of Telemachus is debated in Homeric tradition, and libraries likewise cannot guarantee that their training efforts will always produce future heroes and leaders. However, in mythology as well as in history, every protege is a potential future mentor: let's work together to continue the cycle!

NOTES AND REFERENCES

1. All of the information about Homer's *Odyssey* is derived from the following sources:

Austin, Norman. "The Power of the Word," in *Homer's "The Odyssey"*, edited by Harold Bloom. New York: Chelsea House, 1988, pp. 69-85.
Belmont, David E. "Athena and Telemachus," *Classical Journal* 65 (December 1969): 109-116.
Clarke, Howard W. "Telemachus and the 'Telemacheia'," *American Journal of Philology* 84 (April 1963): 129-145.
Eckert, Charles W. "Initiatory Motifs in the Story of Telemachus," *Classical Journal* 59 (November 1963): 49-57.
Kitto, H.D.F. "The Odyssey: The Exclusion of Surprise," in *Homer's "The Odyssey"*, edited by Harold Bloom. New York: Chelsea House, 1988, pp. 5-33.
Millar, C.M.H. and J.W.S. Carmichael. "The Growth of Telemachus," *Greece & Rome*, ser. 2, 1 (June 1954): 58-64.

2. Quoted from:

Homer. *The Odyssey*. Translated by Robert Fitzgerald. New York: Doubleday, 1961, p. 48.

3. The etymology of the word is found in:

Oxford English Dictionary. 2nd ed. Oxford: Clarendon, 1989, p. 614.

4. Quoted from:

Levison, Daniel J. et al. *The Season's of a Man's Life*. New York: Knopf, 1978, pp. 98-99.

5. For literature on and descriptions of mentorship, see:

Clutterbuck, David. *Everyone Needs a Mentor: How to Foster Talent within the Organization*. London: Institute of Personnel Management, 1985.
Hunt, David M. and Carol Michael. "Mentorship: A Career Training and Development Tool," *Academy of Management Review* 8 (1983): 475-485.
Merriam, Sharan. "Mentors and Proteges," *Adult Education Quarterly* 33 (Spring 1983): 161-173.
Zey, Michael G. *The Mentor Connection*. Homewood, IL: Dow Jones Irwin, 1984.

6. An historical review of what has traditionally been taught in library school about reference librarianship is provided by:

Rothstein, Samuel. "The Making of a Reference Librarian," 31 *Library Trends* (Winter 1983): 375-397.

7. The feelings and thought of the new librarian are described and fictional-ized in:

> Jones, Dorothy E. "'I'd Like You to Meet Our New Librarian': The Initia-tion and Integration of the Newly Appointed Librarian," *Journal of Aca-demic Librarianship* 14 (September 1988): 221-224.

8. The distinction between library school education and in-house training and/or staff development is drawn by:

> Roberts, Anne F. "Myth: Reference Librarians Can Perform at the Refer-ence Desk Immediately Upon Receipt of MLS, Reality: They Need Training Like Other Professionals," in *Academic Libraries: Myths and Realities.* (Proceedings of the ACRL Third National Conference, Seat-tle, April 4-7, 1984). Chicago: Association of College and Research Libraries, 1984, pp. 400-404.
>
> White, Herbert S. *Library Personnel Management.* White Plains, NY: Knowledge Industry Publications, 1985, pp. 114-118.

9. For ease of reading the new librarian will be referred to with the pronoun "he" (to parallel Telemachus) and the department head with "she" (to parallel Athena-Mentor).

10. For a discussion of this role conflict, see:

> Mendelsohn, Henry N. "Role Conflict and Ambiguity in Reference Librar-ianship," in *Conflicts in Reference Services*, edited by Bill Katz and Ruth A. Fraley. (The Reference Librarian, no. 12) New York: The Ha-worth Press, 1985, pp. 179-186.

11. This debate and its implications are summarized by:

> Nielsen, Brian. "Teacher or Intermediary: Alternative Professional Models in the Information Age," *College and Research Libraries* 43 (May 1982): 183-191.

12. One author advocates that library schools change their focus from teaching sources to teaching information transfer services:

> Galvin, Thomas J. "The Education of the New Reference Librarian," *Li-brary Journal* 100 (April 15, 1975): 727-730.

13. The introduction to a previous issue of The Reference Librarian provides an excellent overview of these ethical issues:

> Rothstein, Samuel, "Where Does It Hurt?: Identifying the Real Concerns in the Ethics of Reference Service," in *Ethics and Reference Services*, edited by Bill Katz and Ruth A. Fraley. (The Reference Librarian, no. 4). New York: The Haworth Press, 1982, pp. 1-13.

14. This principle is discussed by:

Beck, Arthur C. and Ellis D. Hillmar. *Positive Management Practices: Bringing Out the Best in Organizations and People*. San Francisco: Jossey-Bass, 1986, pp. 20, 32.

15. See the chapter on the socratic method in:

Hyman, Ronald T. *Ways of Teaching*. 2nd ed. New York: Lippincott, 1974, pp. 91-118.

16. Roberts and the following sources provide descriptions of typical or model content for orientation/training programs for librarians:

Devine, Judith W. "Considerations in the Management of a Reference Department," in *Reference Services Administration and Management*, edited by Bill Katz and Ruth A. Fraley. (The Reference Librarian, no. 3) New York: The Haworth Press, 1982, pp. 61-70.

Isaacs, Julian, "In-Service Training for Reference Work," *Library Association Record* 71 (October 1969): 301-302.

Rolstad, Gary O. "Training Adult Services Librarians," *RQ* 27 (Summer 1988): 474-477.

Stabler, Karen Y. "Introductory Training of Academic Reference Librarians: A Survey," *RQ* 26 (Spring 1987): 363-369.

Young, William F. "Communicating With the New Reference Librarian: The Teaching Process," in *Reference Services Today: From Interview to Burnout*, edited by Bill Katz and Ruth A. Fraley. (The Reference Librarian, no. 16) New York: The Haworth Press, 1987, pp. 223-231.

17. This point is made by Beck, p. 127 and:

Hendley, Margaret. "Role of the Manager in Reference Staff Development," in *Personnel Issues in Reference Services*, edited by Bill Katz and Ruth A. Fraley. (The Reference Librarian, no. 14) New York: The Haworth Press, 1986, pp. 105-117.

18. For a more lengthy discussion of the training implications of conflicting and diversified roles, see:

Kemp, Barbara. "Multiple Roles of Academic Reference Librarians: Problems of Education and Training," in *Personnel Issues in Reference Services*, edited by Bill Katz and Ruth A. Fraley. (The Reference Librarian, no. 14). New York: The Haworth Press, 1986, pp. 141-150.

19. Among the advocates for stressing such socialization are Jones, p. 223 and:

Creth, Sheila D. *Effective On-the-job Training: Developing Library Human Resources*. Chicago: American Library Association, 1986, pp. 4-6.

20. A cynical view of interpersonal skills of beginning reference librarians is provided by Kemp, p. 144.

21. For very readable summaries of the importance of these factors to organizational success, see Beck and Hillmar's discussion and the following story of the establishment of Holiday Inn, Inc.:

> Walton, William B. Sr. with Dr. Mel Lorentzen. *The New Bottom Line: People and Loyalty in Business.* San Francisco: Harper and Row, 1986.

22. Creth, pp. 62-64, advocates this constructive approach to learners' mistakes.

23. Visionary leadership is most articulately described in:

> Garner, Leslie H. Jr. *Leadership in Human Services.* San Francisco: Jossey-Bass, 1989, pp. 8-10.

24. Cargill provides a brief but enlightening overview of the individual's and others' role in one's career development:

> Cargill, Jennifer. "Career Development: It's Your Option," *College and Research Libraries News* 49 (September 1988): 513-517.

25. In addition to Creth, the following sources were consulted regarding general principles for designing training programs:

> Bertcher, Harvey J. *Staff Development in Human Service Organizations.* Englewood Cliffs, NJ: Prentice Hall, 1988.
> Broadwell, Martin M. *The New Supervisor.* 3rd ed. Reading, MA: Addison-Wesley, 1984.
> Casteleyn, Mary. *Planning Library Training Programmes.* London: Deutsch, 1981.
> Nadler, Leonard. *Designing Training Programs: The Critical Events Model.* Reading, MA: Addison-Wesley, 1982.
> Tracey, William R. *Designing Training and Development Systems.* Revised ed. New York: American Management Association, 1984.

26. Garner, pp. 87-88, discusses the importance of efficiency and effectiveness in human service organizations.

27. For a cogent synopsis of reasons to conduct training in libraries, see Creth, pp. 1-2.

28. Among these critics are Roberts, p. 400, Stabler, p. 367, and Young, p. 223.

29. Among advocates for checklists and written training plans are Creth, pp. 49-50, Luccock, p. 17, and Stabler, p. 369.

30. For more information on training methods, see:

> Conroy, Barbara. *Library Staff Development and Continuing Education.* Littleton, CO: Libraries Unlimited, 1978.

Cowley, John. *Personnel Management in Libraries.* London: Clive
   Bingley, 1982.
Gardner, James E. *Helping Employees Develop Job Skills: A Casebook of
   Training Approaches.* Washington, D.C.: Bureau of National Affairs,
   1976.
Luccock, Graham, "Induction Training," in *Handbook of Library Train-
   ing Practice,* edited by Ray Prytherch. Aldershot, Hants, England and
   Brookfield, VT: Gower, 1986, pp. 3-36.

   31. For more thorough discussions of training evaluation, see Conroy, Creth,
and:

   Castelyn, Mary. "Evaluating Training," in *Handbook of Library Training
   Practice,* edited by Ray Prytherch. Aldershot, Hants, England and
   Brookfield, VT: Gower, 1986, pp. 90-125.

   32. Similar arguments are made by Creth, pp. 50-51 and Stabler, pp. 368-
369.